Beyond Agriculture – making markets work for the poor:
proceedings of an international seminar

28 February–1 March 2005, Westminster, London, UK

Edited by

F.R. Almond *and* S.D. Hainsworth

CROP POST-HARVEST
PROGRAMME

Natural Resources International Limited
Park House, Bradbourne Lane
Aylesford, Kent ME20 6SN, UK

PRACTICAL ACTION
Technology challenging poverty

Intermediate Technology Development Group (ITDG)
Schumacher Centre for Technology and Development
Bourton on Dunsmore, Warwickshire CV23 9QZ, UK

2005

Citation

Almond, F.R. and Hainsworth, S.D. (Eds.) 2005. Beyond Agriculture – making markets work for the poor: proceedings of an international seminar, 28 February–1 March 2005. Westminster, London, UK. Crop Post-Harvest Programme (CPHP), Natural Resources International Limited, Aylesford, Kent and Practical Action, Bourton on Dunsmore, Warwickshire, UK. 176pp.

ISBN 0-9546452-3-5

This publication is an output from the Crop Post-Harvest Research Programme (CPHP) funded by the UK Department for International Development (DFID), for the benefit of developing countries. The views expressed are not necessarily those of DFID.

Practical Action is the working name of Intermediate Technology Development Group Ltd., Charity reg. no. 247257

Contents

Opening

Preface

The international seminar *Beyond Agriculture – Making markets work for the poor* was held on 28 February and 1 March 2005 in Westminster, London. The seminar, jointly hosted by the Crop Post-Harvest Programme (CPHP) of Natural Resources International Limited and the Intermediate Technology Development Group (ITDG) provided an opportunity to explore market access issues at a time when the Department for International Development (DFID)-funded Renewable Natural Resources Research Strategy (RNRRS) had just completed a 10-year cycle, and to consider what lessons might be carried forward into the planning of future work. Its origins, however, were rooted in a number of emerging developmental priorities, and in the experience of the CPHP, one of the ten research programmes of the RNRRS.

Donors and policy makers are now re-asserting the central importance of a healthy agriculture sector as a pre-requisite for general economic growth in developing countries; and whilst opinions still vary as to the rate and feasibility of agricultural modernisation in different contexts, the role of the smallholder farmer will continue to be important for the foreseeable future in most countries. There is considerable interest in high-value export markets for agricultural produce, but internal markets are many times greater in value, and their relative importance is set to rise further. There is also general agreement that the removal of the various constraints that hinder increased access to those markets by both producers and consumers must be a policy priority. And nowhere is this all more relevant than in sub-Saharan Africa.

The CPHP has funded a large number of market-related projects over its lifetime, and the knowledge outputs generated suggested a number of key access issues for small-scale producers and members of the market chain. These projects have been comprehensively reviewed[1]. But the CPHP experience also addressed a number of broader issues related to the way in which research knowledge could be put to use by the poor that were also reflected in the seminar content. These issues included:

- How research gaps are identified
- How to engage with the private sector
- How to establish what human and institutional resources need developing
- How to change the perspective of researchers and the private sector in the post-harvest system.

As a result, in its latter years CPHP sought to develop a new way of doing business by shifting its focus from research to innovation, i.e., from knowledge generation to knowledge impact[2]. In essence this new approach set out to form coalitions that combine researchers, the private sector, non-governmental organisations (NGOs) and governments to solve particular problems. The process emphasises the intermediation functions between the producers of new knowledge (whether they be farmers, traders, or scientists) and the users of new knowledge (such as farmers, equipment manufacturers, processors and vendors of agricultural produce).

However, it was felt that an objective consideration of market-access issues needed more than a presentation of those research outputs. The CPHP therefore joined forces with ITDG in order to bring in the perspectives of an international NGO with long experience of the practical application of technologies and policies relating to the rural economy, both on- and off-farm. This linkage, between research knowledge and evidence, and policy and practice, was a central principle for the seminar that aimed to bring together practitioners, policy makers and researchers from around the world.

Despite the declared focus on the challenges of internal markets in Africa, the issues of market access were still too broad to be sensibly covered within a 2-day event, and preparation for the seminar therefore included some additional features. Firstly, an informal consultation was held amongst the network of professionals in order to define a small number of central themes that, in general opinion, represented the key areas of challenge for market access. These emerged as:

- Building linkages and enhancing trust between small-scale rural producers, buyers in growing markets, and suppliers of critical inputs
- Supporting small-scale producers to associate, collaborate and coordinate so as to achieve economies of scale in their transactions with buyers (or suppliers)
- Making channels of information and market intelligence (e.g., about product specifications, market prices) accessible to rural producers
- Enabling rural producers to understand and better satisfy the product, process or delivery standards required by buyers.

Secondly, overview papers were commissioned from acknowledged experts, who were briefed to summarise, in an accessible and not overly academic way, the state of knowledge and the challenges in each of these areas. The four resulting papers were circulated in advance. These, together with a broad overview paper from ITDG, provided the starting point for debate and discussion. During the seminar itself participants were then able to devote as much time as possible to discussion, with additional opportunities for some related presentations and networking.

The material presented in these proceedings is not therefore a consistent statement of knowledge, nor does it necessarily represent the full views and positions of any of the organisations involved. It contains as many hypotheses and unanswered questions as it does firm knowledge and evidence, and as such it provided, and hopefully will continue to provide, a stimulus for further enquiry and debate.

Endnotes

1. Marter, A. 2004. CPHP thematic review: food marketing projects. DFID Renewable Natural Resources Research Strategy, Crop Post Harvest Programme Report. Natural Resources International, Aylesford, Kent, UK. 24 pp.
2. Barnett, A. 2004. From research to poverty-reducing innovation. Sussex Research Associates Limited, Brighton, UK. [Policy leaflet] 4 pp.

Welcome

Jim Harvey (Head, Livelihoods Advisers Group, Department for International Development, London, UK)

I am very pleased to be with you today. It's great to see such a broad gathering and I'd especially like to welcome those of you who have travelled from outside of the UK, including Richard Mkandawire from the New Partnerships for Africa's Development (NEPAD) There are two reasons why I'm pleased to be here:

Firstly, the subject is a very important one. Just a few years ago agriculture had all but fallen off the development map. Now it is really back on the scene again and people are beginning to recognise its importance in poverty reduction all around the world as evidenced by NEPAD, the Commission for Africa, and the policy documents of the World Bank. Agriculture is still the major sector, the major source of income and the major source of jobs in many countries – especially for poor people. And in a rapidly urbanising world that importance is retained beyond what the bare statistics would suggest. Two weeks ago the World Bank published their report *Beyond the City: the rural contribution to development*[1]. This report on Latin American countries, the most highly urbanised in the developing world, found that natural resources and the rural economy were far more important to overall economic growth and poverty reduction than the bare statistics suggest. If that is the case in Latin America, how much more important must it be in sub-Saharan Africa?

But we have to acknowledge that there are sceptics about agriculture and that they have some reason. Whilst trade reforms are clearly vital – and the subject of attention in this '2005 year' – it is already evident in many countries, particularly those in sub-Saharan Africa, that the supply side and all the constraints around it need urgent attention if advantage is to be taken of the new opportunities.

Some of this is pretty basic stuff: roads, rural access, reliable electricity, functioning ports, etc., but some is more qualitative – like the business and investment climates, and the regulatory environment. Some aspects are changing year by year – there is a very fast-moving scene on food and production standards that already influences export markets (as those who live in the UK have seen over the last few days with the Sudan-1 scare and its repercussions) and that will increasingly affect domestic markets[2]. Export markets are important but domestic markets – particularly in sub-Saharan Africa – are likely to be hugely more so over the next 15–20 years.

But it isn't always clear how poor people can benefit from such markets. If they are lucky some can find jobs in the marketing chain, but making markets work for poor people – producers and consumers – is both a slogan and a really urgent need, so I hope we can get under the skin of the issue over the next couple of days.

My second reason for taking great pleasure in being here is that the Crop Post-Harvest Programme is one of the research programmes funded by DFID under our Renewable Natural Resources Research Strategy. I have been associated with this Programme for the past 6 years and have seen its work develop to engage on these issues, so it is great to see that work coming to fruition. I have also had a much looser association with ITDG whom I would like to compliment for being the co-sponsor of this seminar. ITDG is an organisation that both DFID and I hold in a very high esteem and we are delighted to see this partnership here today

I wish you a very successful seminar.

Endnotes

1. *Beyond the City: the rural contribution to development.* World Bank, Washington DC, USA.
   According to the study, while rural natural resource activities only account for 12% of regional gross domestic product (GDP), their effect on national growth and poverty reduction is nearly twice as large due to the forward linkages to other economic activities and their high contribution to exports. For instance, for each 1% growth of the rural natural resource sector, there is a 0.22% increase in national GDP and a 0.28% increase in the income of the poorest families. This represents more than twice the expected 0.12% increase corresponding to the sector's share of GDP.
   In addition, the research found that the rural population in the region is actually 42% of the total, almost double the official figure of 24%, when measured according to the Organization for Economic Cooperation and Development (OECD) criteria for defining rurality, which include both population density and distance to major cities. This means that rural problems, such as poverty, have been highly underestimated and need much greater attention and more adequate public policies.

2. Recent food safety issues such as those related to *E. coli* breakouts, 'Mad Cow' disease, tainted animal feed products, and the contamination of berries and olive oil have contributed to more stringent food safety and agricultural health standards (Sanitary and Phytosanitary Standards, or SPS) in high-income countries. The report: *Food Safety and Agricultural Health Requirements: challenges and opportunities for developing country exports* stresses that these new standards, characterised by the report as a 'double edged-sword,' place particular demands on developing-country producers and exporters of high-value food products, such as fruit, vegetables, fish, meat, nuts, and spices. "In many cases, however, such standards have played a positive role, providing the catalyst and incentives for the modernisation of export supply and regulatory systems and the adoption of safer and more sustainable production and processing practices," says Steven Jaffee, Senior Economist, World Bank. "Countries can use this as an opportunity to differentiate themselves."
   The research, based on a series of case studies in developing countries, reveals that developing country suppliers are not faced with all-or-nothing, comply-or-perish choices. Suppliers should, according to the report 'determine the products and markets in which they can best compete and use diverse approaches to comply with standards.' New private-sector standards will also bring more attention to the entire supply chain.

Opening address

Richard Mkandawire

The New Partnership for Africa's Development (NEPAD) is delighted to be associated with this very important meeting. NEPAD is a programme of the African Union, and I think all of us in Africa agree that it is maybe the last hope for Africa. We are all aware of the continued deterioration of livelihood opportunities in Africa, perhaps the only continent where per capita food production has been declining over the past 40 years. African Heads of State and government are saying that this situation should not be allowed to continue. All of us are familiar with the images of starving children and malnutrition that appear on our TV screens and frequently in the media. That situation is uniquely African and the African leadership are committed to preventing it from continuing. They prioritised agriculture alongside infrastructure at the top of the development agenda, and when they met in Maputo in 2003 they committed themselves to increasing the budget allocation to agriculture by 10% within the next 5 years. There are already indications that most governments are moving towards this commitment and NEPAD is highly delighted that the international community are beginning to acknowledge that something needs to be done to focus attention on agriculture. Within such official development agencies as those of Germany, France and the United States of America I think there is also now acknowledgement that this should be done. Indeed, the World Bank itself is also saying we need to get the agriculture sector moving again. But I think the challenge is how is this going to be done, and where our focus should really be. And this is why I think it becomes extremely important that various knowledge institutions and practitioners on the ground really begin to share information. The NEPAD Secretariat have written to the Minister for Overseas Development, the Right Honorable Hilary Benn, requesting him to ensure that agriculture is placed on the agenda of the Group of Eight (G8) industrialised nations at their meeting later this year that will be chaired by the UK Government. Within the context of the commitment by African leadership to specifically address agriculture, a framework document, the *Comprehensive Africa Agriculture Development Programme* has been prepared and was endorsed in Maputo in 2003. A number of countries and regional economic communities are beginning to align their programmes to this document that was produced through a wide range of consultative processes within Africa and is thus a truly 'home-grown' product – not one from the Food and Agriculture Organization of the United Nations (FAO) or the World Bank – it is a document from Africa that actually brings together various interest groups to pay special attention to common areas of interest. It identifies four 'pillars': land and water, market access and infrastructure develop-ment, addressing full security, and science and technology. So we are very pleased that this seminar is concentrating on market access and infrastructure develop-ment, and we hope to learn what is actually taking place on the ground and about some of the challenges that confront small-scale producers in accessing markets. We know that in Africa the withdrawal of the public-sector parastatals has affect-ed markets and that the private sector has not been keen to fill that vacuum. This is a challenge we need to address. But how? Are there innovative ways of actu-ally ensuring that small-scale producers are linked to markets? There is general agreement that Africa is going to evolve as one of the largest markets for its own products in the next decade or so and it is therefore very important that within Africa itself inter-regional trade is strongly promoted.

NEPAD would like to find out how institutions, particularly in the North can assist us in working together to document what is working on the ground. Despite the picture that has been painted of Africa there are actually pockets of successes out there, but these have not been well documented and perhaps insuffi-ciently explored for scaling up. The work being undertaken by Natural Resources International in this area is commendable and I hope that this meeting will come to a consensus on how these efforts can be continuously supported by documen-tation that enables the exchange of experiences across Africa. NEPAD can play a key role by facilitating mutual learning between regional economic communities, national governments, and institutions in the UK and elsewhere. We would like to make a special appeal to DFID to allocate resources to those institutions that are engaged in the process of documentation, sharing experiences and network-ing because we believe that is one way we can begin to make a difference in Africa. We would like to commend NR International, and the Intermediate Technology Development Group (ITDG) for hosting this meeting and hope to engage further with them because we are committed to partnerships and to the promotion of the best practices that I believe will be shared during this meeting.

From the African side our leadership are absolutely committed to making sure that there is a change in the circumstances of small-scale producers, and to en-suring that there is a new beginning in the way of doing business in Africa, by ad-dressing issues that confront small-scale producers, and by ensuring that various new alliances that are emerging, i.e., that the private sector, non-governmental organisations and other players, begin to make a contribution to raising issues of poverty and hunger in Africa. This meeting will assist us in further articulating a new development agenda in Africa in terms of how best we can improve the well-being of the majority of small-scale producers. I hope that by its end we will be on common ground as to how we can make a difference to the vast majority of the people in Africa who are living under enormous deprivation. And we hope again that the international community will continue to pay attention to these critical issues.

Keynote address

Mandi Rukuni

Introduction

In this keynote address we should bear in mind that there are four main themes to this seminar and that they have been addressed in the papers that were circulated to you.

The four themes are:

- **Building linkages and enhancing trust between small-scale rural producers, buyers in growing markets, and suppliers of critical inputs**
- **Supporting small-scale producers to associate, collaborate and coordinate to achieve economies of scale in their transactions with buyers (or suppliers)**
- **Making channels of information and market intelligence (e. g., about product specifications, market prices) accessible to rural producers**
- **Enabling rural producers to understand and better satisfy the product, process or delivery standards required by buyers.**

When I considered the first theme about building linkages and enhancing trust between smallholders I thought that during our deliberations we should focus on the issues of linkages and trust. The second theme with which the papers are very concerned is economies of scale issues that are extremely important when we talk about collaboration and collective action etc. When considering information and knowledge, if there is one underlying strategic issue, it is the use of knowledge by the groups that we would like to support and this is what I will use as my underlying issue to cut across all the themes. We should not forget that delivery standards include not only infrastructure issues, but also building skills among the smallholders, farmers and dealers that we are trying to help get into the market.

There is strong evidence in the papers that we are trying to help poor smallholder farmers and dealers to help themselves, and that there are three ways of assisting them to do this by:

- Improving collective action
- Building capacity to use knowledge to transform power
- Aligning the groups with global and meta trends.

Core theory of success

Collective action all starts with the quality of relationships we are building in any group or individuals we expect to be effective, either as a commodity association or any other force that is going to take on the market. The quality of relationships is not always a numbers game because the higher the quality of relationships then the higher the quality of collective thinking. It is not always collective action but collective thinking that counts, and collective thinking is dependent on high-quality dialogue and interaction. High-quality collective thinking leads to high-quality action and therefore high-quality results. To achieve success in building strong collective action credibilities, we need to start by understanding how relationships lead to success.

Collective action is one of the silent themes that came through all the papers. Is it the economic interests of groups that make up the primary force that leads to powerful cohesive groups, or is it social and/or political issues? The evidence seems to support the idea that economic interests are more likely to coerce groups together much more quickly and much more strongly, so that they are able subsequently to deal with social and political issues.

At the Kellogg Foundation we have put a lot more emphasis on supporting commodity groups and commodity associations rather than farmer's unions that tend to be a lot of political hot air! Farmer's unions can be pretty powerful, they can open doors, they can go to the Minister and the Minister will pay attention, but quite often they don't understand the business or the market. When we are talking about increasing the competitiveness of these commodity groups, reducing their transaction costs and helping them to understand better how to add value, I would say very strongly that it is not always going to be possible nor desirable to try to get into the external markets, because charity begins at home and if there is a lot more exchange of goods and services at the village level this kindles understanding and the local market will help to grow the competencies of these budding businesses.

If one compares Africa and South Asia, I think the extended family is being under-utilised as the primary business force in Africa where we only use it for funerals and weddings. At least the Asians still use it for business, and they are very astute. It is not just about getting information, or knowledge about the markets, it is about actually building real practical skills to be able to do so many of the tasks necessary to be good players of the market. People need to understand both the formal and informal rules that apply in the market. This is possible with collective action. It is not a numbers game, most of us here work for non-governmental organisations and government and so on, so we hold certain values and we are not always comfortable dealing with commercial entities, particularly when they are fairly aggressive. It is a dog-eat-dog world, not pretty for most of us, but it is the world we live in. When we talk about the ability of a group of individuals to actually understand and have the knowledge and information and capacities to deal with the market, it is not always going to be because of the numbers, it is a knowledge issue. That is why I am emphasising knowledge, and when it comes to knowledge, certainly the majority is not always right, otherwise we would still believe the world was flat!

So – even if it is a tough world – we are still trying to empower these groups, and starting again with a simple model, there are only four sources of power in the world:

- Violence
- Politics
- Money
- Knowledge.

Among these violence is unfortunately the most widely used, and then politics is the next – and those of you who really know will agree that politics is a form of official and organised violence Money is the third most important source of power and finally, knowledge is the fourth. But as you all appreciate, knowledge is the only source of power that does not diminish when you share it. Everything else, if you share you lose something – that's why at the end of the day knowledge is the most powerful force.

Here are a few insights on the transformative power of knowledge from the circulated papers that are dealing with issues not in terms of case studies, findings and insights but right at the cutting edge.

- We need to move from tacit to explicit and systematic knowledge
- Learning how to learn is vital
- Learning is largely a social process (participation).

One of the issues that we face is – How do we quickly move from tacit knowledge to explicit and systematic knowledge? Because most of the papers are loaded with what I would still consider tacit knowledge, i.e., knowledge that exists mostly in the heads of people but has not yet been translated to prototypes. How do you actually mass translate this type of knowledge for ordinary people who want to use the information? Although we may be pre-occupied with 'information and knowledge' when we translate this to the groups we are trying to assist, we actually need to know how we build their capacity to learn fast so they can get from information to knowledge through the following steps:

- From 'frameworks ' to 'prototypes '
- From 'first generation ' to 'second generation ' knowledge
- Action learning–outcome-based learning (information–knowledge–skills–values).

I don't think it is how much information such groups can access all the time, it is about how they learn and re-learn quickly, building their capacities to learn, and once again acknowledging that learning is largely a social process; that is why in most of the papers there is a mention of participation. Participatory process are discussed in the papers, and as I said earlier participation, for us in the non-profit world is soothing – it makes us feel we are being democratic, it is part of value-based leadership and inclusive. But at the end of the day if you are going to make it in the market you also need results-based leadership, so the social process must encompass both capacity to embrace and be democratic as well as capacity to allow great ideas to surface and move the groups forward. That is why it becomes important to separate political organisation from business leadership of groups, otherwise if you mix the two you will have problems.

We have to move from information to knowledge because knowledge is the application of information and a lot of information that exists in developing countries today, certainly in rural groups, is very difficult to translate into action.

Information needs to be packaged in a way that allows those who take action to move from frameworks and concepts to prototypes. This is a way of simplifying the way that knowledge is applied because if we can build one or two prototypes, even from the knowledge that we have in this meeting, at least two or three good prototypes could be built. If you want to build a successful commodity association these are the proven steps you should take.

It is then necessary to move from first-generation to second-generation knowledge, because with only first-generation knowledge you don't have the confidence to recommend or replicate. In our discussions we should identify what comes through most of the cases presented that leads us to confidence in making a recommendation.

Also coming through the papers strongly is that action learning as an important way for farmers to learn. Most of you will be familiar with this framework for knowledge, basically it is arguing that since we are spending most of the time in the top left-hand column sharing and networking, a lot of the tacit knowledge is just not documented. It needs to be documented in a fashion that allows those who are likely to use it to: bench-mark, compare, contrast, and combine it with what else they have, so that it can be translated into forms that go into skills development.

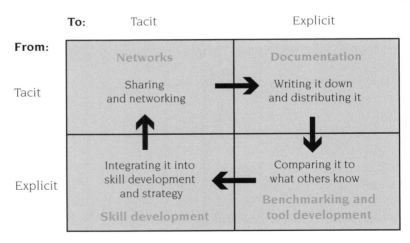

Basis of understanding markets and deal-making

Strategic use of knowledge

There are three levels of progress. When it comes to the market a lot of people in Africa, I think, are the worst marketeers in the world. We are the most brilliant artists, we make great things, but we struggle when it comes to marketing them. One of two things happens: either we fail to establish a production process that allows us to replicate the products to specific standards that are required by the market, or if somebody succeeds with their product locally then everyone tries to go for the same thing!

By **strategic use of knowledge** I think we need to move to what I'm calling improvement change, in other words, how do we actually make maximum use of the existing knowledge that these farmers already have in trying to get to the markets from the known to the unknown?

At the second level we are trying to build their capacity for intelligent borrowing, at that stage it is really 'copying from the best in the class.' It's the quickest way to get to the top, but we know that some people are more intelligent at borrowing than others, and I think here the Asians have been better than Africans, so we need to see more intelligent borrowing in Africa.

At the highest level is the mindset change, being able to move from the known to the unknown.

Arbitrage

Arbitrage involves information – knowledge – skills – rules/values, e.g., for cross-border trading. In traditional societies it requires a lot of self-confidence to believe that you can see the world differently from the way you did not so long ago, and that you can go from these ideas to the markets and can ultimately be the best. In terms of the market, no matter how sophisticated your ideas, marketing boils down to arbitrating because if there is a deficit over here but there is a surplus over there, and I can go and pick it up from over there and bring it over here and make money, that's marketing!

This is the basis of understanding markets and deal making and deal-making skills and it is extremely important for these groups that we are trying to promote. We could build a lot of other skills, but I often find in the work that I am doing in southern African that these groups lack the capacity to structure deals and enter into heavy-duty contracts.

The golden triangle

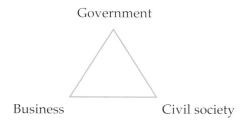

In the developing regions, quite often government and business don't see eye-to-eye on what needs to be done for the development agenda for poor people. And then civil society quite often doesn't trust either government or business. So as long as government policies are tentative because they really don't understand what is happening – the government then becomes schizophrenic so that during the day they will say all sorts of populist things about "Well they don't really believe in the market forces....they need to moderate," they just kind of get a bit mushy, but some of them believe in the market and they will be doing their deals at night, so no one is getting anywhere! I believe that some of the ideas we are talking about require hard-nosed dialogue between these three groups and between the countries and the regions and I think the network process will help us to make progress towards this.

Trends in public spending on agriculture in Africa

The trend is still downwards in terms of public-sector spending on agriculture in Africa. It decreased from 7.5% to 6% between 1980 and 1998 so in spite of all the declarations such as the Lagos Plan of Action in 1980 that said: 'Take it up to 10%' it is still going down and the share of agriculture expenditure in total government expenditure has also decreased from 6.27% to 4.88% during the same period. If you look at the Asian countries that managed to pull themselves out of poverty, they were averaging 15.4% of total government expenditure into agriculture in 1972, so we do have a long way to go in Africa. Just as an example on infrastructure, if we look at the road densities that we have to achieve in Africa to be at the same stage India was in the 1950s, for some countries a 10-fold increase is needed. Africa is a larger continent than Asia geographically, distances are greater, but we have the lowest rural road densities so how do we get to the markets?

Some of the meta trends do work in favour of poor farmers who are trying to get to the market, cultural diversity elements, the growing demand of natural products in the world, and the realisation – even in the United States whose government refuses to sign the Kyoto agreement – that big business is now able to prove that sustainability pays. So it should be possible in future for organic agriculture and environmentally friendly products and services to get our poor farmers into the big markets.

In conclusion

I am going to leave you with a couple of African philosophies for collective action. The thing about development, particularly building capacity and competence to play hard on the market does not happen overnight, you really just have to be patient and go for the long haul, because things take time and that's what termites have done. Termites are masters of collective action, they can bring down a building and you don't even know it. They get organised, they've got great leaders, they know exactly where to go and you think you've got a big beautiful building but one day you make the mistake of leaning on a wall..... and everything falls down! So I think we need a lot of hard work, the termite philosophy, and to identify the long-term investment issues that we need to make these endeavours a success.

Then lastly there is the African feast – termites are the competitive side of collective action – but then there is a nicer side. The African feast is the exact opposite. The whole community knows that on Saturday there is to be a great feast at such and such a location. Every household brings something. You bring what you have and take what you need. This is how knowledge is going to help, transform and empower the poor people of the region.

So we should build linkages and trust, but should beware of the conspiracies of silence – because if people don't trust you they may not tell you everything that you need to know to help them. Because they are used to being disadvantaged, rural people and poor people can sometimes conspire not to speak. I have emphasised economies of scale as opposed to economies of size just to ensure that although I believe that big business has a large role to play, we have to distinguish how we scale things up for small-scale producers as opposed to economies of size, which are more important for the larger firms. Coupled with enhanced networking, deal-making skills and technologies for delivery, we have many contributions to bring to the feast.

Theme papers

Building linkages and enhancing trust between small-scale rural producers, buyers in growing markets and suppliers of critical inputs

Rupert Best, Shaun Ferris and Antonio Schiavone

Introduction

There is growing consensus that agricultural growth is critical to meet the ambitious Millennium Development Goal of eradicating extreme poverty and hunger. Global studies highlight that the distribution and incidence of poverty is predominantly a rural problem and that it is increasingly concentrated in South Asia and sub-Saharan Africa. Likewise, the United Nations Millennium Project's Task Force on Hunger (2005) estimate that half of the world's 852 million chronically or acutely malnourished population live in smallholder farming households, two-tenths are landless, one-tenth are pastoralists, fisherfolk, and forest users. The remainder, around two-tenths, live in rapidly spreading urban slum areas.

In sub-Saharan Africa where poverty is increasing in many countries, the Food and Agriculture Organization of the United Nations (FAO) estimate that 64% of the total population are directly involved in agriculture as their primary source of income and livelihood. Projections by the World Bank to the year 2015 show that the people living in absolute poverty in sub-Saharan Africa will increase by 25% from 315 million in 1999 to 404 million in 2015 (World Bank, 2003).

The achievement of agricultural growth in general, and smallholder agricultural growth in particular, requires a balanced set of measures at all levels from international trade to national, and household levels. Peacock et al. (2004) in their report on Investment in Smallholder Agriculture in sub-Saharan Africa identify and focus on four core and priority components needed to develop farmers' capacity to respond to new opportunities and thereby provide the foundations for a 'pathway out of poverty.' These are:

- Empowered and enabled rural poor
- Access to land and water resources
- Effective and efficient front-line support services
- Improved and accessible rural infrastructure.

The concern for the provision of 'effective and efficient front-line support services' is mirrored in the sixth of seven recommendations made by the UN Millennium Project's Task Force on Hunger (2005), which urges governments to 'increase incomes and make markets work for the poor' through a series of interventions that are oriented primarily to improving the availability and access of rural communities and their enterprises to a range of essential services. Finally, the Rural Economic and Enterprise Development (REED) framework developed by a working group of donor and international technical assistance institutions, also identifies 'access to effective and efficient support services and resources' as one of the ten cornerstones for successful intervention that seek to promote economic rural growth (GTZ, 2003).

From the foregoing it is evident that:

1. Concerted efforts need to be made to address poverty and hunger, and that efforts up to now have not been sufficiently effective, particularly in Africa
2. Market orientation to agricultural production is vital if the growth necessary to improve the livelihoods of the rural poor is to be achieved
3. A key component to establishing and strengthening the links of farmers with markets is the provision of a range of effective and efficient support services.

The agreement that market orientation is vital presupposes that smallholder farmers have unreserved access to market opportunities. In reality, trade liberalisation and the increasing concentration and vertical integration of markets means that, even if smallholder farmers target domestic rather than international markets, agricultural and trade policies in third countries, and particularly developed countries, affect the opportunities open to smallholder farmers. In addition, there are many sensitive domestic political and social reasons in developed countries for avoiding changes in the status quo. For example, opening more favourable markets for developing countries in Organization for Economic Cooperation and Development (OECD) markets will lead to a loss in jobs, cause significant changes in rural economies and possibly to increased food and agricultural product prices.

Whilst the authors recognise the major inequities with market access at the meso and macro levels, this paper starts from the premise that promotion, establishment and strengthening of rural agro-enterprises are essential components of both local and national development. They believe that success in agro-enterprise development will improve household food security, income and employment. If correctly managed this approach will empower rural communities to increasingly become agents of their own change and contribute towards a shift from risk to resilience. The paper focuses on building local entrepreneurial and leadership skills, improving social linkages and enhancing trust among actors and between stakeholders involved in development.

The situation analysis provided by the papers mentioned earlier and the interventions recommended suggest that the agricultural research and development (R&D) community knows *what* needs to be done to move forward. The question that now arises is whether it knows *how* to move forward and achieve at different levels – macro (political), meso (institutional) and micro (farmer–market) – changes in practice, attitude and behaviour that will lead to the interventions having the desired outcomes in terms of reducing poverty and hunger. The authors' focus is on the 'how' of implementing change in development situations, based on their experience, and to the extent possible, to compare and contrast such experience with that of others.

What are the challenges?

There are many and varied challenges to growth in smallholder agriculture, among them are the following:

- **Low-value goods.** The majority of farm families have been accustomed to producing basic staples for their own subsistence, with a little surplus for sale to provide them with the cash to buy clothes, food items that they cannot produce themselves, and to access essential health and educational services.
- **Market pressure.** Since the collapse of government-led agricultural support programmes in the 1970s, structural adjustment and market liberalisation has meant that smallholder farm families in developing countries face the ever-increasing imperative of incorporating themselves into the market economy in order to generate sufficient cash income that will allow them to access essential basic needs and thereby improve their livelihood.
- **Undermining existing markets.** At the same time that governments have reduced their role in the food market, relief agencies have significantly increased their supply of free or highly subsided imported food into developing countries. In a bid to avoid criticism for not meeting the needs of food-insecure communities, agencies such as the World Food Programme (WFP) have become formidable procurement agents that are able to react to food needs and raise cash more rapidly than local private sectors. In many cases this has meant that local marketing structures and systems are being bypassed and eroded by the very agents that aim to assist developing countries.
- **Oversupplied markets.** The success of many international development programmes at the production level has led to oversupply of many global commodity markets. Support to new entrants in the coffee market led to the virtual collapse of economies in Eastern Africa and there are no immediate market options for the farmers who relied on these markets for their income and the governments who relied upon the taxation of such goods for their support and debt-repayment programmes.
- **Decline in commodity prices.** Even so-called 'cash crops' have experienced price declines in real terms over the past two decades. Trade liberalisation and globalisation, coupled with the improved production efficiency of medium- to large-scale producers and oversupply of such major commodities as coffee, cotton, palm oil and rubber, some of which are important smallholder crops, has led to an increasingly harsh and competitive marketing reality. Prices for the top-10 traded tropical agricultural commodities are currently at a 40-year low and many farmers are removing perennial tree crops because prices have fallen below production costs.
- **Inconsistent policy.** There is growing evidence that attempts to alleviate poverty and hunger through interventions targeted at improving staple cash-crop production are also flawed. Government programmes to increase the productivity and production of such staples as maize, through the provision of seed, fertilisers and credit have proved that it is possible to increase production when agro-climatic conditions are favourable. However, the partial nature of these interventions, with no medium- to long-term vision or support for the development of sustainable local or regional markets, or adequate and transparent management of strategic grain reserves, result in a quick reverse of seemingly

positive outcomes in terms of productivity into situations where farmers loose money and are unable to repay loans and countries continue to require food aid, as evidenced in Ethiopia in 2000/1 and 2001/2 and in Malawi in 2001–03 (G.Gray, Catholic Relief Services, personal communication; Government of Malawi, 2004).

- **Lack of market information.** Most farmers receive no information about changes in the value of their products, whereas traders have reasonably rapid access to such trade-based information. This skew in access to basic market information has been cited as a major impediment to empowering farmers to negotiate for better prices and thus to build market confidence and trade links. Despite the low cost of such services few governments are investing in them to support the farming community.
- **Poor organisation.** Farmers in many countries are poorly organised. This lack of scale means that trade suffers from poor quality, low volume, and weak links and is often uncompetitive because of the consequent high transaction costs. The lack of organisation within the agricultural sector in many developing countries, and particularly in Africa, is often blamed on the collapse of the government-led co-operative systems, through poor management and lack of marketing skills. In many countries this has led to a long-term distrust of farmers working together.
- **Declining infrastructure.** Farmers are finding it increasingly difficult to compete in national and regional markets due to their poor access to such infrastructure as roads, storage facilities, power and transportation. As poverty increases in many parts of Africa, these facilities are decreasing and therefore many communities are less able to engage in more distant markets than before.
- **Shocks.** Some of the most severe constraints to developing growth markets in many developing countries are based on natural and civil shocks. These severe impediments are caused by: drought, floods, war, political and religious disputes, the devastating effects of a host of diseases such as HIV/AIDs and malaria, and by attacks from such pests as locusts and grain borers.
- **New trends in the wholesale and retail sectors.** In addition to all of these major hurdles to growth in the small-scale sector, there are also significant changes in how goods are traded and the regulations that restrict access to these rapidly growing markets. At the wholesale level, consolidation or merging of buyers has meant that market power has shifted out of the hands of producers to the large corporations who bulk buy goods. In the retail sector, the rise of the supermarkets has also meant that it is now possible to monitor supply chains and contracts are only given to those producers who meet increasingly stiff international food-safety standards.

Meeting the challenges

Despite the worrying nature of these challenges there are many examples of smallholder farmers confronting them through projects that work in a systematic manner to address the basic problems in engaging the marketplace. The strategies used in these projects typically employ the following approaches:

- Increasing competitiveness through achieving economies of scale and value addition by collective action and improved production, post-production handling and processing, and marketing. An example is provided in Box 1 that describes the creation of a new market for cassava in the northern coastal part of Colombia that required innovations in production, processing and marketing.
- Diversifying their production, by incorporating higher-value crops or livestock activities that have an identified demand. Box 2 summarises the experience of the Usambara Lishe Trust in bringing together small-scale farmers to produce and market a wide range of vegetable crops to satisfy the needs of a particular segment of the Dar es Salaam market in Tanzania.

Box 1. Cassava chipping and drying in the northern coastal area of Colombia

Over the period 1981 to 1989, the Integrated Cassava Research and Development (ICRD) Project of Colombia's Integrated Rural Development Programme was implemented in northern Colombia as an inter-related set of institutional, organisational and technological interventions designed to link small-scale cassava farmers, with and without land, to expanding markets. By 1993, 101 small, farmer-run cooperatives and 37 private individuals had established cassava chipping and sun-drying plants for the production of dry cassava chips for the animal feed industry. These plants annually produced 35,000 mt of dry cassava valued at US\$ 6.2 million. It is estimated that 36% of small-scale cassava farmers in the region sold cassava to drying plants and that 15% of such farmers belonged to a cooperative. A study undertaken in the year 2000 assessed the project's impact on participating communities in terms of poverty alleviation, and identified the avenues by which the project was able to bring about positive changes. The study shows that agricultural R&D interventions can contribute tangibly to poverty alleviation when the following conditions are met:

a. Market and post-harvest technology R&D are integrated with production-oriented R&D
b. Inter-institutional partnerships are developed whereby different institutions with complementary expertise, comparative advantages and mandates collaborate to respond to the demands of local community organisations and individuals
c. Existing social and human capital is used to create intimate networking among institutions, local social organisations, and individuals.

Source: Gottret and Raymond, 2003

These examples of farmers moving from a subsistence, or household food security orientation to a greater level of market orientation illustrate the significant and major changes that are required in terms of how farmers and their communities see the world, relate to each other and interact with other actors beyond their communities. These changes mean that farmers must take on new skills to:

Box 2. Production and marketing of high-quality vegetables for the Dar es Salaam market

The West Usambara Mountains are located in the Tanga region of north-eastern Tanzania. Altitudes range from 450 to 2,400 masl, average annual rainfall is 600–2,000 mm, with temperatures between 16 and 22°C. In 2002, the total population of the area was estimated at 460,000 with farm sizes of 0.5 to 2.5 ha. Traditional staple crops were maize, beans and bananas; coffee and tea were introduced in the colonial era and missionaries introduced the first vegetable seeds. Over a 20-year period, from 1981 to 2000, the Soil Erosion Control and Agro-forestry Project (SECAP) supported by Deutsche Gesellschaft für Technische Zusammenarbeit (GTZ) GmbH promoted integrated, holistic, soil and water conservation approaches in selected watersheds using participatory forest management for village and local authority forest reserves. In 1993/4 consultants carried out a marketing survey in major urban centres and identified the potential for vegetables and fruits. Supported by SECAP, 100 farmers in 4 village 'societies' initiated production of 9 types of vegetables and in 1996 a first delivery of 300 kg was made to the Sheraton Hotel, Jangwami Sea Breeze Hotel and Masudi grocery in Dar es Salaam. When SECAP ended in 2000, 60 farmers, of whom 16 are women, established the Usambara Lishe Trust (ULT) as a non-governmental organisation (NGO). Today ULT produces over 100 different vegetable and fruits and markets 5–6 mt every week to 16 speciality market outlets in Dar es Salaam. ULT has established a reputation for producing high-quality vegetables and its legal status has facilitated access to credit. Major constraints to growth include weak horticultural extension, input and research services, especially for fruit trees where market opportunities are unrealised.

Source: Rimoy, 2003

- Identify the right product for the right buyer at the right price and time
- Establish production systems that make efficient and sustainable use of existing financial, human and natural resources
- Incorporate post-harvest handling, and possibly processing techniques so that their products meet buyers' requirements
- Improve business and marketing and organisational schemes that improve competitiveness by reducing costs and increasing marketable volumes
- Strengthen relations and links among market-chain actors
- Improve access to flows of both market-based information and new production and post-harvest handling technologies and financial services.

This transition for the majority of farmers, especially those located in more marginal areas and distant from markets, requires orientation and mentoring from development organisations, access to a range of public and private services (inputs, transport, information, finance, etc.) and a set of government policies that provide an enabling environment that supports business in remote locations (see the Market Map of Hellin et al., this volume, which clearly distinguishes between these levels). The REED framework mentioned earlier and the approach being used by the Centro Internacional de Agricultura Tropical's (CIAT) 'Territorial Approach to Rural Business Development', places these components within a defined spatial area, or 'territory'[1].

The territorial approach proposed by CIAT seeks to contribute to the development of local capacities to facilitate rural enterprise development in a flexible, dynamic and coordinated fashion (Lundy et al., 2005). This approach includes the following components (Figure 1):

1. The identification and strengthening of an interest or working group composed of diverse local organisations with common goals and strategies for rural enterprise development
2. Identification, management and development of market opportunities available to the region
3. Participatory production to market chain analysis, consensus building with diverse actors along the chain and design of a shared strategy to increase chain competitiveness
4. The implementation of the selected options that were identified and negotiated by the actors in the previous step
5. Identification and promotion of appropriate and sustainable business development services and markets for these services for the region.

Figure 1. Components of a territorial approach to rural business development

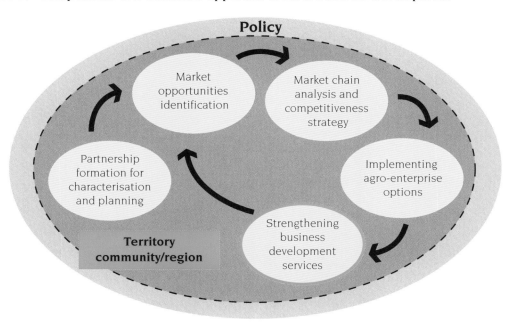

---

[1] A territory is here used to represent a geographical area bounded by administrative or agro-ecological limits. The minimum expression of a territory is the community or village. The maximum expression of a territory is usually determined by the reach, or radius of action of the support institutions or local government.

The entry point for this approach is the identification and consolidation of the local interest group. The other components are then subsequently developed in collaboration with that group. During the process, a number of policy – or enabling environment-related issues will be identified, and the local interest group needs to progressively incorporate these into their strategy and plan of action for the territory.

This example of an approach to agro-enterprise development is used to illustrate that at different stages of the process, relationships, linkages and trust need to be established among different actors. The principal instances are:

1. Formation of the interest group that seeks to develop a shared vision, strategy and plan of action for promoting agro-enterprises in the territory
2. Development and subsequent implementation of a shared strategy among market-chain actors to increase the competitiveness of one or several selected supply chains
3. Establishment of linkages between the demand and supply of business development services that may be delivered by providers from within or outside the territory.

In this paper, attention is principally concentrated on the second of these: the development and subsequent implementation of a shared strategy to increase the competitiveness of supply chains. In the concluding section, the relationships between other stakeholders that are important for the support to the agro-enterprise development process are briefly considered.

Linkages and trust: facilitators and champions

An important tool that is used in the analysis of market chains is the 'Market Map'. Figure 2 shows a market map drawn by producers, processors, traders and service providers belonging to a coffee market chain in Yorito, Honduras (see also Box 5). The map identifies the different actors, the linkages between them and values of coffee at different stages in the chain.

Market-chain analysis such as the one depicted, case studies by Rottger (2004) and Santacoloma and Riveros (2004) and support from the analysis of supply chains (Woods, 2004), identify two key actors in the process of enterprise development: the market or enterprise facilitator and the chain champion. The market facilitator role can be undertaken by a person from a local government or non-governmental organisation (NGO) belonging to the territory whose task – as the name suggests – is to facilitate processes that build relationships and increase trust between the different actors in the process of developing shared plans and identifying opportunities for long-term cooperation (Woods, 2004). In many respects the facilitator is seeking to improve the efficiency and value of goods supplied by a community within a given territory.

The chain champion on the other hand is a higher order player within the supply chain of a given sub-sector selected for intervention. The chain champion needs to have a vision of the opportunities that could arise from closer collaboration and is someone with the energy to organise and drive processes of relationship

Figure 2. A market map prepared by producers, processors, traders and service providers to the coffee market chain in Yorito, Honduras

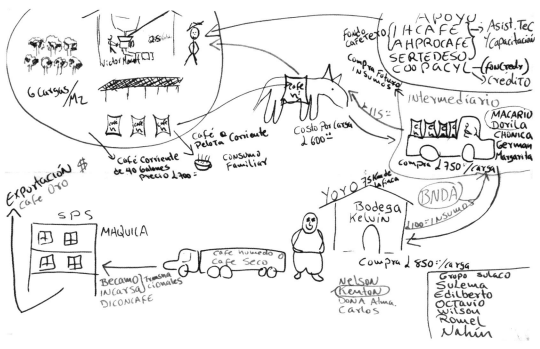

building (Woods, 2004). Ideally this person is from the private sector and has self-motivated incentives to achieve enhanced chain performance. Whereas the market facilitator has to be present right at the start of the enterprise development process, it is likely that a chain champion will only emerge once there becomes a clearer idea of the specific actors involved in the selected supply chain whose performance and operational effectiveness it is intended to improve. The chain champion need not necessarily reside in the territory. Box 3 illustrates typical roles of market facilitators and chain champions. The following section examines the steps in the agro-enterprise process and the part played by these two actors.

Building linkages: the development process

The partners in an interest group for agro-enterprise development need information on which to base sound decisions to make best use of and combine the territory's assets in order to exploit natural resources in a way that benefits the local economy. The inherent risks associated with adopting a market and enterprise orientation can be significantly reduced if time is spent in both generating appropriate information and subsequently planning actions based on the analysis of this information. Three major decision points can be identified:

Box 3. Market facilitators and chain champions

A facilitator: Africare and the Nyabyumba potato farmers

Since 2001in its Uganda country programme Africare, the international NGO, incorporated an explicit market and enterprise component into its activities in Kabale District, in the south west of the country. The objective was to build the capacity of their target communities in the identification of market opportunities, and the selection of attractive options that could then be built into enterprises. The Nyabyumba farmers, with whom Africare had been working in improving seed potato production through a farmers' field school, were anxious to assure a market for their seed potato by improving the market for ware potatoes. Supported by Berga Lemaga of the Association for Strengthening Agricultural Research in Eastern and Central Africa (ASARECA)'s Regional Potato Network, Stephen Tindimubona of the Ugandan National Seed Potato Producers' Association, Charles Musoke of Africare facilitated the process by which the group identified Nandos, the fast food chain, as a market that they could access. Since mid-2003 the Nyabyumba farmers have been able to supply consistently high-quality potatoes directly to this niche market. Africare and other service providers have facilitated the farmer group in the signing of contracts, the design of production and delivery mechanisms, the strengthening of the management of their organisation and through access to improved varieties and other inputs. As yet, a chain champion is not evident, and the nurturing of the gains achieved to date probably depends on the identification of such a person.

Source: Musoke et al., 2004

A champion: Tropical Wholefoods and dried fruit production and marketing

Tropical Wholefoods, under the direction of Adam Brett, is a small privately owned company, which focuses on fair trade. It has been successfully selling fairly traded products in the UK since 1992 and has been growing progressively ever since. The key products are dried tropical fruits and vegetables. The company works directly with farmers and farmer groups and presently they are importing from small fair-trade producers in Uganda, Burkina Faso, Pakistan and Zambia. The company identified the opportunity and characterised the demand for dried fruit in a wide range of products and selected the most promising for development. Tropical Wholefoods supports their drying enterprises through helping them to access technical assistance, training and credit.

Source: Tropical Wholefoods. 2003. E-guide and resource pack. CD-rom

A champion: Uganda Grain Traders Association

In 2002, the maize sector in Uganda reached a critical juncture. In that year, the country experienced a bumper maize grain harvest, which was intended to supply the food relief markets and to be sold into Kenya. However, in 2002, Kenya, which normally experiences a 200–300,000 mt annual maize deficit, had an unexpected surplus. Prices crashed and farmers were left unpaid. At this point, John Magnay, the chief executive of a local family input supply business, stepped in, set up a local consortium of grain traders and asked the Government of Uganda to provide an emergency line of credit to buy up to 50,000mt of grain. Facilitated by the Ministry of Trade, Magnay then set up a series of meetings with government representatives from Malawi and Zambia, countries that had experienced severe drought and crop failure. A deal was struck and 30,000mt of grain was sold in Zambia. The effect was to take the slack out of the Ugandan market and rebuild confidence amongst the farmers.

Since that time, Magnay has formalised the traders' consortium under the Uganda Grain Traders logo, UGT, and has continued to buy and sell on behalf of this group in the East African region. John has led several campaigns to improve marketing of grains, among them: a. improving national storage, with a US$ 3M state of the art storage facility in Kampala, b. supporting the Regional Agricultural Trade Intelligence Network (RATIN), c. sensitising informal and formal traders on grain quality, particularly for export, and d. establishing a risk fund to support more formal regional trading of Uganda maize grain. Magney represents Uganda Grain Traders at regional and national forums. He is thus becoming a chain champion for maize, beans and rice trading in Uganda, seeking to make these more formal and lucrative sub-sectors for the producing and trading communities.

Source: S. Ferris, CIAT, personal communication

1. At the outset: what to produce, where to produce and with whom to produce; this determines the sub-sectors and products with which to work
2. Once sub-sectors have been chosen: what actions and activities need to be undertaken to develop or strengthen them
3. Once enterprises are up and running: what needs to be done to maintain and enhance their competitiveness.

    Information can be gathered and socialised in different ways, and a distinction is made between 'contracted' information gathering and the use of participatory methods where the beneficiaries of the enterprise development play a key, if not central, role in the information collection and analysis process. In the former – contracted studies – experts are hired, sometimes to work with local counterparts and sometimes in total independence, to collect and analyse the information required. Both means are equally valid when they are used in the correct context and at the right hierarchical level. Participatory processes, if well applied, generate ownership of the results by the intended beneficiaries, introduce new skills and capacity, and build the confidence of the participants, which in turn leads to empowerment. The use of experts has the advantage that since information gathering is extractive in nature, the studies can usually be undertaken more quickly, and they can go to greater depth and breadth. In any situation it is likely that a combination of the two approaches will be required.

Selecting products and sub-sectors: matching market opportunities with assets and skills

The selection of products and sub-sectors with which to intervene is a critical and highly strategic step. It involves three inter-related sets of activities:

1. Having a clear understanding of the livelihood assets (natural, physical, human, social and financial) of the communities that make up the territory object of the intervention, placing special emphasis on our target client groups, (their social ranking, investment options, leadership and business skills, traditions and aspirations).
2. Having knowledge of the opportunities afforded by markets within the territory itself, in adjacent territories, extending from the local to the regional, country, and in some cases to the international level.
3. The selection of attractive enterprise options for subsequent development into supply chains balancing the following criteria:
   - Strength of market demand in terms of volumes and prices
   - Production feasibility in the territory given the biophysical conditions, infrastructure, access to productive resources and existing livelihood strategies
   - The interest to the smallholders who are to benefit by the interventions
   - Profitability versus investment and risk of the enterprise, ensuring compatibility with the means and aspirations of the target population.

Working together to initiate the information gathering process: the interest group

In a highly competitive market environment, the selection of sub-sectors is key to both developing sustainable competitive advantage for the territory (and the farmers involved) and for making sure that benefits can accrue to the more marginalised in the community. Local facilitating organisations, including local government, should work together in developing an appropriate rural enterprise strategy for a given territory. Too often local development agencies work independently and at times compete against each other, and adopt perverse practices that hinder enterprise development. Peacock et al. (2004) highlight the need for coordination among service providers and Lundy et al. (2004) have developed a sequence of steps by which the interest or working group of like-minded research and development practitioners can arrive at a common vision and plan of action for promoting enterprise development in a territory. The opportunity for working together to develop a common strategy has the added advantage of identifying complementarities in the skills of different institutions, while at the same time breaking down institutional barriers and building levels of trust. The process has to be catalysed and initially convened by an institution that sees the potential benefits for achieving the goals of the institution through partnership.

Characterising assets and potential beneficiaries

Methods and tools used for the characterisation of livelihood assets are well documented (Scoones, 1998). Often characterisation includes wellbeing or wealth ranking to profile rural inhabitants. For agro-enterprise-related interventions a profiling of smallholder farmers and other agriculturally related actors such as processors, according to their relative level of market orientation and organisation is needed. It can be helpful to categorise rural producers according to four agro-enterprise development phases based on: their degree of organisation, the level of integration with the market, the types of technology employed, and their access to support services. Table 1 shows for each stage some of the pre-conditions that can orient the enterprise-development process. The underlying assumption of this profiling is that smallholders need to form groups to effectively access markets. Internal cohesion and trust within groups and between groups of farmers, and building their enterprise orientation are major challenges (see Biénabe and Sautier, this volume).

In any territory it may be possible to identify groups of farmers and other rural actors that correspond to all four development phases. In the poor and more remote rural areas, it is likely that the majority of farmers will be in the subsistence and early stages of the development gradient. However, it should be noted that the most vulnerable sector of the population will be landless – this sector does not appear in this scheme, but they probably derive their livelihood from selling labour to enterprises that are in development stages 2, 3 and 4.

Identifying market opportunities and selecting products

Methods and tools for market opportunity identification and evaluation that can be used to select sub-sectors are less well known or employed. Often only secondary information and local knowledge are used to draw up a long list of options that are then subjected to evaluation using pre-determined criteria (Lusby and Panlibuton, 2002). This approach has the risk of: a. being over influenced by supply side criteria, b. overlooking emerging market opportunities, or c. basing decisions on out-of-date information. Ostertag et al. (2004) provide a method for market opportunity identification that can be designed to meet the specific needs of a particular territory. It involves a rapid market survey followed by an evaluation of each of the most promising products identified against market, production and financial criteria. The options that do not meet these criteria are discarded. The products that remain are then subjected to participatory evaluation to identify those that are most attractive to the target farmers, based on the criteria that the farmers themselves consider to be most important.

This method requires that the persons undertaking the study have skills in conducting market surveys, have basic crop and livestock management knowledge, and are capable of undertaking simple financial analysis. When this type of study is conducted in urban centres that access food supplies from different areas, it will provide information useful for a number of territories and not only the one that is the target of the intervention. In Kampala, the method was employed to identify market opportunities for urban and peri-urban farmers (Nyapendi et al., 2003), and then expanded to provide the National Agricultural Advisory Services (NAADS) with market information on the products selected for development by NAADS-assisted farmers from different districts during their preferred enterprise selection process (Nyapendi et al., 2004).

The principles of the Ostertag method can be adapted for use by a market facilitator at the community level where levels of farmer or other rural producer participation can be increased (Best, 2003; Sanginga et al., 2004a). In this case, it is usual for the community or farmer organisation to elect a group of 4 to 6 farmers to represent

Table 1. Evolutionary stages, or profiles, of smallholder farmers and the degree of maturity of their agroenterprises

Stage	Characteristics	Pre-conditions to enterprise development
1. Subsistence	Individual farmers producing predominantly for their own consumption, selling small surpluses to local markets. Precarious to non-existent access to services and no use of purchased inputs. Low asset accumulation, most vulnerable.	This type of community may require specialist intervention that can be considered as pre-enterprise oriented. Many agencies supply such communities with support processes such as re-stocking assets after a social/natural shock. This may include provision of: a. food aid, b. seeds, tools, livestock, inputs, c. conflict resolution, d. safety-net clauses and interventions.
2. Early stage	Small-scale rural enterprises with low levels of value addition and weak business orientation and incipient social cohesion among group members. Access to services is incomplete and irregular which limits enterprise growth prospects.	Communities at this stage are well positioned to benefit from enterprise-oriented interest groups, i.e., co-ordination of agencies that have a common interest in market-oriented processes. Service providers should review their competence and staff profiles to ensure quality of marketing services.
3. Developing	Commercially oriented enterprises with higher levels of social cohesion that have incorporated value adding, handling and/or transformation processes, and product diversification. Selling into local, regional and national markets. Have access to appropriate services that permit enterprise growth.	These groups will require specialist support in areas of enterprise growth. Service providers and their interest group members should develop strategies that bring specifically needed skills to bear. This may include such aspects as market information, finances, new product development, etc.
4. Mature	Farmer enterprises are fully integrated into supply chains producing products that meet market demands in terms of quality and frequency of supply, both nationally and for export. Are capable of identifying and paying for required business development services.	These groups will require support in areas of business management and are likely to be interested in risk capital ventures that will provide them with a forward looking edge in the marketplace. Increasing use of information and communication technologies (ICTs) to support enterprise development and growth.

Source: IFDC, 2003

them in undertaking the market opportunity identification and enterprise selection process, periodically providing feedback and consulting with the larger group.

Because of the logistic and cost implications of facilitating farmers to undertake this type of market research, the analysis is typically narrower, focusing on fewer product categories and market outlets, than the more formal survey described above. However, it has proved to be a powerful tool for expanding the horizon of farmers, opening their eyes to opportunities that they had never previously imagined. For many farmers it may be the first time that they have visited markets beyond their immediate locality and with a view to compare and contrast products rather than simply to negotiate prices for sale. When well conducted, the process of participatory market research and enterprise selection enhances farmers' understanding of the major purchasing conditions and requirements with respect to price, quality, volumes and frequency of delivery etc. It should also provide important contact information with traders who could in the future become purchasers of their produce, and is therefore a first step in forging potential market linkages. Box 4 describes how this process was undertaken with a community in Kabale District, Uganda.

Achieving balance among selection of sub-sectors

The selection of products and sub-sector(s) for development need to explicitly address how the selected farmer groups will benefit from either: a. establishing new, or b. increasing the operational effectiveness of existing productive activities, through improved market linkages. A strategy for a territory may focus on groups of farmers at a particular development stage, or may attempt to achieve benefits across development stages. Opportunities for directly incorporating the landless can be explicitly addressed. These might include activities that can be undertaken in reduced spaces, such as the rearing of small animals, production of mushrooms, herbs or medicinal plants. Alternatively, the strategy might be to develop new or existing enterprises, which through growth can provide employment opportunities for those without land. A dynamic local agricultural sector should provide opportunities for growth in local service provision (Poulton et al., 2001).

Planning for increased enterprise and supply chain competitiveness

Market chain and sub-sector studies

Following product selection, a more in-depth analysis of the supply chain or sub-sector[2], for the selected product(s) is required, through which specific actors are

---

[2] In this paper the following definitions are used: A sub-sector refers to all the actors and services that are financially and socially linked as products, information and finances flow from producers through intermediaries to consumers for a particular commodity. Usually a sub-sector analysis is undertaken at a national level. A market chain has a similar definition, but may be undertaken at more local level and provide a partial view of the total commodity sub-sector. Supply chains are market chains with a greater level of social and business integration between partners along the chain.

Box 4. Participatory market research for enterprise selection in Muguli B community, Kabale District, Uganda

Muguli B is a community of 47 farmers located in the hills of south-western Uganda that is supported by Africare. In 2001, the community initiated an integrated process to improve their capacity to identify and develop income-generating enterprises and improve their household food production through market research to select attractive options coupled with field experimentation of cash and food crops. The community selected five of their members to represent them in a marketing committee. This committee, facilitated by Africare, pre-selected six products on which to undertake market research: coffee, potato, pyrethrum, eggs, pork, and cabbages. These six were selected for their present cash income- generating potential (potato, cabbages) and because the farmers had observed that other farmers in the area were profitably producing the products (pyrethrum, coffee, pork and eggs). For each product, the members of the committee visited market outlets and gathered information on prices, volumes and frequency of delivery, quality requirements and payment conditions. Similarly they also visited farmers who were already producing the products commercially to collect information on production practices, inputs and costs. Armed with this information on markets and production, they calculated the cost–benefit ratio for each product. The results of the visits and the economic analysis were shared with the whole community who discussed and used their own criteria to evaluate the options. The community eventually selected pyrethrum and eggs for enterprise development. The advantages that they saw in these products were:

For pyrethrum:
• Its production and sale are economically attractive
• A local company purchases pyrethrum flowers. The company provides seed, technical assistance and collects the dried flowers at collection centres close to the areas of production
• Pyrethrum can be grown on high ground and in soils that are not so suitable for food crops, on farmers' lots that are under-utilised at present
• The women of the communities were favourably disposed to pyrethrum as they see it as an opportunity for men to become more engaged in agriculture, and hopefully spend less time in such unproductive activities as brewing and drinking.

For eggs:
• Their production is economically attractive and there is high demand for local eggs
• Poultry is an activity that can be undertaken close to the house and is easy to control
• The enterprise will provide an income-earning opportunity for women.

identified and characterised, relationships among actors are understood, bottle-necks are identified and actions for overcoming them proposed.

The area of market chain and sub-sector analysis has received considerable attention over the last decade and many methods and techniques are available (see the *Guide to Developing Agricultural Markets and Agro-enterprises* on the World Bank web page http://www.worldbank.org). The majority of methods are designed to be undertaken by professionals, and should capture information that characterises all three levels of the ITDG Market Map: the market chain itself, the business and extension services, and the factors in the enabling environment that affect the performance of the sub-sector (Hellin et al., this volume). Some methods, such as Holtzman (2002) provide the steps for generating information, but do not go into details of how to prioritise bottlenecks or constraints for subsequent implementation. The method described by Lusby and Panlibuton (2002) provides tools for prioritisation and pays special attention to business service assessment. These methods rely principally on secondary information, key informants, structured and semi-structured interviews and focus group discussions. They stress the need for 'a multidisciplinary person or team skilled in economic analysis, business needs assessment, participatory workshop facilitation, and enterprise development' (Lusby et al., 2002), and 'knowledgeable analysts' (Joss et al., 2002), with a 'cross-country comparative perspective' (Holtzman, 2002). The outputs are recommendations on:

- Policy and regulatory reforms
- Innovations in technology, institutional arrangements, and organisation or coordination of marketing functions
- Further, more focused research.

In East Africa, over a period of 5 years from 1999 ASARECA's FOODNET programme built a capacity for undertaking these types of studies and completed them for the major commodities of the region. There are plans to strengthen the capacity of the major agricultural universities in the region in the use of these techniques (S. Ferris, CIAT; personal communication).

If resources are available to undertake them, market chain/sub-sector studies provide a more complete picture of how the sub-sector operates. Such analyses provide a broad vision of the many different market opportunities and market chains that function for a particular product. These, options can be used to select the most appropriate market chain for the target beneficiaries.

The methods mentioned above are by and large extractive in nature and provide a bird's-eye perspective of a sub-sector. As such they characterise linkages between actors and at best observe whether trust exists or not. Supply chain management (SCM), a concept that has gathered pace over the past 15 years, goes beyond market chain or sub-sector analysis to look at 'the management of relationships between the businesses responsible for the efficient production and supply of agribusiness products from farm level to consumers, as a means of reliably meeting consumers' requirements in terms of quantity, quality and price' (Woods, 2004). The methods employed in SCM explicitly consider what is termed 'relationship marketing' with its three key constructs: satisfaction, trust and power-dependence (Batt, 2004). These constructs are considered in more detail in the following section on trust.

Table 2. Comparison of three participatory approaches to market chain analysis

Market analysis and development (FAO–CFU, RECOFTC, 2000)	Increasing the competitiveness of market chains for small-scale rural producers (Lundy et al., 2004)	Participatory market chain approach (Bernet et al., 2004)
Phase 1. Assess the existing situation • Identify the target group • Determine the financial objectives of the target group • List existing resources and products • Identify key constraints of the existing market system • Shortlist a range of products • Raise awareness of the benefits of working together **Phase 2. Identify products, markets and means of marketing** • Analyse the four areas of enterprise development • Select the most promising products • Create interest groups for selected products **Phase 3. Plan enterprises for sustainable development** • Examine the business environment of the selected products/enterprise • Define the enterprise mission, goal and objectives • Develop strategies in each of the four areas of enterprise development • Formulate the action plans to implement the strategies • Calculate financial projections for the enterprise • Obtain financing as specified in the capital needs statement • Initiate the pilot phase and training • Monitor progress and deal with change	**Phase 1. Preparation** • Select a market chain • Plan and execute a rapid market survey • Identify and convene key actors in the market chain **Phase 2. Information gathering** • Analyse participatory market chain • Form working groups by function • Map the market chain • Evaluate business development services • Document market chain history • Evaluate organisation strengths **Phase 3. Design, planning and negotiating** • Analyse critical points in the market chain and prioritisation of interventions • Negotiate among actors the strategy and interventions required to increase competitiveness • Monitor market chain's competitiveness	**Phase 1. Diagnostic research to understand key actors** • Identify market chain actors • Characterise activities, interest, ideas and problems • Prioritise and select opportunities **Phase 2. Definition and analysis of business opportunities** • Undertake participatory in-depth market and enterprise analysis of each identified opportunity **Phase 3. Implementation of joint market innovations** • Execute interventions that may include: – Design, development and launching of new products – Introduction of new technologies that increase efficiency – Establishment of new institutions or services in support of enterprise development

Participatory approaches to market chain analysis and project design

Development practitioners – i.e., market facilitators – in the field, need practical methods that can be applied by them, if possible without resorting to the contracting of outside experts. In recent years, participatory approaches have been developed for gathering information on the market chain through facilitated meetings with actors within the chain, and as a means of converting the information into concrete action or business plans while building trust among the different actors involved (FAO–CFU, RECOFTC, 2000; Lundy et al., 2004; Bernet et al., 2004; van de Hayden and Camacho, 2004).

Table 2 compares three of the four methods cited above. They show certain commonalities, but with each placing different emphasis on certain areas. The approaches of FAO-CFU, RECOFTC and Lundy et al. initiate the process by selecting among sub-sector options, whereas in the approach of Bernet et al. the sub-sector has been selected a priori. In the methodology proposed by Lundy et al. the characterisation of formal and informal support services in terms of quality and cost is more explicitly addressed. The method of FAO–CFU, RECOFTC (2000) that was developed specifically for tree and forest products, and that of Lundy et al. (2004) have been used quite extensively under a wide range of conditions and by different development and research practitioners. The authors of this paper are unaware of any documented cross-country or cross-commodity assessment as to the advantages and disadvantages of the respective methods, or how different practitioners may have adapted them to local circumstances. The method of Bernet at al. (2004) is still under validation in Bolivia, Peru and Ecuador. All methods are intensive in the use of time and recognise the need for facilitation by persons with an appropriate level of technical knowledge and social skills. They also stress that the approaches do not guarantee success, but have proved in practice a useful tool to strengthen processes of rural enterprise development. Some of the limitations (Lundy et al, 2004; Bernet 2004) include:

- Their use can lead to a merely descriptive exercise if processes of negotiation and planning between the actors, and sound financial analysis are not incorporated
- They require certain facilitation abilities, technical knowledge and an entity or group that leads the process
- They depend on the willingness of the chain actors to negotiate and collaborate for common gain. Dominance by a key actor is unlikely to achieve the desired results
- It takes time to build trust-based relationships between chain actors, especially if a history of mistrust exists.

Boxes 5 and 6 describe two cases where the use of participatory processes brought different actors together to determine means of identifying new opportunities and for overcoming bottlenecks and constraints, and which have resulted in income increases for the participating farmers and building of confidence to engage in the market.

As mentioned above, ideally if resources permit, formal and participatory methods of market chain analysis should be combined. Formal studies can provide greater depth and more quantitative results upon which to base decisions; they may

Box 5. Coffee farmers in Yorito, Honduras

Despite the depressed market situation, coffee producers in Yorito, Honduras have found a means of making their coffee more profitable. The Agro-industry Committee of the Consorcio Local para el Desarrollo de la Cuenca del Rio Tascalapa (CLODEST), a local consortium of farmer organisations, facilitated the participatory market mapping of the existing coffee chain bringing together producers, processors and traders. This helped identify critical points and enhance communication between the coffee farmers and the local trader. A short-term outcome has been the negotiation of higher prices with an existing trader, and a medium-term outcome was the decision to seek organic certification. Since November 2001 a smaller group of 12 farmers have been selling their coffee to the local trader at 500 lempiras per quintal (US$0.69/kg) while non-participating farmers receive 250 lempiras per quintal (US$0.34/kg). The trader not only provides marketing services but also technical assistance and credit for capital investments needed to improve quality. Recently, the coffee from 45 households was certified as 'transition' (transition from traditional to organic production) and negotiations are in progress with a coffee cooperative, which exports organic beans for the German market, to sell this transition coffee at a premium. These results have been achieved without a formal project and have been brought about through a process that has improved communication and trust between producers and the trader.

Source: Wheatley and Peters, 2004; Lundy et al., 2005

also be able to gain greater understanding of the factors in the enabling environment that are favouring or hindering rural enterprise development. They may also, if made explicit in the studies, offer an opportunity to identify a chain champion. This aspect has probably not received the attention it deserves and has led to over-emphasis being paid to developing farmers groups to the exclusion of identifying and supporting a chain champion who may provide the demand pull so essential for enterprise success. Participatory approaches, on the other hand, will generate ownership of the process by the intended beneficiaries and strengthen their capacity to introduce innovations into their activities in the future, and they also initiate a process of trust building among actors. Bingen et al. (2003) compare approaches to human capital development in projects for linking farmers to markets and conclude that those with an explicit emphasis on developing community skills are likely to prove more sustainable when projects terminate. At present there are relatively few field-level development practitioners with the required skill set to be able to facilitate the process of participatory market chain analysis and the subsequent development of interventions to enhance a supply chain's competitiveness.

Participatory market chain analysis explicitly concludes with the development of an action or business plan that is negotiated among the actors and service providers. The implementation of the business plan requires the continued mentoring and support provided by the market facilitator and other service providers. For

Box 6. Market analysis and development method applied to non-timber forest products (NTFPs) in Tabanani Village, Central River Division, The Gambia

At the end of 2000, the Gambia Forestry Department adopted FAO's market analysis and development (MA&D) approach to assist communities in the creation of income-generation activities from community forests. The objective was to train Forestry Department personnel in MA&D methodology in order for them to facilitate the development of community-based enterprises utilising products, resources or services from community forests. Within a year of introducing the MA&D approach, six villages decided to coordinate their approaches, with the purpose of establishing a stronger position for access to information and for negotiating the sale of their forest products. An important result of the MA&D approach has been the identification by villagers of new and more valuable uses of NTFPs. For example, the leaves of the rhun palm are normally used as fencing material, mostly for on-farm use. Rhun palm splits (made by splitting the palm bole into 16 pieces which are used to replace 10x10 cm timber) were sold previously at GMD 15 (US$ 0.51) a piece to buyers who resold the same split for GMD 80 (US$ 2.71) on the market. Within a year, the villagers had established a selling point in the market and were selling their splits for GMD 70 (US$ 2.37). Rhun palm is now also used to build furniture, which is also sold in the market. Other villagers have become aware of these results and the potential income-generation opportunities offered by forest management. Twenty-six villages have adopted the MA&D approach and this new way of thinking is now being extended to the marketing of other resources (crops, fruits, etc.). Villagers realise that they have much stronger bargaining power when they are well organised and better informed.

Source: http://www.fao.org/forestry/site/25490/en

example, in the Nyambyumba potato case (see Box 3) the relationship with the purchaser Nandos very nearly broke down because of misunderstandings brought about by communication problems. The facilitator needed to be on hand to help sort out problems. There is little written about the length of time that a small rural enterprise requires mentoring. Experiences in urban settings where private-sector companies volunteer to mentor small-scale businesses that are getting started suggest that a 3-year period is required, over which time the intensity of mentoring gradually diminishes (S. Street, independent consultant; personal communication). This is a factor that is seldom appreciated by development organisations, which for reasons of funding and programming have to move on from supporting specific farmers groups after a certain period.

Strengthening services for enterprise growth

Historically it has been common practice for donors and governments to intervene in the market for business development services (BDS) by financing public provision or permanently subsidising services delivered by others, such as NGOs. This has had the consequence of development organisations stepping in to provide services (transport is a good example) that, because they are financed by donors, are unsustainable once project support is terminated. This approach has the effect of crowding out commercial providers of services (Committee of Donor Agencies for Small Enterprise Development, 2001).

While development organisations may be aware of the negative effect of these practices, they lack expertise to facilitate alternative approaches that seek to promote sustained increases in both the demand for and supply of services. This paradigm shift in the role of development organisations – from a provider to a facilitator of services – is a major challenge since it requires a change in the attitude, behaviour and roles of donors, governments and development practitioners. In the transition, major contradictions and conflicting responses to development needs can be observed, with organisations espousing a market orientation for farmers, while in different parts of the same organisation attitudes and practices continue to support an interventionist policy with respect to service provision.

Assessment of business development services (BDS)

If a development objective goes beyond the linking of selected farmers producing one particular product to one particular market, then it will be necessary to assess BDS needs and subsequent interventions on those critical services whose improvement will benefit the widest number of target beneficiaries. There are a number of services that are not sub-sector specific, such as market information, business management and legal services, finance etc. whose improvement can benefit a wide range of rural producers. FOODNET the regional marketing network in East Africa, supported the development of market information, as this was considered to be an equitable way in which to support a number of enterprise options (Ferris and Robbins, 2004).

Current thinking on the provision of BDS for small-scale enterprises is championed by the Small Enterprise Education and Promotion (SEEP) Network (http://www.seepnetwork.org/bdsguide.html). The SEEP network provides an overview of the methods that can be used to make an assessment of services by sub-sector and across sub-sectors. Techniques that are described include: sub-sector and market chain analysis, rapid appraisal techniques, general small enterprise surveys, specific BDS market-assessment tools, needs assessment through clusters and networks, etc. As well as these formal information-gathering methods, action research, or what is termed an 'incremental approach', can be employed, which lays emphasis on learning and developing in-depth relationships with the enterprises with which a facilitator is working and learning together in an incremental fashion about service provision needs (Hileman and Tanburn, 2000). For a market facilitator immersed in a local enterprise-development situation, he or she will need to adapt and combine methods to suit the particular circumstances and resources available.

Trust in supply chains

Supply chain management (SCM)

The previous sections have concentrated on the process of agro-enterprise development with the purpose of identifying the moments when opportunities for linkages become evident and the role of the market facilitator in catalysing relationships between market chain actors becomes clearer. Earlier in this paper, the emergence of the SCM concept that examines the relationships between businesses as a mean of better meeting consumer requirements for products and services (Woods, 2004) was discussed. SCM is about implementing practical improvements to allow a supply chain to be more competitive and more responsive to consumer demands. It requires active management initiated by one or more members of the supply chain: the chain champion. The study of SCM draws on several disciplines, one of which is relationship marketing. Relationship marketing recognises the importance of commitment and trust in business-to-business relationships, and that such relationships are dynamic and can only develop over time (Woods, 2004).

Batt (2004) summarises the advantages for both suppliers and customers arising from long-term relations and concludes that the greatest benefit is the reduction in uncertainty on both sides. The key positive constructs of relationship marketing are satisfaction and trust, and these manifest themselves in the following ways:

* Satisfaction has to do with the degree to which a preferred supplier's performance meets the customer's expectations. Satisfaction increases when performance exceeds expectations and vice versa
* Trust in a relationship is considered critical in situations where there is risk and incomplete buyer information with respect to the quality or performance of the product or service being supplied.

The differentiation of trust at three levels made by Sako (1992, see Batt, 2004) helps categorise behaviour that is readily observed in rural agro-enterprise situations. *Contractual trust* is an expectation that the exchange partners will abide by their written or oral contractual obligations and act according to generally accepted business practice. A common complaint often levelled against small-scale farmers is their habit of 'breaking' agreements to sell to a particular trader or company, if higher prices are offered by others. *Competence trust* is derived from the assumption that the entrusted firm will carry out the activities competently and reliably. Both farmers and the private sector often have little faith in the ability of, for example, the public sector to deliver quality and reliable extension services or to provide an enabling environment for business transactions to proceed smoothly. *Goodwill trust* arises where both parties have developed mutual expectations that the other will do more than what it is formally committed to perform. This is the ultimate in trust category in that it accommodates an understanding that if things go wrong for either party, there will not be an immediate breakdown in the relationship.

Functions of social capital in rural agro-enterprises

Johnson et al. (2002) help to place trust in the wider perspective of the role of social capital as an input into the process of agro-enterprise development. In a study of 50 rural agro-enterprises in Colombia they identified three principal functions played by social capital:

- Acquisition of information via information networks
- Reduction of uncertainty and monitoring costs through trust-based relations
- Establishment and maintenance of collective action.

On making a comparative analysis across and within enterprises, it was found that the use of the different functions of social capital were highly correlated and that social relations do perform an economic function within enterprises, as measured by revenue per worker. This suggests that enterprises do benefit from broadening their networks and by strengthening their existing relations with other actors in the supply chain. Johnson et al. postulate that the fact enterprises use personal relations for professional objectives is a sign of market failure. They surmise that the extent to which technological or institutional innovations can reduce the reliance on personal relationships and promote the emergence of alternative suppliers and markets for services that are currently provided through social capital, both efficiency and equity are likely to increase. Johnson et al. recommend that, when assessing BDS and the design of interventions to strengthen their provision, careful attention is given to what types of BDS are currently being provided by which types of relationships and why.

Conclusions and implications

There is increasing evidence that building skills and social capital are critical elements for improving business opportunities. It is also clear that if farming communities are not to sink further into poverty greater investments are required to assist this community to develop their skills, expand their linkages within the marketing environment and build trust-based relationships with different actors.

Process

Heavy emphasis has been placed on the *process* of enterprise development. That process is important because firstly, it helps define the situation as it is now and the desired situation in the future, and secondly, it makes possible the identification of possible steps that need to be taken to achieve the desired situation. This was illustrated using the territorial approach to rural agro-enterprise development that involves a sequence of steps and important elements including:

- Interest group formation and characterisation of a territory
- Organisation of farmers
- Identifying markets and chain analysis
- Developing a strategy and a business plan with chain actors
- Strengthening support services for selected market chains
- Advocating for policy changes

Each step involves different stakeholders (partners, actors, service providers, policy makers, etc.) and is therefore a mechanism for identifying the potentially useful links that need to be established to achieve success. These links can be highly beneficial for business development but as investment and or risk increases, the need for mutual respect and trust will play an ever-increasing role. The challenge with respect to frameworks and approaches to agro-enterprise development is to make them sufficiently clear, flexible and uncomplicated so that they can be understood and adapted to different situations by local development practitioners and communities.

Facilitators and champions

Those in the field that observe trust-building processes know that: they take time, will not occur over night, and require facilitating and championing. What are the implications?

Development practitioners – both from government and NGOs – now have to more clearly define their roles: are they facilitators of development or are they providers of services? Their natural tendency has to be service providers who have, perhaps unwittingly, distorted market mechanisms by substituting for potentially private service provision. For most institutions this paradigm shift is not easy and is unlikely to be achieved without buy-in and support from senior management. It requires changes in attitudes and behaviour, and the learning of new skills. This suggests that there is a great deal still to be done in advocating the need for change among development practitioners and in providing support for organisations that want to make this shift.

Moving toward a market and enterprise orientation means that the skills of front-line field facilitators have to be upgraded and complemented. An increasing minority have the required characteristics, but to make a real dent in the magnitude of the challenge, especially in Africa, requires a very large investment in capacity development. Understanding market and business principles, placing emphasis on profitability (US$/ha) rather than levels of production (t/ha), and quality rather than quantity are important elements. In addition, skills are required for identifying stakeholders, understanding their motivations and facilitating interactions between them. In many cases development institutions will need to build in-house capacity in these areas, either through retraining or hiring in personnel with appropriate backgrounds, to mentor and support field-level facilitators. Experience has shown that capacity building is not a one-off event, but a process that requires iterations of learning, field-level practice, analysis of what has been achieved, and further learning, practice and analysis cycles (Remington et al., 2005).

As discussed, champions of supply chains are likely to be private sector actors from within the supply chains themselves or from associated services. Their appearance may be fortuitous and spontaneous or it may be that in existing market situations champions may be 'sleeping', and require external facilitation for them to awaken and play the role for which they were destined. The question is how can potential champions be identified early in the agro-enterprise process, and then champions be facilitated and supported in their role? Is the existence of a chain champion a precondition for the eventual sustainability of an intervention once project funds have run out? How can it be determined that levels of linkage and trust are at a sufficiently high level such that external facilitation is no longer required? This is an area ripe for further research to provide guidance to field facilitators on how to mobilise different actors in support of improved chain performance.

Linkages and trust

The natural tendency when referring to linkages and trust is to confine this to the actors within a supply chain. However, it is evident that the concept of linkage and trust also applies to relations among different stakeholders at different stages of the agro-enterprise development process. This paper has only summarily addressed these needs for relationship building, so some critical, and perhaps less-evident linkages are highlighted

Among facilitators and service providers at a territorial level. It is advocated that local institutions and community organisations should come together to develop their vision and strategy for agro-enterprise development. This is easy to say but less easy to achieve. The process of bringing partners together requires a convener and facilitator who is able to convincingly argue the case for working together to achieve a common goal and who, whilst having a clear idea of the what requires to be done, has the ability to build a consensus among group members. The potential partners have to understand that working together will require give and take, and possibly changes in the way that they do things. There needs to be a feeling that interaction, sharing responsibility and learning from each other in promoting local agro-enterprise development will be a mutually beneficial experience and will achieve their own institutional goals more effectively and efficiently than by working alone.

Within and among farmers' groups. Establishing and consolidating farmer groups is obviously key to the agro-enterprise process outlined (see Biénabe and Sautier, this volume). There is much empirical experience on forming groups and organisations that have become experienced in facilitating group formation processes. At the same time there are many examples of failures from which to learn. Generating among members a sense of ownership and commitment to their organisation require particular leadership and managerial skills that are often lacking in rural situations.

Between public and private service providers and the farming community. Just as there can be high levels of confidence and trust between communities and their service providers, so the opposite can occur. The various stages of the agro-enterprise process are oriented toward characterising these relations through canvassing the opinions of users of the services and identifying appropriate means of making service provision more effective. The expectation is that as rural communities' capacity to manage their own change increases, so they will become effective at demanding and accessing the services that are useful to them, and in reaction to this, service providers will become more responsive to the needs of their clients.

Between research and development institutions and the private sector. The relationship between research and development has been largely hidden in this discussion, as those that provide research services and those that provide more development-type services have been considered together. Striving for and maintaining competitiveness and relevance requires that businesses and institutions innovate. The process of innovation needs to be continuous. Processes of innovation can occur at any level, they do not necessarily require great investments in either highly qualified personnel or resources. However, they can be greatly enhanced by access to information and new knowledge. So, establishing productive relations, trust and mutual respect between research and development institutions and between these and the private sector that are focused on resolving the constraints and bottlenecks to the competitiveness of supply chains will be a further key to achieving better rates of success (Hall et al., 2003).

Between civil society organisations, government policy-makers and donors. This leads to the connection between micro- and meso-level interventions and the macro- or policy-related issues that are likely to favour or hinder success on the ground. However good institutions may be at developing frameworks, approaches, methods and tools, all these are likely to have limited impact if relations with decision makers, whether they be those that make policies or provide the resources that make development work possible, are weak and affected by high levels of scepticism and lack of confidence from either side. In many developing countries, and particularly in Africa, governments have a poor reach among rural people, they are viewed as being less than competent and officials are often corrupt. These conditions lead to less than satisfactory levels of confidence and trust in these institutions either at a local or national level. The same applies to the donor side. Confidence is strained when conflicting approaches are espoused among and even within donor and lead technical assistance agencies. This is compounded by what appears to be a lack of commitment by developed countries to confront and find solutions to some of the root causes of the huge inequalities that exist between rich and poor, if to do so goes against their own interests. These are global issues and need to be tackled at that level by those whose mandate it is to do so: the World Bank, the United Nations system, the World Trade Organization, the political bodies that represent developed and developing countries, and the international research and development community. Moving towards achieving higher levels of mutual understanding and agreement about what the problems are and possible options for resolving them, and greater levels of trust and mutual respect among these various actors is as important as achieving progress at the micro and meso levels.

Interrelatedness of interventions

The challenges of making markets work for the poor are significant, but there is a wealth of experience and knowledge that has been accumulated over the years. There are globally, and to a certain extent regionally and nationally, strong institutional structures through which to work and on which to build future interventions. There are initiatives that are in progress or being conceptualised, that should be strengthened or supported so that they eventually achieve their desired impact. Just three as examples of these initiatives related to linkage of farmers to markets that are relevant when considering future directions are presented.

1. **The review of the Strategic Priorities of the Consultative Group on International Agricultural Research (CGIAR).** The CGIAR has had, and still has, a predominantly food-production orientation. However, the Group now recognises that improvement of smallholder farmers' livelihood cannot depend alone on the production of food staples. The Group is examining the most appropriate way of incorporating research on smallholder production, processing and marketing of high-value products. In other strategic priority areas emphasis is being placed on smallholder competitiveness, institutional capacity building and farmer organisation. A first challenge is to acknowledge the need for interconnectedness in the components that make up a strategy for linking farmers to markets. The second challenge is to achieve much greater levels of complementarity among the system of semi-autonomous research centres with respect to market and enterprise development research. The topic merits a system-wide or challenge programme approach to harness synergy and generate innovative approaches and to encourage partnership with others who can provide complementary expertise.

2. **The Food and Agriculture Organization of the United Nations (FAO)** has invested considerable resources and time to developing a **Global Post-harvest Initiative**: Linking Farmers to Markets in collaboration with the Global Forum on Agricultural Research (GFAR) and the Post-harvest consortium (P*h*Action). The strategic framework for this Initiative, which was developed through an exhaustive consultation among stakeholders in five regions, espouses a forward-looking market and enterprise orientation for smallholder production that considers the integrated nature of producer to consumer linkages, and the need for interventions to be based on wide stakeholder participation in decision-making and implementation. Taking the strategy from the design to implementation phase requires a high level of integration within and between the individual organisations that are the key proponents. If successfully managed, the initiative could provide an important vehicle for raising awareness among international and national government policy makers and an integrating function among interventions at meso level across regions.

3. **Regional and sub-regional agricultural research forums.** Almost without exception, regional and sub-regional agricultural research forums have identified

post-harvest and agribusiness research as high priorities. Competence and experience in sub-sector approaches and market chain studies and analysis varies from region to region, and largely the smallholder sector has not been the focus of attention in terms of enhancing supply chain performance. With the gradual incorporation of civil society organisations (NGOs and farmer organisations) into decision-making processes of the forums, the voice of the smallholder is becoming more evident. This is leading to a demand to address this particular vacuum and presents opportunities for investing in the reorientation and strengthening of the capacities of national agricultural research organisations to focus on resolving constraints and bottlenecks to supply chains market in which smallholders are key actors.

These are just three initiatives that could be harnessed, strengthened and built upon. The situation in rural areas with respect to poverty, and especially Africa, is serious. If, as projected, sub-Saharan Africa slips even further behind over the next decade, and other regions continue to gain in competence, services and infrastructure, apart from being a disaster for humanity, it could mean the collapse of market solution for smallholder farmers' livelihoods. If the proposal is to turn the situation around, development agencies are going to need to be inventive in research and development, but also forceful in supporting those that are advocating for changes in the enabling environment that will make market solutions work for the poor.

References

Batt, P.J. 2004. Incorporating measures of satisfaction, trust and power-dependence into an analysis of agribusiness supply chains. In: Johnson, G.I. and Hofman, P.J., eds. 2004. Agriproduct Supply Chain Management in Developing Countries. Proceedings of a workshop held in Bali, Indonesia, 19–22 August 2003. ACIAR (Australian Council for International Agricultural Research) Proceedings No. 119, 194pp.

Bernet, T., Devaux, A., Ortiz, O. and Thiele, G. 2004. Participatory market chain approach. In: Participatory Research and Development for Sustainable Agriculture and Natural Resource Management: a Sourcebook. Centro Internacional de la Papa (CIP) – Users' Perspective with Agricultural Research and Development (UPWARD). Lima, Peru.

Best, R. 2003. Farmer participation in market research to identify income-generating opportunities. Centro Internacional de Agricultura Tropical (CIAT), Kampala, Uganda. 2pp. (Highlights: CIAT in Africa No. 9). Available at: http://www.ciat.cgiar.org/africa

Bingen, J., Serrano, A. and Howard, J. 2003. Linking farmers to markets: different approaches to human capital development. Doi: 10.1016/j.foodpol.2003.08.007

Committee of Donor Agencies for Small Enterprise Development. 2001. Business Development Services for Small Enterprises: Guiding Principles for Donor Intervention. 2001 Edition. Small and Medium Enterprise (SME) Department. World Bank Group. Washington, DC. USA. 21pp.

FAO–CFU, RECOFTC (Food and Agriculture Organization of the United Nations – Community Forestry Unit, Regional Community Forestry Training Center). 2000. Community-based Tree and Forest Product Enterprises: Market Analysis and Development. Booklets A, B, C, D, E and F. Forestry Department, FAO, Rome, Italy.

Ferris, S. and Robbins, P. 2004. Developing Marketing Information Services in Eastern Africa. The FOODNET Experience. Final report. Association for Strengthening Agricultural Research in Eastern and Central Africa (ASARECA) FOODNET; Commodity Marketing Information Services (CMIS). Kampala, Uganda. 38pp.

Gottret, M.V. and Raymond, M. 2003. An analysis of a cassava integrated research and development approach: has it really contributed to poverty alleviation? Pages 205–226 *in:* Mathur, S. and Pachico, D. (eds) Agricultural Research and Poverty Reduction: Some Issues and Evidence. Centro Internacional de Agricultura Tropical (CIAT). Cali, Colombia. 268pp.

Government of Malawi. 2004. Report of the Presidential Commission of Enquiry into the Management of the Strategic Grain Reserve, Lilongwe, Malawi.

GTZ (Deutsche Gesellschaft für Technische Zusammenarbeit) (ed.). 2003. Guide to Rural Economic and Enterprise Development. Working Paper edition 1.0, November 2003. GTZ, Eschborn, Germany.

Haggblade, Steven J. and Gamser, M. 1991. A Field Manual for Sub-sector Practitioners. GEMINI Publications Series. Development Alternatives Inc. Bethesda, Maryland, USA.

Hall, A.J., Yoganand, B., Sulaiman, R.V. and Clark, N.G. (eds). 2003. Post-harvest Innovations in Innovation: Reflections on Partnership and Learning. Crop Post-harvest Programme (CPHP), South Asia, c/o International Crops Research Institute for Semi-arid Tropics (ICRISAT), Patancheru, Andra Pradesh, India.180pp.

Hileman, M. and Tanburn, J. 2000. The Wheels of Trade – Developing Markets for Business Services. Intermediate Technology Publications, London, UK.

Holtzman, J. S. 2002. Rapid appraisals of commodity subsectors. *In:* A Guide to Developing Agricultural Markets and Agro-enterprises. World Bank, Washington DC, USA. 14pp. (available at: http://www.worldbank.org)

IFDC (International Fertilizer Development Center). 2003. A strategic framework for African agricultural input supply development. *In:* Crawford, E., Kelly, V., Jayne, T.S., and Howard, J. (eds). 2003. Input use and market development in sub-Sahara Africa: an overview. Food Policy 28: 277–292.

Johnson, N., Suarez, R. and Lundy, M. 2002. The Importance of Social Capital in Colombian Rural Agro-enterprises. CAPRi Working Paper No. 26. CGIAR Systemwide Programme on Collective Action and Property Rights. International Food Policy Research Institute (IFPRI). Washington DC, USA (Available at: http://www.capri.cgiar.org)

Joss, S., Schaltenbrand, H. and Schmidt, P. 2002. Clients First! A Rapid Market Appraisal Tool Kit. Theoretical Background and Experiences from RMA events. Experience and Learning in International Co-operation. Publication No. 3. Helvetas. Zurich, Switzerland. 50pp.

Lundy, M., Gottret, M.V., Cifuentes, W., Ostertag, C.F., Best, R., Peters, D. and Ferris, S. 2004. Increasing the Competitiveness of Market Chains with Smallholder Producers. Field Manual No. 3. The Territorial Approach to Rural Agro-enterprise Development. Centro Internacional de Agricultura Tropical (CIAT), Cali, Colombia.

Lundy, M., Ostertag, C.F., Best, R., Gottret, M.V., Kaganzi E., Robbins, P., Peters, D., and Ferris, S. 2005. Strategy Paper: A Territorial Approach to Rural Agro-enterprise Development. Rural Development Project. Centro Internacional de Agricultura Tropical (CIAT), Cali, Colombia.

Lusby, F. and Panlibuton, H. 2002. Sub-sector/Business Service Approach to Program Design. Report submitted to: Office of Microenterprise Development, United States Agency for International Development (USAID/G/EGAD/MD), Washington DC, USA.

Musoke, C., Byaruhanga, J., Mwesigwa, P., Byarugaba, C., Kaganzi, E. and Best, R. 2004. Linking farmers to markets: the case of the Nyabyumba potato farmers in Uganda. Paper prepared for the Conference on Integrated Agriculture Research for Development. 1–4 September 2004. Entebbe, Uganda. National Agricultural Research Organisation (NARO), Kampala, Uganda (unpublished).

Nyapendi, R., Kaganzi, E., Best, R. and Ferris, S. 2004. Identifying market opportunities for small-holder farmers in Uganda. Uganda Journal of Agricultural Sciences 9 (11): 64–76.

Nyapendi, R., Jagwe, J. Ferris, S. and Best, R. 2003. Identifying market opportunities for urban and peri-urban farmers in Kampala, Uganda. Centro Internacional de Agricultura Tropical (CIAT), Kampala, Uganda. 8pp.

Ostertag, C.F., Lundy, M., Gottret, M.V., Best, R., Peters, D. and Ferris, S. 2004. Identifying and Assessing Market Opportunities for Small Rural Producers. Manual 2. The Territorial Approach to Rural Agro-enterprise Development. Centro Internacional de Agricultura Tropical (CIAT), Cali, Colombia.

Peacock, C., Jowett, A., Dorward, A., Poulton, C. and Urey, I. 2004. Reaching the Poor, a Call to Action. Investment in Smallholder Agriculture in sub-Saharan Africa. FARM-Africa. London, UK. 30pp.

Poulton, C., Al-Hassan R., Cadisch, G., Reddy, C., and Smith, L. 2001. The Cash Crop Versus Food Crop Debate. Crop Post-Harvest Programme Issues Paper No. 3. Department for International Development (DFID), NR International, Imperial College at Wye, UK. 6pp.

Remington, T., Best, R., Lundy, M. and Ferris, S. 2005. CRS and its learning alliance with CIAT and FOODNET: Building sustainable R&D partnerships for more efficient generation and delivery of new knowledge to improve the livelihoods of the rural poor. Catholic Relief Services (CRS) and Centro Internacional de Agricultura Tropical (CIAT). Nairobi, Kenya.

Rimoy, M. 2003. Production and marketing of high quality fruits and vegetables: the Usambara Lishe Trust experience. Presentation delivered at the Community Agro-enterprise Development Workshop held in Lushoto, Tanzania, 24–28 March 2003. Centro Internacional de Agricultura Tropical (CIAT), Kampala, Uganda.

Rottger, A. 2004. Strengthening Farm–Agribusiness Linkages in Africa. Proceedings of an Expert Consultation. Nairobi, 23–17 March 2003. AGSF Working Document No. 5. Agricultural Management, Marketing and Finance Service (AGSF). Agricultural Support Systems Division, Food and Agricultural Organization of the United Nations (FAO). Rome, Italy. 66pp.

Sako, M. 1992. Prices, Quality and Trust: Interfirm Relations in Britain and Japan. Cambridge University Press, Cambridge, UK.

Sanginga, P.C., Best, R., Chitsike, C., Delve, R., Kaaria, S.and Kirkby, R. 2004a. Linking smallholder farmers to markets in East Africa. Mountain Research and Development 24 (4): 288–291.

Sanginga, P.C., Best, R., Chitsike, C., Delve, R., Kaaria, S. and Kirkby, R. 2004b. Enabling rural innovation in Africa: an approach for integrating farmer participatory research and market orientation for building the assets of the rural poor. Uganda Journal of Agricultural Sciences 9 (11): 934–949.

Santacoloma, P. and Riveros, H. 2004. Alternatives to improve negotiation and market access capabilities of small-scale rural entreprenuers in Latin America. AGSR Working Document No. 4. Agricultural Management, Marketing and Finance Service (AGSF). Agricultural Support Systems Division. Food and Agricultural Organization of the United Nations. Rome, Italy. 78pp.

Scoones, I. 1998. Sustainable Rural Livelihoods: A Framework for Analyisis. Working Paper No. 72. Institute of Development Studies (IDS). Brighton, UK.

Tropical Wholefoods. 2003. E-guide and resource pack. CD-rom. Natural Resources International Ltd, Aylesford, UK.

UN Millennium Project. 2005. Halving hunger: it can be done. Summary version of the Report of the Task Force on Hunger. The Earth Institute at Columbia University, New York, USA. 32pp.

van der Heyden, D. and Camacho, P. 2004. Guía Metodologica para el Analisis de Cadenas Productivas. Ruralter. Centro Internacional de Cooperación para el Desarrollo Agrícola (CICDA), Intercooperation (IC), Servicio Holandés de Cooperación al Desarrollo (SNV). Lima, Peru. 91pp.

Wheatley, C. and Peters, D. 2004. Who benefits from enhanced management of supply chains? *In:* Johnson, G.I. and Hofman, P.J. (eds). Agriproduct Supply Chain Management in Developing Countries. Proceedings of a workshop held in Bali, Indonesia, 19–22 August 2003. ACIAR Proceedings No. 119, Australian Council for International Agricultural Research (ACIAR), Canberra, Australia. 194pp.

Woods, E.J. 2004. Supply chain management: understanding the concepts and its implications in developing countries. *In:* Johnson, G.I. and Hofman, P.J. (eds). 2004. Agriproduct Supply Chain Management in Developing Countries. Proceedings of a workshop held in Bali, Indonesia, 19–22 August 2003. ACIAR Proceedings No. 119, Australian Council for International Agricultural Research (ACIAR), Canberra, Australia. 194pp.

World Bank. 2003. World Development Indicators. Washington DC, USA.

Market information needs of rural producers

Alan Marter

Introduction

The aim of this paper is to assess the importance of market information and the scope for improving information systems for small-scale producers, especially the poor, in sub-Saharan Africa The paper begins by briefly reviewing the factors that cause or exacerbate poor market information. This review enables a more effective identification of the means to tackle such constraints and also shows that there is no simple or uniform solution – problems and solutions will often differ and may be complex. Information is also only part of a package of requirements that are needed to improve marketing – producers often need additional components in order to take advantage of the information on offer. The institutional context of producers – market linkages, producer bodies, etc. may also be important parts of the package.

The study covers both agricultural and non-farm livelihoods and markets. However, the ongoing importance of agriculture in sub-Saharan livelihoods, and the strength of interaction between non-farm and agricultural activities, means that agriculture remains a key sector of concern. It is estimated (Delgado, 1997), that 80% of cultivated area in Africa is either remote or of low potential, and the focus of the paper is therefore especially upon both the poor and areas of poor access. The inherent uncertainty of agricultural production (especially for rainfed systems) also emphasises the need for information and understanding (including market information) that can reduce, but not eliminate, such uncertainties.

The importance of market information

The importance of market information and access to such information on the part of small-scale –producers and the poor has long been recognised. Poor information is linked to a number of critical problems in marketing including: low or inequitable producer incomes, weak or uneven supply responses to price signals, low market efficiency, etc. Whilst the focus has often been upon output markets, those for inputs for small-scale producers are also frequently negatively affected by lack of information that is often equally critical to their livelihoods.

Sound market information can enable producers to make effective production decisions, take advantage of new market opportunities, improve spatial distribution, etc. (Shepherd, 1997 quoted in Goodland and Kleih, 1999). The importance of such information relates in part to its value in reducing (but not removing) risk e.g., to avoid selling at a time of market over supply. It can also inform alternative locations of sales (or purchases) further along market chains (although these may be offset by costs, including labour/marketing time, and additional risks). Negotiation with traders can be facilitated e.g., at farm-gate level though knowledge of prices in destination markets. Information also enables more effective decisions on storage (where perishability is not an over-riding issue) e.g., in respect to relative costs and risks against seasonal price variation. It can also inform similar decisions with respect to off-season production (Coote and Wandschneider, 2001)

What is needed and by whom – producers' (and traders') priorities

A market information system can be defined as having the following characteristics – the ability to: collect, process, and analyse market data systematically and continuously and to ensure delivery of information on a timely basis to all market participants (Poon, 1994 quoted in CTA, 2001). To this could be added the need for systems to be driven and ultimately operated by stakeholders, notably small-scale producers (CTA, 2001)and to be affordable. Whilst considerable emphasis is placed upon the need for timeliness in market data, this only relates to a portion of information needs, notably pricing, whilst other areas such as quality requirements, etc., are less time-sensitive. The degree of perishability of produce is another key factor impacting upon the need for timeliness.

Producers' (and traders') priorities will vary depending upon circumstances but, whilst market constraints are often stated as the first priority by small-scale producers, it is important to recognise that market information as such is not necessarily their first concern. Studies by members of the Natural Resources Institute (NRI) (Kleih, 1999; Kleih et al., 1999b; Kleih et al., 1999d) indicate information as the second priority in Uganda and only the fourth in Malawi. In both these countries the road network and transport access are of equal or higher concern (although this may be partly because the areas under study were remote regions).

Whilst market information needs have often been a pre-occupation of development agencies it is also important to understand the views and needs of producers themselves – with respect to both the relative importance of information constraints as a whole, and their priorities for specific needs that should be addressed. One of the problems with past initiatives has been the failure to fully identify such needs (Robbins, 1998), or to engage producers in the design of appropriate information systems.

Producers' own priorities for specific information are illuminating – a case study in Mali (Kleih et al., 1999c) provides an example:
- Coverage of both food and (grain) cash crops
- Information on supply and demand as well as prices
- Information on inputs (including transport, equipment and fertiliser), prices, availability and quality
- Availability and conditions for credit
- Demand for processed products.

In this example, the diversity of needs (including food crops and input market data) goes well beyond the information provided by many existing information systems. For those with the most limited exposure to markets, information on relevant prices for the main crops in major markets may be an effective starting point. However, many producers will have needs that extend beyond this. Whilst most are concerned with domestic markets, there are differing requirements, e.g., between local and urban, perishable and non-perishable products. A minority may also supply external markets, e.g., regional formal (and informal) trade and international markets – the latter being particularly demanding. Producers may be interested in information on traders themselves, notably their trustworthiness (Robbins, 1998), and in the dynamics of markets, e.g., in changes taking place in terms of products and market location, etc. (Lynch and Ashimogo, 1999). Finally, gender may be an important factor, since both men and women may have similar information needs, but perhaps more often these will differ (Janowski et al., 2003), e.g., because women may cultivate and/or sell different crops/products and women are often (much) more constrained in access to information and information sources.

Given this diversity of interests, those promoting information systems have begun to emphasise a growing package of information components. This may include:
* Location of buyers (or suppliers for input markets)
* Buyers requirements (variety, quality, packaging, delivery, timing)
* Availability and cost of alternative transport to and from differing rural and urban assembly, wholesale and retail markets
* Potential for product loss (or input deterioration), current prices in alternative markets per variety or input, quality and volume
* Seasonality and evolution of real price over time (Coote and Wandschneider, 2001).

Development practitioners are also increasingly emphasising the importance of business skills and the capacity to analyse markets as much as market information itself. These ideas are often linked to associated organisational and institutional development, notably promotion of producer organisations (see the following section).

Although the focus of this paper is on producers, traders may also have needs for information, and supplying these may, in fact, be mutually beneficial to both producers and traders. Smaller-scale traders in particular may have more limited access to information, and confront relatively high market risks hence they may share a degree of common interest with producers (Robbins, 1998). Traders may be particularly interested in information that relates to spatial and arbitrage decisions and also in new market opportunities (Wye College, 1999).

Factors impacting on producers' access to information
Post-liberalisation policy and the macro environment. The post-liberalisation environment in developing countries that has been characterised by a withdrawal of the public sector from market support and intervention has highlighted

information access needs. The decline or collapse of public-sector extension services, especially in Africa, has also emphasised the need for alternative systems of information provision, especially for the poor and in more remote locations. In many areas the private sector (including those components that might provide embedded information services), has developed to only a limited degree, thus raising issues of the level of competitiveness in markets and with consequent implications on information needs and information flows. Overall transactions in marketing can entail a variety of costs, and it is now recognised that an understanding of this institutional context is critical in the development of effective market interventions (for a discussion of the key components of the New Institutional Economics see Poole in CTA, 2001).

Economic and locational characteristics of producers. The level of poverty of many small-scale producers is of fundamental importance because not only does it limit access to information in a variety of ways, it also limits the capacity to use information even where it is available. The poor often lack the resources (and capabilities) to cover the search costs for information other than that to be found in their immediate locality (Poole, 1999). Limited access to information arises in the context of: lack of market contacts and the tendency of smallholders to sell at the farm gate or in local markets, poor literacy levels and the lack of access to modern media, as well as the absence of effective information services.

The needs of the poor may be magnified by geographical/locational factors since they may live in remote areas, or areas with limited access to infrastructure, especially roads and transport. Such remoteness limits their access to traders, diminishes access to information and hence their capacity to bargain. These limitations can be exacerbated by credit links and ties between producers and traders.

Social characteristics. Social characteristics interact with and may re-enforce limitations imposed by economic circumstances. Ethnicity or the effects of social and political disruption may have wider negative impacts on marketing (Marter and Wandschneider, 2002), and access to market information. Gender is of particular importance coupled with general intra-household relationships. There may be conflicting interests between men and women in households such that, for example, women choose to sell without the knowledge of men who are likely to expropriate the income from such sales. In these circumstances information access (for both men and women) is constrained (Lynch and Ashimogo, 1999). Female-headed households may face particular constraints in their capacity to access both markets and market information.

In more general terms there are issues of awareness and confidence amongst disadvantaged groups (the poor, women, youth, etc.) and associated needs for empowerment to be coupled to market interventions, including provision of information. Such awareness may be partly a function of levels of education, where women are again often disadvantaged (CTA, 2001).

Organisational and institutional issues. In 'institutional' terms (i.e., in the wider sense of the rules of the game), relationships between producers and traders may have a key impact on the scope for interchange of market information. These issues revolve around, for example, the levels of repeat dealing, exclusivity, trust and reputation (Poole, 1999; Poole in CTA, 2001). In terms of organisations, the existence, e.g., of producer bodies can have major implications for both the capacity of small-scale producers to access and to use market information (see Biénabe and Sautier, this volume). The number and capabilities of non-governmental organisations (NGOs) may be of importance, given their scope to interact with producer bodies either alone or in combination with the private sector (Marter and Wandschneider, 2002). The public sector may also offer some scope for interaction depending upon the overall policy environment and levels of public-sector institutional presence (e.g., via decentralised bodies).

Differing marketing systems. Differing categories of market may require differing levels of information and analysis. On domestic markets, those supplying perishable products will be in particular need of up-to-date information (Poole, 1999; CTA, 2001), whilst relatively sophisticated urban markets may require more comprehensive data, perhaps because of market regulations, or more complex and demanding specification of products, etc. Export-market requirements, especially those in developed countries, are generally even more demanding, and there are a variety of differing categories, each with differing information needs, e.g., the larger commodity markets including semi-processed items, specific needs for perishable exports (notably seafood and horticultural produce), and niche options such as organics and ethically traded items. Requirements in major commodity markets may be exacting, with those for perishables and niche markets even more demanding. As a result, unless there are very sound market intermediaries, i.e., bodies that can access and interpret market needs and translate these into activities and procedures that can be managed by small-scale producers, many of these markets are beyond the means of the poor both in terms of information, specifications, regulation and requirements. Regional markets (for formal trade) are sparsely catered for, even where regional bodies exist (Robbins, 1998), still less where trade is largely informal in nature (Coote et al., 2000).

Donor activity and the literature on market information has focussed upon markets for outputs – but it is often the case that there are similar needs for information on inputs, with inputs taken to include pre-harvest practices and technologies that are linked to subsequent marketing strategies (Coote and Wandschneider, 2001).

Information systems – needs and opportunities

Who currently provides ?

Farmers/producers. Other farmers, neighbours, family, friends and 'contact farmers' are often the main source of information for small-scale producers, (Poole et al.,

1999), especially for the poor (Bagnall Oakeley and Ocilaje, 2002 quoted in Janowski, 2003), and/or in remote areas. Similarly, local public meetings and/or group meetings can be an important information source, especially for women (CTA, 2004). Middle- income and more wealthy farmers are more likely find other sources more important e.g., via extension services, agribusiness, NGOs and local government.

However this type of interpersonal source has many limitations – the better-informed farmer may not share all the information, and the information itself may be partial, inaccurate, or out-of-date. Social relationships, notably those based upon age and gender and within the household may act to constrain available information, particularly to women (Lynch and Ashimogo, 1999). The value of such information also depends upon how it is used, e.g., if farmers are 'active', keeping records and hence able to discern trends, etc. (Wye College, 1999)

Traders – the local private sector. Traders may also represent a source of information, although this is less common because of the mistrust between producers and traders that is prevalent in many areas (Poole et al., 1998). The latter is especially the case where few traders operate or there is generally limited competition. However, where there is common interest traders may play a significant role, e.g., where there are opportunities to expand sales, where new opportunities arise, and where market specifications including quality is important (Coote and Wandschneider, 2001).

As with farmer-based information however, that derived from traders may not always be accurate, timely or complete. This is partly because traders themselves, especially small-scale traders, often have only limited access to information. It is also the case that better-off or relatively wealthy farmers can benefit from such information whilst the poor are much more confined to local small-scale traders/the village environment. The gender bias against women also arises with this source, since it is often men who are the most active and/or have the most access to traders in pursuing market information (Lynch and Ashimogo, 1999).

Government. The collection and distribution of market information has often been retained as a function of government even where liberalisation policies have been pursued with vigour. Part of the reason for this is that information can often be regarded as a public good – since the market will not provide information to dispersed small-scale producers on an equitable or regular basis. However, it can be argued that in some instances information is also a private good e.g., in the context of traders' informal networks where information has both a cost and value, and hence may not willingly be shared (Poole in CTA 2001).

The expense of gathering such information has often contributed to the decline or collapse of public-sector systems (Kleih, 1999). Additional problems include a focus on price data alone, where even this is seldom adequate due to delays or failure to collect prices of most relevance to producers. Depending upon the specific market, price data may in any case be very variable, especially for perishable items, with large changes occurring over the day, or even hour. Further problems include weakness in analytical capabilities and lack of appreciation of commercial needs.

Such information systems and services may be linked to (agricultural) extension as conduits of information and complementary advice (e.g., on production and, less frequently, on marketing). Activity under the National Agricultural Advisory Service (NAADS) as part of the Plan for the Modernisation of Agriculture (PMA) in Uganda provides an example of attempts to link information services and more effective extension. Other dissemination media for information via government programmes include radio services, but in all cases coverage is often patchy. Extension services may not have (adequate) access to information on distant markets, they may in any event lack resources to cover their designated rural areas, and also lack both appropriate training and motivation (Coote and Wandschnieder, 2001).

Non-governmental organisations (NGOs) and donors. A number of international NGOs [e.g., the Cooperative League of the USA (CLUSA), Technoserve and CARE] plus some local NGOs have engaged in the development of marketing and information services, sometimes working in collaboration with government agencies, but often in the absence of the latter. The depth of information provided and coverage of such systems has been variable, and sustainability (especially because of costs) has often been problematic. Many NGOs, especially in the past, were not focussed upon marketing as such and lacked expertise, since their main concern was, and sometimes is, upon development and production activities (Marter and Wandschneider, 2002). However, NGOs can be effective, especially where they have generated sound working links within communities, including the promotion of local self-help or producer groups.

Community-based organisations (CBOs) – producer bodies. Many of the cooperative bodies that were prevalent prior to liberalisation have collapsed or substantially diminished in scale (for a variety of reasons, including competition with the private sector). However some cooperatives remain, especially in export crop sectors, and recently there has been a revival of interest in the potential role of producer bodies in a variety of production and marketing functions including information systems. Promotion of or support for producer bodies, and systems such as outgrowers, is quite widespread, but their coverage and capacity remains open to question (see Biénabe and Sautier, this volume)). Capabilities of such bodies specifically with respect to market information systems have not been assessed to a great extent, although there are indications that they can be effective, especially where linked to international NGOs (de Vletter and Hills, 2004).

Agencies concerned with international trade. The more demanding nature of information requirements in international markets (in terms of: specification, quality, delivery, packaging, contractual arrangements, foreign exchange and finance, certification and documentation, etc.), and the consequent need for intermediary bodies was noted earlier . These agencies include: producer bodies, local export-ers/traders, or outgrower schemes, some of which may be operated by importers or their agents. In addition (local) government, sometimes with donor assistance, separate donor-funded agencies and selected NGOs may also play a part.

Public-sector export agencies have been relatively ineffectual since they of-ten lack marketing and commercial skills. NGO activity is often geared to specific export-market niches e.g., ethical trade outlets and organics, both of which may be quite demanding. NGOs also quite frequently lack the marketing and commercial capabilities to effectively advise small-scale producers on realistic market potential and requirements (Marter and Wandschneider, 2002) Private-sector agencies may be more effective, but there can be concerns over their strength in terms of bargain-ing power over (client) producers.

All these bodies (public, private and NGO), may draw upon internation-al agencies concerned with market information, the best-known being the Market News Service operated by the International Trade Centre (ITC) (Robbins, 1998). Media used in international market information systems are often more diverse and sophisticated than those for domestic markets and include dedicated agencies, publications, broadcasts, phone services and internet sites.

Options to improve systems

Residual roles for central government. The model where public-sector agen-cies gather and distribute market information may still be effective where servic-es remain well resourced and extension staff are well trained and motivated (e.g., as was found to be the case in Zimbabwe a few years ago – Poulton et al., 1999). However in many African states extension services are now in a poor condition (e.g., Ghana and Tanzania, Poole et al., 1999; Wye College, 1999). Innovations to improve public-sector provision of information focus broadly upon two areas, firstly, more-appropriate and efficient data collection (and analysis), and secondly, the development of more-effective data distribution.

On the data-gathering side the focus has been upon ensuring the collection of more-relevant, regular and timely information and upon securing effective funding. Information needs normally extend beyond price data to include market alternatives, channels and specifications, and there is also a need for more-con-sistent data sets from main wholesale markets and for historical price analysis (Wye College, 1999). One option could be the development of collaborative links to provide effective systems with donors. Involvement of the private sector is also possible, but may be more feasible at micro level working with producer bodies where there is local mutual interest (see Producer bodies). Notionally some of the funding needs for information collection could be derived from small-scale pro-ducers, but in practice it would be costly to collect payment and, in any case, likely to be ineffectual through unwillingness to pay (NB the public-good issues dis-cussed earlier, Poole, 1999).

Proposals for data distribution include strengthening resources for exten-sion capability and motivation, but more particularly the pursuit of options either through local/decentralised government, or the private sector, NGOs, or CBOs. These ideas are also often linked to the use of alternative media, particularly radio. Greater emphasis on analysis as part of information services has also led to proposals for private-sector participation in this area. Options for alternative institutions working alone or in collaboration, and the use of alternative media, are examined in the following sections.

Decentralisation – opportunities and limitations. Decentralisation of government has been implemented in an increasing number of African states with the aim of improving accountability and the quality of services to local communities. In practice the process has had distinctly patchy success, depending upon: the degree of real authority that is delegated, the resources allocated to local bodies (and their capacity to raise revenue), the capabilities and motivation of local administrative staff, and political participants in the process (James et al., 2001).

In terms of information systems, local authorities are seen as a potential partner in the distribution of information gathered (and perhaps analysed) by central authorities. Such activity could also be supplemented by collection and distribution of local market data. The latter could be much more demand-driven if linked to needs assessments conducted amongst producers/farmers themselves, whilst local extension services could act as the intermediary between producers and the district administration (Kleih, 1999) An alternative to extension services where these are weak could be the involvement of NGOs or even the private sector. It is also suggested that further institutional components are required e.g., involving local chambers of commerce and/or farmers associations (Kleih, 1999). In terms of media, in addition to extension, radio is generally identified as the most appropriate, operating either through commercial FM or community channels (Goodland and Kleih, 1999, see also Alternative media).

Overall the success of such initiatives will depend firstly on the capacities of local administrations (and extension services), which may be partly an issue of funding resources. Much will also depend upon the location of markets and on telecommunications capacity. It could also be argued that more could be done to integrate such initiatives with those developed at community level; especially by producers' bodies and even local traders.

Development of human capital – training. Education and/or training are seen as means of enabling producers both to develop their own record-keeping where feasible, and to be able to use information from external sources more effectively. Primary education and basic literacy can play an important if long-term role (Kleih, 1999), and may be particularly important in relation to gender. Female access to education and levels of literacy is often more limited, and particularly so with respect to modern technology. Women's economic roles and hence information needs are often not fully understood or taken into account during the development of appropriate training. Support to raise confidence may be important given men's attitudes towards women's participation in marketing.

Whilst education has underlying importance, most of the emphasis by development agencies is on training producers themselves that can generate more immediate results. Some agencies such as CLUSA focus upon functional literacy as an essential precursor to more specific activities and on enterprise development, including production, marketing or market information initiatives (de Vletter and Hills, 2004). It is reported that such functional literacy can be supplied at relatively low cost (although requiring a fairly long time period for implementation), and can be 'spun off' to local agencies once established. Farmer-to-farmer extension is an option that has been found low-cost, and effective for production-related activity (e.g., by the Intermediate Technology Development Group (ITDG) in Peru), but it remains to be seen if this can also be applied to market activity and market information. (Hellin et al., 2004; Cuello et al., 2004)

Training can cover both the acquisition of information and development of record keeping. This can be extended to the development of analytical skills with respect to calculation of production and marketing costs, the development of historical price charts as means of assessing the relative returns between differing production opportunities, and a deeper understanding of the marketing process more generally. (Wye College, 1999; Coote and Wandschnieder, 2001). Increasingly it is recommended that producers (even the poorest) should be charged for such services since it is generally found that subsequent use of training skills is significantly greater. (Wye College, 1999).

Visits and exchanges in various forms can be means of developing required understanding and skills, e.g., visits to successful producers who have penetrated specific markets, as well as visits to markets themselves. Additionally it may be feasible to encourage traders and/or processors to visit producers. Farmer/producer forums have been found to be effective means of information exchange for production related topics (Matsaert, 2002), whether the same applies for marketing and market information remains less clear. NGOs as well as public-sector bodies are often seen as having a major role in such training and visits, together with farmer organisations (at community level).

Training has also been given on group marketing and producer group formation (Kleih et al., 2004). This initiative is linked to the use of FM radio for both market information and promotion of group marketing, which are discussed in the following section.

Alternative media – modern technologies and radio. There are a very wide (and growing) number of media that can be used for market information systems, but a considerably smaller number that are accessible to the majority of poor, small-scale producers. Media such as mobile phones and internet access remain out of the reach of the majority because of expense and limited coverage. Mobile networks are still largely confined to main urban centres and transport routes. Mobiles themselves are costly, e.g., around US$100 in Tanzania and US$270 in Kenya, and expensive to run, e.g., around 20–40cents per minute (Jensen, 2002). Unsurprisingly therefore ownership of mobiles is generally very small, e.g., between 0% and 6% in rural areas of Uganda (Janowski et al., 2003), with more general ownership in sub-Saharan Africa estimated at around 3% (Jensen, 2002). Internet access remains even more constrained e.g., with around one person in 250–400 having access, compared for example with 1 in 30 in Latin America. Internet connection is generally quite costly, with the exception of francophone West African states (Jensen, 2002). Overall, users of modern media to date have mainly been traders (especially larger-scale traders), and more wealthy producers.

Thus whilst modern technology will undoubtedly play a growing role for more wealthy producers and producer groups, using, e.g., satellite phones, wider use is likely to remain constrained. Such access might be improved by public-sector interventions, e.g., to assure better coverage, promotion of community acquisition or support to the poorest. Other options include further investment in communications infrastructure and differential phone charges (e.g., to subsidise remote areas). (Wye College, 1999). Recent developments in East Africa (Ferris and Robbins, 2004) also indicate potential for satellite-based systems to provide coverage in (rural) areas where internet access is not available, working with producer groups and the private sector. These initiatives include an array of technologies including use of short message services (SMS) linked to mobile phones. However actual access to the latter in rural areas to date appears limited because of limited ownership of mobile telephones (Kleih et al., 2004).

In terms of access to 'modern' technology there are particular limitations arising for women. These include the effects of women's activities that limit access time, difficulties in using public access community facilities, and limited income to pay for access. There is also a tendency for men to hijack information technology (IT) overall. Some exceptions do arise, e.g., via the Academy of Environmental Development (AED) Ghana and the use of telecentres in Uganda designed for illiterate women (CTA, 2001), but these are the exception rather than the rule.

Other media involving the printed word can be constrained by limited literacy that persists amongst adults in many areas, language issues, and limited coverage of, for example, newspapers in rural areas. Even where the latter are produced, circulation may be slow, especially in remote areas where the need for up-to-date information is greatest (Janowski et al., 2003). In rural Uganda it was also found that readership amongst women is especially constrained partly because of lower functional literacy (with, e.g., 25% of men but only 3% of women reading newspapers).

Overall radio is therefore generally rated as the most accessible media currently available, partly because ownership and/or access is often widespread, e.g., with over 80% of rural households owning radios and most others having some kind of access in rural Uganda (Janowski et al., 2003). However, listenership has been found to vary on a gender basis, which arises where men control ownership and/or access (e.g., in Uganda) Much current interest is focussed upon commercial FM radio and on community radio, but FM radio operated on commercial lines may be expensive, e.g., in terms of programme slots covering market information). One option is to promote sponsorship, e.g., through banks, credit agencies and input suppliers (Poole, 1999; Poole et al., 1998), but difficulties may arise because sponsors' interests predominate rather than those of listeners (Bagnall Oakeley and Ocilaje, 2002).

An alternative to FM radio is the development of community stations – these in fact may be the only option in remoter or poorer areas where there is insufficient return to support FM radio. Community stations are often sponsored and supported by donors or NGOs, but as a result may confront problems in terms of long-term sustainability. The level of professionalism on offer may also be limited, and participation in programme making difficult to sustain over time.

As is the case for some other sources, information-based programmes put out by radio sometimes lack up-to-date or reliable content. Part of the solution lies in close consultation with listeners in terms of type of programme, language, specific information content, number/repeats, and timing of programmes – the latter being especially important. Consultation with listeners in Uganda indicated the importance of these points and also raised suggestions, e.g., for greater participation by listeners, advertising of timing of programmes, and focus upon analysis of market issues, storage and transport.

Listeners have been found to have positive views towards educational/information programmes. Radio may act as a tool for both market information and also to promote group activity, especially where it is combined with local training inputs. Assessment of existing services in Uganda shows that radio (especially combined with training, e.g., via Foodnet and other local agencies), can lead to more effective marketing activity, e.g., in terms of negotiation with traders, accessing alternative markets and adopting storage strategies to sell at times of better prices (Kleih et al., 2004).

Formalisation of market linkages – contractual aspects. To a degree producers already obtain market information via traders, but this is often constrained by lack of mutual trust (see Best et al., this volume). A measure that could generate or improve mutual trust between producers and traders is via the development of standard contracts. This could also be done in the context of other measures to improve relationships, e.g., encouragement of private-sector interaction with producer bodies by intermediaries such as donors and NGOs. One example of this approach is provided by CLUSA where farmer's organisations are linked via apex bodies to 'reliable' traders.

Contracts as such can perform a variety of functions (Poole, 1999; Poole et al., 1999) e.g., clarifying and formalising obligations and enabling a means to adjust these, plus rights of stakeholders involved where there are unavoidable contingencies. In theory they also provide a means of formal redress where there are problems, but in practice it may be more satisfactory to rely upon informal or traditional norms. Over time such contractual systems can therefore become a means for building institutional (in its widest sense) components founded upon trust, and hence contribute to the business-enabling environment.

For the trader such contracts may provide greater assurance of supply especially for women traders, for example, those in Ghana (Poole et al., 1999). In more general terms benefits can arise via increased flows of market information, reductions in transaction costs and the interlinkage of information, input, credit and output markets (Wye College, 1999). Improved/standard contractual arrangements can be applied as much to input as output markets and may be especially applicable where these are otherwise problematic, e.g., as in Ghana and Tanzania (Poole et al., 1999; Lynch and Ashimogo, 1999).

Systems for 'sophisticated' (mainly export) markets. Intermediary bodies and institutions are of special importance in sophisticated/export markets, given the complexities of markets themselves and hence their associated information needs. Measures to improve the performance and interaction between agencies and market participants are therefore a key area. For some, notably NGOs, the need is often to improve their own understanding of niche markets in order to develop realistic views of potential and of support services, including information provision, that may be needed. Although mainly focussed upon traders, systems using the internet, satellite links, SMS and mobile phones such as those being developed in East Africa (Ferris and Robbins, 2004) can also offer opportunities to farmers groups given sufficient resources and capabilities. The systems developed in East Africa also cover formal and informal regional markets.

An additional component for many intermediary agencies is to improve access to and use of media, notably services offered by international agencies such as ITC. The United States Department of Agriculture (USDA) agricultural information service also covers some international markets (especially in Europe) as well as the US market and agencies such as the Europe-Africa-Caribbean-Pacific Liaison Committee (COLEACP) and the Commonwealth Secretariat can offer some assistance (Robbins, 1998). It remains the case however that the greater part of information from such sources concerns more mainstream commodity and product export markets. It could be argued that the latter may represent more appropriate markets in any event for agencies with limited trading experience.

A common option is to develop vertical linkages between developing country bodies and those in importing countries (Best et al., this volume). In some markets importers or their agents will insist upon such linkages and provide comprehensive information and technical advice for production, handling, and marketing – especially for perishable items, e.g., horticultural produce. These types of initiative include the development of out-grower schemes. For the latter there may be a need to assure safeguards to ensure fair treatment of producers including equal access to market information (see Biénabe and Sautier, this volume).

Government agencies may have a residual role and there are many examples including those operating with donor support. [e.g., the United States Agency for International Development (USAID)-funded Initiative for the Development of Export Agriculture (IDEA)].

The significance of producer organisations. Producer bodies are the topic of a separate paper (see Biénabe and Sautier, this volume), but it is worth noting that these bodies can play significant roles with respect to market information, including their interaction with other options, e.g., new media systems and contracting.

Producer bodies are increasingly being supported and promoted, and in theory at least can provide a means both to share costs of information search and to promote more effective use of information. They may enable producers to share the costs of contacts, e.g., with major wholesale markets and/or key traders in larger markets, hence improving information access, especially in poorer or remote areas. They may also provide scope for accessing more sophisticated/modern media, e.g., mobile phones or even internet services.

As noted earlier there are also initiatives to deliberately link group development (e.g., via training inputs), with more accessible media, notably radio (see Kleih et al., 2004; Ferris and Robbins, 2004). The latter have experimented with FM (and community) radio linked to promotion of communal marketing as a deliberate package. Initial feedback from the approach has been positive and respondents have indicated that more interactive approaches between groups and those developing programmes would be productive.

Producer groups developed with significant international NGO assistance (e.g., those assisted by CLUSA), have been shown to be sustainable, for example in Mozambique (de Vletter and Hills, 2004). Members of groups supported by both CARE and CLUSA have been found to have a wider range of market information sources than individuals, as well as deriving benefits from information supplied more directly via NGO assistance.

Conclusions

Information – its significance in wider market development

Experience indicates the importance of taking account of differing needs of stakeholders in the design of information systems, e.g., producers concerns with input as well as output markets, with food crops as well as cash crops, and with information that can diminish risk in both production and associated marketing activities. Local markets are often of key concern. This implies at least some involvement of producers themselves in the identification of areas of information need and the design of means to meet such needs. Information generally is only of value if it can be effectively used, and it seems likely that a part of the information package needs to be the development of producers' own analytical capability. This can be done on an individual basis (e.g., through training) or, perhaps more efficiently via producer groups where these exist. Similarly, another part of the package may be the development of confidence and negotiating skills that can improve both marketing capability and the degree of self-sufficiency in information acquisition and analysis. The latter is likely to be particularly important for women and the poor.

At the outset of this paper it was noted that market(ing) information is only one of several concerns of small-scale producers. Other priorities clearly will vary, but more obvious areas include access to 'hard' infrastructure, especially roads/transport, as well as other elements of 'soft' infrastructure, notably security, and financial institutions for both savings and credit. Small-scale producers will generally require more than information alone, e.g., training in production, or processing; and/or improved access, e.g., to inputs or to credit or savings promotion schemes, etc. Hence whatever the information package adopted, it is evident that there is likely to be a need for a similarly tailored package of additional components (see Hellin et al., this volume)

Sustainability of systems – coverage and cost-effectiveness

Regardless of quality of services, public sector and NGO-sponsored information systems have frequently collapsed due to financial constraints. Financial sustainability may be inherently a problem given the (semi) public good nature of information for many stakeholders. Payment systems for information for small-scale producers will in any case be difficult to operate due to the large numbers and their dispersed location (Kleih, 1999). However it is apparent that information can also be a private good and that there may be scope to charge specific categories of stakeholder, e.g., larger producers, processors associations, etc. (CTA, 2001). This may imply the need for a deliberate strategy to have multiple stakeholders in market information systems since small-scale producers alone may be too dependent upon subsidised systems. Where subsidies are involved in information systems these need to be affordable, explicit, finite, and as limited as possible. Alternative funding options could also be feasible, e.g., the scope for endowment funds which could be established initially with donor funding (CTA, 2001).

Several further strategies/conclusions stem from problems with sustainability. Firstly it is important to build systems that minimise the level of information gathering, analysis and distribution needed by focusing on key requirements of stakeholders. Secondly to use media that provide the best coverage and value for money – at present radio appears the best option in this respect, although experimentation with more sophisticated media, working with, for example, producer groups and group marketing may also have potential.

Integration with other marketing initiatives

Institutional development will remain a key component in information systems (CTA, 2001), e.g., there may be scope to link information systems to group approaches and to the encouragements of capacity to analyse markets on the part of producers (bodies) themselves. Linkage between different agencies – especially producer bodies and local and international NGOs may add to such capacity. Hybrid bodies, notably companies limited by guarantee, may be able to play the part of 'honest brokers' between producers and the private sector and be more attuned to commercial issues (Marter and Wandschneider, 2002). Experience in Asia, (India, Bangladesh) indicates that such companies can also provide training to producers that includes development of producers analytical capacity. Producers' capacity to cover fees for such training may be an issue indicating a possible role for initial NGO support to be withdrawn as producers resources develop (e.g., via savings initiatives).

Producer bodies may also facilitate approaches that seek to promote market linkage. This can be at a general level by providing a forum for greater interaction with the private trading sector (perhaps assisted via companies limited by guarantee), in order to identify areas of common interest including information exchange. There is also scope for more specific interventions e.g., development of standard contracts (Poole, 1999) that be effective both at the individual trader/producer level and help to improve the wider business and commercial environment.

The combination of a variety of approaches to improve both marketing and market information access and use has been illustrated by the use of training and FM radio coupled to producer group development and activity (Kleih et al., 1999 a; Kleih et al., 1999b). The approach used has been based upon participatory techniques and local institutions (e.g., local radio and training via Foodnet and other local agencies). Future options might be to progressively build in private trading sector participation to such initiatives.

Some issues to be resolved

Whilst considerable progress has been made in the development of more effective market information systems, e.g., through greater involvement of producers, institutional innovations and the use of more cost effective media, etc., there remains a range of issues to be resolved. Some of the questions arising from this paper include:

- How fundamental are producer bodies in enabling (poor) small-scale producers both to afford market information access and to use it effectively?
- To what extent will modern media play a role in information systems relevant to (poor) small-scale producers? – and over what time-frame?
- How important is human capital development as a precursor to effective use of market information, especially for women?
- Do media such as radio really require additional interventions (e.g., training, linkage to communal marketing or producer bodies) in order to be effective?
- Is remaining public-sector support to market information systems best focussed at the national level or to decentralised or local systems?
- Given their resources can NGOs play anything more than a relatively marginal role in systems designed to meet the needs of the majority of small-scale producers?
- What combinations of agencies and institutional relationships work best in the development of effective information services – and how much private sector participation is desirable or feasible?

References

Bagnall Oakeley, H. and Ocilaje, M. 2002. Development of procedures for the assessment and management by farmers of their agricultural information networks and needs at the sub-county level in Uganda. National Agricultural Research Organisation/Department for International Development (NARO/DFID) Natural Resources Institute (NRI), Chatham, UK.

Coote. C. and Wandschneider, T. 2001. Training manual on NGOs and agricultural marketing: principles, interventions and tools. A report produced for CARE Bangladesh. Natural Resources Institute (NRI), Chatham, UK.

Coote, C., Gordon, A. and Marter, A. 2000. International Trade in Agricultural Commodities: Liberalisation and its Implications for Development and Poverty Reduction in ACP States. Policy Series No. 5. Natural Resources Institute (NRI), Chatham, UK. 79pp.

CTA (Technical Centre for Agriculture and Rural Cooperation). 1999. Information and communication technologies: A remarkable revolution. SPORE No. 79. CTA, Wageningen, the Netherlands.

CTA (Technical Centre for Agriculture and Rural Cooperation). 2001. Gender and Agriculture in the Information Society. Technical consultation on the integration of statistical and agricultural market information services for CTA workshop held in Wageningen the Netherlands, November, 2001. CTA Working Document No. 8026. CTA, Wageningen, the Netherlands.

Cuello, J., Rodriguez, D. and Hellin, J. 2004. The Kamayaq farmer-to-farmer extension in the Andes AgREN, Overseas Development Insitute (ODI), London, UK. 49pp.

Delgado, C.L. 1997. Africa's changing agricultural development strategies. Brief No. 20 International Food Policy Research Institute (IFPRI), Washington, DC, USA. 42pp.

de Vletter, F. and Hills, S. 2004. The CLUSA rural group enterprise programme in Mozambique. Presented at the Rural Incomes and Employment Workshop held in Canterbury, UK, July 2004. Aga Khan Foundation (AKF) Geneva, Switzerland. (unpublished)

Ferris, S. and Robbins, P. 2004. Market Information Services, Quality, Governance, Sustainability and Use of ICTs. (mimeo)

Goodland, A. and Kleih, U. 1999. Community access to market opportunities – Options for remote areas: a literature review. Natural Resources Institute (NRI), Chatham, UK.

Hellin, J., Rodriguez, D. and Cuello, J. 2004. Sustainable farmer-to-farmer extension. Appropriate Technology 31(1).

James, R., Fancis, P. and Pereza, G. 2001. The institutional context of rural poverty reduction in Uganda: decentralisation's dual nature. University of East Anglia, Norwich, UK.

Janowski, M., Kleih, U. and Okoboi G. 2003. Baseline study carried out in five sub-counties on farmer's livelihoods, and needs and sources of information. NRI Report No. 2766. Natural Resources Institute (NRI), Chatham, UK.

Jensen, M. 2002. The African internet: A status report African internet connectivity internet site, 2004. http://www3.sn.apc.org/Africa (accessed January 2005)

Kleih, U. 1999 Community access to marketing opportunities: Final Technical Report. Natural Resources Institute (NRI), Chatham, UK.

Kleih ,U., Jumbe, C., Kergna, A. and Odwongo, W., 1999a. Community access to marketing opportunities. Paper presented at the workshop on Improving Smallholder Market Access in Remote Areas, held at Wye College UK, 1999. (unpublished)

Kleih, U., Jumbe, C. and Tchale, H. 1999b. Community access to market opportunities – Options for remote areas. Malawi case study. Informal project report. Natural Resources Institute (NRI), Chatham, UK.

Kleih, U., Kergna, A. and Sanono, O. 1999c. Community access to market opportunities – Options for remote areas. Mali case study. Informal project report. Natural Resources Institute (NRI), Chatham, UK.

Kleih,U., Odwongo, W. and Ndyashangaki, C. 1999d. Community access to market opportunities – Options for remote areas. Uganda case study. Informal project report. Natural Resources Institute (NRI), Chatham, UK.

Kleih, U., Okoboi, G., Janowski, M., Omony, G., Taiwo, B. and Bisase, D. 2004 Synthesis evaluation survey in seven sub-counties of Lira, Apac and Soroti districts. Informal project report. Natural Resources Institute (NRI), Chatham, UK.

Lynch, K. and Ashimogo, G. 1999. Overcoming informational constraints: improving horticultural marketing and technical information flows to smallholders: Tanzania country report. Informal project report. Wye College, University of London, UK.

Marter, A. and Wandschneider, T. 2002. The role of NGOs and CBOs in marketing in Uganda: The potential in remote regions and in reaching the poor. NRI Report No. 2699. Natural Resources Institute (NRI), Chatham, UK.

Matsaert, H. 2002. Institutional analysis in natural resources research. Best Practice Guidelines No. 11, Natural Resources Institute (NRI) for Department for International Development (DFID), London, UK.

Poole, N. (ed.). 1999. Overcoming informational constraints: improving horticultural marketing and technical information flows to smallholders: Summary project report. Wye College University of London, UK.

Poole, N. 2001. Market information in theory and practice: institutional perspectives. In Technical consultation on the integration of statistical and agricultural market information services CTA workshop held at Wageningen, the Netherlands. Imperial College of Science Technology and Medicine University of London, London,UK.

Poole, N., Kydd, J., Loader, R., Lynch, K., Poulton, C. and Wilkin, K. 1998.Overcoming informational constraints: improving horticultural marketing and technical information flows to smallholders: Literature review. Wye College, University of London, UK.

Poole, N., Seini, W. and Heh, V. 1999. Overcoming informational constraints: improving horticultural marketing and technical information flows to smallholders: Ghana country report. Wye College, University of London, UK.

Poon, B. 1994. FAO Agrimarket Guide. Food and Agriculture Organization of the United Nations, Rome, Italy.

Poulton, C., Chaonwa, W., Mukwereza, L., Loader, R., Mariga, K., Masanganise, P. and Sanyatwe, D. 1999. Overcoming informational constraints: improving horticultural marketing and technical information flows to smallholders: Zimbabwe case study. Wye College, University of London, UK.

Robbins, P. 1998. Review of market information systems in Botswana, Ethiopia , Ghana and Zimbabwe A study commissioned by Technical Centre for Agriculture and Rural Cooperation (CTA). Wageningen, the Netherlands.

Robbins, P., Bikande, F., Ferris, S., Hodges, R., Kleih, U., Okoboi, G. and Wandschnieder, T. 2004. Advice manual for the organisation of collective marketing activities by small-scale farmers. Natural Resources Institute (NRI), Chatham, UK.

Shepherd, A.W. 1997. Market information services. AGS Bulletin, Food and Agriculture Organization of the United Nations, Rome Italy.

Whiteside, M. and Gouveia, F. 2003. The role of groups and associations in agricultural livelihood development in northern Mozambique – Experiences from CARE projects. Consultants report. Gloucester, UK. (unpublished)

Wye College. 1999. Overcoming informational constraints: improving horticultural marketing and technical information flows to smallholders: Final Technical Report. Wye College, University of London, UK.

The role of small-scale producers' organisations in addressing market access

Estelle Biénabe and Denis Sautier

Introduction

Marketing through rural producers' organisations can be a way to overcome the constraints faced by individual small-scale farmers. Farming systems around the world are very diverse, yet dominated by small-scale family farming. About 75% of the 1,300 billion people working in the farming sector worldwide (3 billions with their families) still practice manual agriculture. Half of them do not use any inputs (fertilisers, seeds, etc.) because they lack the means (Mazoyer and Roudart, 2002). Only 2% of the world's farmers have a tractor and annually produce more than 1,000 mt/worker; 66% of the world's farmers annually produce less that 10 mt of grain equivalents/worker (Mazoyer, 2001). In addition to farmers' generally low incomes and lack of capital, marketing agricultural products tends to be hampered by such market imperfections as lack of information in rural areas, that is reinforced by the geographic dispersion of agents, and by poor infrastructure and communications. These characteristics are particularly vivid with the withdrawal of the state from productive and economic functions when the private sector is under-developed or when the market is not sufficiently attractive. Collective action can therefore be a way in which to address these obstacles and mitigate transaction costs, granted a dynamic market is identified. In the context of globalisation, characterised by more instability and competition, small-scale farmers are confronted with an increased need to enhance their competitiveness, and hence their productivity and ability to take advantage of economies of scale. Organisation can enable them to do this.

Small-scale farmers face new constraints from the rapid changes in the organisation of marketing channels that are arising in the developing world. Public marketing boards are being dismantled, wholesale markets are loosing space; and supermarkets chains are spreading in Latin America, East and South-East Asia, Central Europe and Eastern and Southern Africa (Reardon et al., 2003). Food product characteristics tend to be no longer determined by producers, but by traders, supermarkets and agro-industries that set their own standards. These private standards often substitute for missing or inadequate public enforcement of safety norms, and are used in the competition with the informal sector to claim superior food product quality (Reardon and Berdegue, 2002; Balsevich et al., 2003). Furthermore, the rise of supermarkets tends to result in most countries in the establishment of centralised buying and distribution centres, with: (i) concomitant shifts from traditional brokers to new specialised/dedicated wholesalers and (ii) a decline of traditional wholesale systems (Dries et al., 2004).

Small-scale producers generally lack the knowledge, information and re-sources to meet quality standards and formal markets' specifications. And the usual lack of formal contractual arrangements may be a disincentive for them to invest to meet these requirements. Furthermore, these requirements (quality, respect of standards and sanitary norms) are often beyond the technical and organisational capacities of such organisations. Support is then needed but it must be well thought out.

Small and competitive: the role of different association and co-ordination patterns and strategies

One of the main questions in addressing farmers' market access capability is how to improve their competitiveness. Competitiveness can be defined as the capac-ity to improve a market position (Bourdanove and Martos, 1992). It rests on the one hand on cost-reduction strategies that can be achieved through economies of scale, either in terms of input provision, technical assistance or commercial logis-tics and hence, through farmers' organisations. On the other hand, competitive-ness also relies on such non-price factors as reputation, commercial efficiency, or specific quality attributes. These aspects can also be enhanced through farmers' co-ordination.

A second important issue is the lack of power and negotiating capacity of most small-scale farmers in their relationship with downstream agents. Negotiating skills, power and political representation are also critical if small-scale farmers are to participate in the improvement of their institutional environment and in setting up a realistic regulatory framework. Without a strong environment, producers and producers' organisations alone may lack the capacity to anticipate market tends and changes. All these issues can be dealt with through farmers' organisations and collaborative networks, which can take very diverse forms.

There are several ways to achieve economies of scale between smallhold-ers. Aggregation of production, processing, or marketing activities into bigger economic units is just one of them. This aggregation does not always lead to better performance, as is clearly proven by the failure of many over-sized or badly run production or processing units, such as the under-utilised industrial milling units in West Africa. Williamson (1985) gained wide academic recognition for his dem-onstration that economic organisation and governance depend on those structures that reduce transaction costs. Unified governance within one integrated economic unit tends to substitute for the market in those particular cases when transactions are frequent and a high level of uncertainty makes external contracts hazardous. Richardson (1972) actually identified three co-ordination mechanisms for econom-ic activities: hierarchy (direction), market (prices), and co-operation.

Horizontal co-operation as a strategy for achieving economies of scale in-cludes producers' formal associations. But other collaborative configurations also merit consideration. A significant example is the application of the industrial clus-ter approach to agro-food activities.

Local agri-food systems

An array of recent theoretical approaches including endogenous growth analysis, economic geography, or global value chain analysis, has stressed the idea that competitiveness in world markets rests on specific national or local conditions (Requier-Desjardins et al., 2003). These conditions are not solely defined by the availability of cheap labour or natural resources. They also include human capital, externalities linked to branch specialisation, and the competitive advantage stemming from the clustering of specific activities (Krugman, 1991; Porter, 1990). Such factors are also applicable at local levels.

The theoretical framework of cluster analysis (or local productive systems dynamics) is based on Alfred Marshall's work, which stresses the part played by geographical proximity as a diffusion factor of specific technological externalities (qualified workforce, innovation diffusion, etc.). In the 1970s, 'neo-Marshallian' economists, studying localised networks of small and medium enterprises (SMEs) in central Italy – the so-called 'Italian industrial districts' – (Beccatini, 1979), gave further insights into these externalities. They showed that sharing common values, habits, and historical experience induced a common identity and social basis among local entrepreneurs.

Within local productive systems, the proximity of values and behaviours may allow for a lowering of transaction costs, thus fostering improved efficiency of market transactions and greater productive flexibility. The existence of a tight network of relationships also creates a favourable background for collective action, with positive impacts on knowledge diffusion and innovation (Requier-Desjardins et al., 2003).

Clustering is a significant feature of the industrialisation process of developing countries (Nadvi and Schmitz, 1999). Clustering allows small-scale businesses to challenge some of the constraints hampering their development: lack of finance, lack of economies of scale, inability to take risky steps, etc. This is because collective action capacity can be an endogenous 'specific asset' of clusters that goes beyond the mere existence of cost-sharing and agglomeration externalities (Requier-Desjardins et al., 2003). Nevertheless, while clustering can be a path to industrialisation in developing countries, industrialisation is not necessarily an outcome.

Clusters exist in agri-food commodity chains as in electronics, textile or other sectors. However, cluster analysis has as yet hardly been applied to the agricultural or agribusiness sector. It could prove to be a very useful approach for SMEs such as, for example, those in rural food-processing industries in Latin America, that are embedded in rural areas where they contribute to rural livelihoods (see Box 1).

Many other clusters of rural agro-industries can be identified throughout Latin America, and in other parts of the world. They process and market such products as fruits, sugarcane, coffee or cassava, directed mostly to distant urban or export markets (SYAL, 2002; ARTE, 2004). The integration of such clusters into social and local networks can give producers flexibility and enhance their original skills. It facilitates learning-by-doing and learning-by-using and hence, the emergence of

Box 1. Cheese-processing clusters in Latin America

Cheese-processing units are concentrated in some dairy cattle breeding areas through-out Latin-American countries, for example, Ubate in Cundinamarca (Colombia), the hills of Santa Cruz de Turrialba in Costa Rica, the department of Cajamarca in Peru, or some specific areas in Brazil. In Peru, the department of Cajamarca hosts 12% of all national-al cattle and produces 16% of the country's milk, 30% of which is processed into cheese by thousands of small units located in the south of the department around the city of Cajamarca. A significant part of this cheese production is marketed outside the region (mainly in coastal cities), through a cluster of some 80 shops located in the same area of the city of Cajamarca (Boucher, 2004). Similarly in the state of Sergipe in north-eastern Brazil, a geographical concentration of 147 *fabriquetas* (small commercial cheese-process-ing units), along with traders, can be found in the semi-arid area of Nossa Senhora da Gloria, while the surrounding municipalities have very few of these units (Cerdan and Sautier, 2001).They market their product in neighbouring cities and states such as Bahia and Pernambuco. Each cluster consists not only of cheese-producing plants, processing milk bought from cattle-breeders, but also road carriers specialising in milk or cheese trans-port, and various input and equipment (ferments, moulds, etc.) suppliers; a manufacturer who adapts equipment to the specific needs of the *fabriquetas*; and various specialised traders. As a result, the number of milk products has expanded, from the original *queijo de coalho* to new varieties such as *precozido* and *mussarella*; and a large number of small- and medium-scale cattle-breeders have managed to maintain their access to markets.

innovations. Sharing the same historical experience and regional identity, and build-ing on local social capital, these local agri-food systems can, under some conditions, generate economies of scale, minimise transaction costs and trigger collective action, resulting in more sustainable market access for small-scale producers.

Farmers' organisations as a means to achieve economies of scale and access to markets

The development of producer's organisations (POs) enables the pooling of such different resources as credit, information, labour, and transport for selling prod-ucts or buying inputs. Thus, it usually leads to economies of scale. The POs can assume several functions in the commodity chain, including: collection, grading, post-harvest processing and storage. They include a wide range of organisations, such as self-help groups, farmers' associations, and cooperatives (Bosc et al., 2003; Perret and Mercoiret, 2003). Through bulk purchase and/or selling, they can in-crease individual farmers' bargaining power.

To what extent does the search for economies of scale justify the promotion of large groups? Large groups do indeed enable economies of scale with limited mo-bilisation of capital per member and greater scope for pooling risks. Yet as group size increases, so will transaction costs. Larger groups are likely to encompass more divergent interests and asymmetric sharing of information and power (Jaffee and Morton, 1995). Moreover, in small groups, members are likely to receive a higher share of total benefits and to more easily promote member commitment and knowledge of each other. As pointed out by Stringfellow et al. (1997), 'there is often a trade-off between economies of scale and group cohesion, and group cohesion is a critical factor for sustained success'. The efficiency of developing farmers' groups to achieve economies of scale can be counterbalanced by farmers' lack of cohesion and the associated risks of free-riding behaviour. As noted by Stringfellow et al. (1997), small size and homogeneity, which favour group cohesion, are much more important for activities that imply the management of shared assets than for those concentrating on securing transactions with a buyer or a supplier. Indeed, the ability to undertake complex activities by farmer organisations such as operating jointly owned assets requires higher commitment, skills and experience than just coordinating marketing or procurement activities. For marketing activities alone, larger groups can be set up to benefit from economies of scale. Selection of group members is often a key element in creating necessary trust among members. But organisations with restrictive membership conditions tend to create more unfavourable and unstable market conditions for non-member farmers.

In addition to size issues, other key elements affect building an efficient economic organisation oriented towards accessing markets. When discussing the keys for success of POs in accessing markets, elements can be drawn from the San Francisco de Axis cooperative in Nicaragua; an example of the successful development of commercial relationships between a PO and a formal market (supermarket channel) (Rondot et al., 2004). In 1992, the cooperative began with 25 members, selling fresh milk to Prolacsa-Nestlé y La Perfecta. Today, with 141 small- and medium-scale producers as members, the cooperative has diversified its products, with 30% of its revenues now coming from the sale of various types of cheese to supermarkets, 10% from cheese exports to El Salvador and Honduras, and the remaining 60% still coming from selling fresh milk. Milk purchase prices may be lower than those of other cooperatives, but for members, the main advantages are stable prices and a guarantee that the cooperative will buy everything they produce..

To become a supermarket supplier, this cooperative overcame a number of obstacles that can be grouped into three categories:

1. **Barriers to milk processing:** legal status and sanitary certification; environmental compliance certification; commercial registration
2. **Barriers to becoming a supermarket supplier:** a registered brand for cooperative products; proper packaging with bar codes, nutrient data, and optimum purchase dates for the product; renting supermarket shelf space
3. **Requirements to remain a supermarket supplier:** regular product supply; product advertising; 15–30-day delayed payments; obligation to lower prices (10–15%) at special times during the year such as Christmas (while the supermarket margin remains the same: 32%); 1 month's notice before a price increase.

The success of this small-scale producers' cooperative in becoming a supermarket supplier relies on three major elements:

1. **Performance of the cooperative.** Its governing bodies function well and provide accountability and transparency. There is a strong leadership and a clear division of functions between the president of the cooperative and the chairperson of the audit committee. Instead of redistributing gains, the cooperative provides social services that are not otherwise available and that promote a positive image for the cooperative. There is a clear separation of functions between the leadership of the cooperative and the management of the processing factory. Finally, coordination need is higher and collective action works best when dealing with a product that is highly perishable and has high added value.

2. **Ability of the group to identify market opportunities and exploit them.** The cooperative was able to recognise when some of their initial products were not doing well, and quickly made a decision to drop them.

3. **The group's commercial portfolio strategy.** They remained in the traditional market of supplying fresh milk, while diversifying their products and their buyers.

Not only was the organisation able to answer the technical and financial requirements for supplying supermarkets, but it could also identify market opportunities and draw up efficient marketing strategies. It stands out from this example that successful market access development can be reached, provided that both an efficient management and clear marketing strategies exist.

Search for quality: a driver for an efficient organisation and sustained commercial relations

Competitiveness in food production can also be achieved through product differentiation. Small-scale farmers can have comparative advantage in supplying differentiated supply chains based on specific quality, be it in terms of specific location, traditional know-how, or low production costs. According to Moustier (case study in Rondot et al., 2004) the ability to deliver 'safe product' labelled vegetables was a determinant in the choice of supermarkets in Hanoi for their supply from small-scale farmers' cooperatives. Restrictions to the reliance on local production supply arise from the absence of an independent quality-control system that emphasises the importance of an enabling institutional environment.

Developing a partnership with well-organised small-scale producers can be more efficient for down-stream, specific-quality, supply-chain actors, than to work with larger-scale producers whose commitment to enforcing all the required standards may be lower (Roche et al., 2004).

Relying on their experience in setting up a differentiated cocoa supply chain in Ecuador, under the label 'Bio Equitable' (that combines principles from organic agriculture and fair trade), Roche et al. (2004) suggested that a complete and efficient process of involvement in a quality-oriented supply chain for a PO may last about 10 years, from the start of information exchange with PO leaders and local technical staff up to a sustained commercialisation of the product. The learning process for all actors (producers, collectors, exporters, technical assistance staff and buyers) is rather slow. Hence, for high quality to be reached, and given the length of the initial steps, it is essential that long-term mutual agreements be made.

A key to success is ensuring that all supply-chain actors' expectations are communicated to, and understood by, the other actors. Furthermore, the objective of achieving a high-quality product must be shared by all actors and must be kept in mind. There is a need for repeated and frequent communications and negotiations to establish trust. Quality requirements must be understood and remembered by all supply-chain agents at all times. Bosc (case study in Rondot et al., 2004) reports that the building of a sustainable commercial relationship between the SA4R, a French autonomous society specialising in Aveyron-origin labelled veal from southern France, of which the producers are the shareholders, and Auchan, a huge French supermarket chain, was made possible by repeated exchanges. These supported the adjustment and finalisation of the concrete rules and conditions of the commercial relationship, i.e., meat appearance, the quality of the cut and of the packaging. This led to the involvement of a slaughterhouse, Bigard, in the partnership and to the definition of a tripartite charter between Auchan, SA4R and Bigard. Periodic meetings are still organised to: supervise the organisation of relations between the three partners, define a joint promotion policy, and to monitor such activities as: demands planning, development actions and price forecasting. Visits from Auchan department managers to SA4R as well as from producers to the stores for promotional activities are organised regularly.

These principles of intense communication and fine-tuning of co-operation rules and relationships remain valid for quality products, whatever the local context. It is really important for producers to clearly understand their responsibility and tasks within the supply chain and to receive fair remuneration for their efforts. By the same token, support to their quality-control manager must be a priority for the PO.

To support building a trusting relationship with downstream actors, selection criteria for the entrance of new producers may be necessary. In the SA4R case, the entrance of a new breeder as a SA4R supplier is conditioned by a probationary period of 6 months prior to the breeder being given a delivery reference. This delivery reference is revised each year to account for producers' behaviour and to guarantee the reliability of their engagement.

To develop a quality-oriented supply chain, essential technical and organisational changes must be devised and adopted. And to be successful and cost-effective, care must be taken in designing a processing scheme that minimises the technical and social changes linked to producers' current practices (Roche et al., 2004).

Producers' organisations and negotiation processes

The POs responsible for marketing functions need to be efficient economic organisations, and external stakeholders often argue that specialisation is a good way to promote efficacy and efficiency. Stakeholder support to POs may therefore be tailored to make this happen. Actually, a PO usually performs a wide range of activities and functions: economic but also social, representation (advocacy and voice), information sharing/capacity building, and coordination. Economic functions include: the supply, production, processing, and marketing of goods and services and the management of such production factors as: water, land, labour and agricultural equipment. Social functions, benefiting members and/or the local community can include: cultural, education, training, health, drinking water and mutual support. Representation includes defence of group interests and advocacy at the local, and sometimes regional and national levels (before government, firms etc.). Information sharing includes communication, both internal and with other actors, and capacity building. Finally, co-ordination is a key role since POs are in a position to establish linkages at both local and global levels and to integrate the functions cited above.

The need for negotiation capabilities to equilibrate the balance of power with downstream actors and to favour mutual trust and transparency in exchanges is real, and calls for reinforcement of the advocacy function of POs. A balance has thus to be struck in organisations between economic specialisation and non-economic roles. PO specialisation obviously also depends on the local availability of social and economic services.

In most cases, the economic and advocacy functions cannot be considered separately. The grouping of economic operations by POs might be a good start. Nevertheless, it remains necessary for local farmers' groups to scale up in order to gain real bargaining power. Indeed, they need to attain a critical mass if they are to negotiate with traders and the authorities for better prices and a more favourable environment. However, it is worth mentioning that bargaining power does not rely exclusively on production scale. A higher-quality product also enhances the producer's voice, because buyers for speciality markets are much more supplier-dependent than those of commodity products.

POs can play a role in negotiating with other stakeholders changes in the institutional environment according to small-scale farmers' interests. Stockbridge et al. (2003) argue that POs are a good candidate for solving coordination problems since they can build up the internal and external relationships of trust that are required to secure credible commitment forms, and to cooperate in order to realise mutually beneficial actions and investments.

Inversely, the control of economic functions by POs is an indispensable step in the process of building their capacity to assume advocacy functions. Basically POs can defend farmers' interests and improve their participation in three domains: (i) decision-making processes over programmes and projects, (ii) policy-making processes about market access reinforcement and market environment enhancement, and (iii) prospective reflection about the role of family agriculture in a liberalised and global environment – the challenge being to propose and defend general policy orientations that would be more consistent with small-scale farmers' objectives, strategies and specific constraints.

Linkages between economic and advocacy roles may be internal to a multipurpose organisation, or be developed through co-ordination between several organisations. They remain, in any case, an important strategy for combining short- and longer-term competitiveness for small-scale farmers.

How can successful co-operation between small-scale producers be supported and promoted?

Integrating organisation with empowerment through flexible capacity building is the key message to successful support. This can be translated into five basic functions for governments, non-governmental organisations (NGOs) and the private sector.

1. Taking on board the diversity of organisations

First of all, it is now widely recognised that provision of outside support should be aimed at supporting small-scale farmers in implementing their own strategies. Real care needs to be taken about the way to support farmers' organisations because such support may induce an over-dependency on external aid and weaken the existing organisational pattern. The creation of externally driven farmers' groups induced by project developers may be harmful to their viability, because it generally does not take enough account of the underlying patterns of social and economic organisation. Delion (2000) points out the need to involve social specialists in project preparation to analyse the different layers of local organisations (small informal groups, large professional groups...) and to identify clearly the role of different kinds of rural groups at different levels. Biénabe et al. (2004) report the case of the Programme de professionnalisation de l'agriculture (PPDA) in Madagascar which, in 1994, intended to create a new body aimed at representing farmers' organisations at the national level, but failed because this new body did not have any legitimacy among existing grassroots farmers' groups. On the other hand, local productive arrangements, such as the clustering of rural SMEs who have legitimacy based on shared values and social networks but are not always represented by a formal economic organisation, deserve to be better recognised and supported.

Different types of training and capacity building may be required to strengthen POs according to their different needs and opportunities (ODI–CIRAD, 2001). Capacity building can aim to improve the internal structure and functioning of the organisations (decision-making processes, membership rules, internal circulation of information, member compensation for services) in order to facilitate mechanisms of internal consultation and representation. It can focus on access to information such as market functioning (price fluctuation, operators' power, consumers' requirement, etc.) so that POs can develop well thought-out points of view and informed strategies. Another important field for capacity building is improving management capacities, particularly in relation to implementation processes and control over products. And finally, capacity to negotiate and develop proposals is crucial to building new coordination modes and contractual relations.

In remote rural areas, producers' co-operation and organisation needs are likely to differ from those in peri-urban contexts where market connections and opportunities are more diversified. Producers' organisations in remote areas tend to assume a multifunctional role integrating several economic, representation and advocacy activities, with a strong cohesion and a strong link to local development issues.

Obviously, seriously taking on board the need to adapt support strategies to the diversity of organisations implies the development of participatory approaches. For instance, the AVAL project (Action de valorisation des savoir-faire agro-alimentaires africains) that aims to promote of women's food-processing and catering activities in West African cities, promoted a new training concept called 'Ecoles pratiques' (practical schools). Instead of having standard business-support modules delivered by instructors in a dedicated building and over a short period, these schools negotiate the training contents, place, frequency and schedules with each women beneficiaries' group and focus on their dominant economic or commercial activity. Experienced local practitioners ensure follow-up during and after training periods (Devautour et al., 2001). On the whole, training programmes for groups and entrepreneurs that are traditionally based on codified knowledge should provide spaces for apprenticeships in order to augment tacit knowledge, since innovation processes generally arise from a combination of both types of knowledge.

2. Adapting capacity building to POs' structuring stage

Capacity building is a dynamic process that involves a large array of actions. To support the creation of a regional farmers' organisation requested by farmers' representatives to broaden their representation, a regional development project that has been working in Madagascar since 1994 supported by the French Ministry of Foreign Affairs and Agriculteurs français et développement international (AFDI), ran an extensive awareness programme in the villages, together with literacy training, and information and farmer exchanges. This project fostered the emergence of a network of farmers able to participate in public debates and the creation of the Maison des paysans (MdP). Ten years later, the MdP and its local representatives constitute a network of 250 elected small-scale farmers, representing 29 districts. The MdP has two functions: representing the producers, and supplying services to them (advice/information, on-farm trials, experience-sharing, etc.).

Particularly in the early stages of a PO's development, external aid can play a facilitative role. But particular focus should be put on developing the organisational capacities of farmers' groups in order to ensure the PO's autonomy and sustainability. The experience of the NGO Formation paysanne et promotion des organisations professionnelles agricoles (FERT) in Madagascar provides key insights on how to accompany such processes with adapted capacity-building programmes. FERT started work in 1985 with unorganised farmers at community level and set up small, informal groups to organise bulk purchase of inputs or credit supply through small village banks, storage, trading, etc. The primary purpose was to: guarantee the availability of inputs and the quality of products, reduce operational costs (transport, storage, collecting), and increase farmers' bargaining power. Once these activities were working efficiently, each small, specialised group–with technical assistance from FERT–was formalised into an association that took up new activities and grew in size. The associations then scaled up into regional unions, and later on into a national federation.

This gradual support stretched over more than 15 years. An operational 'learning-by-doing' approach was adopted to ensure the viability of the promoted changes. Farmers were given responsibilities from the beginning within small informal groups, while at the same time being given support to assess their needs for training, assistance, etc. Hence, FERT's ongoing support to the capacity-building process was adjusted to the expressed needs of the groups. FERT gave support to: productive activities with local groups, advocacy training and market studies with organisation leaders, and through study trips inside and outside the country in collaboration with local and international institutions. Farmers' groups were also entrusted with some funds to strengthen their abilities to take responsibilities.

It is obvious from this project that an operational learning process is a key element in fostering farmer-driven initiatives and that the creation of an effective farmers' organisation is a long and difficult process. Adopting the learning-by-doing approach over a long period and adapting it gradually to evolving needs appears to be successful. This project also shows the relevance of a support project to articulate a continuum from farmers' grassroots technical activities up to POs' institutional and policy-level capacities, thus reinforcing the farmer representatives' credibility.

This raises the key question as to what sort of 'support' is needed to establish POs. If it takes such a long commitment to ensure that the POs are sustainable, it may be a role that only an NGO or a government can play. To what extent can the private sector oversee a similar role to that of FERT in Madagascar? Some outstanding support and training work has been done through the private sector to empower POs through participation in cash-crop supply chains, e.g., for cotton in Mozambique (Bonnal and Sautier, 1998) and in Mali. However, these actions still generally rely on public or international funding. The private sector logically restricts its focus to those associations that have a direct functional role in the considered supply chain. Finally, support actions channelled by the private sector are in jeopardy when markets are declining, or when firms are merged or re-engineered.

3. Building capacity to efficiently take on economic functions

Ensuring an economic function works efficiently through collective action – such as efficient access to inputs for farmers – is highly demanding in terms of PO skills and capacities. Support has to be carefully designed, as shown by the Projet de centres de prestation de services (PCPS) developed for business services in Mali. This project assisted a federation of service centres, involving a total of 157 POs, to call for tenders with the main input traders and to obtain cheaper inputs for its members. Farmers' groups received support to access market information and to understand the characteristics of markets (price fluctuations, control exerted by larger operators, etc.). But the federation still cannot ensure input supply satisfactorily, due to problems of delayed delivery and lack of input quality because insufficient stress was put on: financial management, stock management and punctual deliveries, respect of quality norms, transparency, etc. Supporting these collective organisational capacities is a key factor for POs if they are to effectively and efficiently assume economic functions.

When producers join an organisation, they usually expect to benefit rapidly from their participation in collective action. Members' immediate payment when delivering their product can help POs tackle the potential problem of free riders. But it presupposes that financial capacities are planned ahead of marketing activities, and that downstream contractual arrangements have been developed. This highlights the need for training to develop and pilot new institutional arrangements between companies, banks and smallholders that are mutually acceptable in terms of risk sharing and the distribution of benefits.

Planning and risk assessment must then precede the choice and implementation of economic functions by POs. As pointed out by Stringfellow et al., (1997), "donors wishing to promote farmer cooperation should refrain from rushing the process of group formation or from overburdening groups with too many or too complex functions". Hence, Lucey and Pesche (1995) urge the construction of new relations arising from step-by-step approaches and the use by governments and NGOs of clear, fixed-term contracts drawn up in conjunction with farmers' organisations.

4. Reasoning support according to different market linkages types

Following Stringfellow et al. (1997), linkage-dependent and linkage-independent groups can be distinguished according to their relationships with the private sector. This distinction is meaningful both for conceiving support to improve farmer access to new market opportunities and for devising capacity building to strengthen existing farmer linkages to markets.

Linkage-dependent groups are characterised by a strong arrangement between the group and an 'outside agency' that has a central role in market access and frequently takes on supervisory activities concerned with the group's commitment to deliver its product under predetermined terms and conditions. This type of farmers' group has a low bargaining power, but it can access markets without requiring high managerial and entrepreneurial skills. On the contrary, linkage-independent groups have much more freedom of action to define their conditions of access to markets. But support to these groups is more demanding in terms of training and capacity building. Indeed, linkage-independent groups face a managerial challenge since they have to make quicker and more frequent decisions in relation to investments (with whom to do business, under what terms and conditions, etc.) while achieving participation and being accountable to their members. Finally, determining the most appropriate arrangement for POs clearly depends on the conditions under which they operate. When they have relatively little experience with formal cooperation and where markets are thin, linkage-dependent approaches seem to offer considerable advantages.

Entering into new commercial relationships and marketing activities necessarily entails more complex and intense learning processes. Linkage-dependent groups may then benefit from an external agency that can facilitate technical compliance of contracts in contract-farming schemes, or play the role of commercial intermediary between local partners and the international market. This is the case of the Biodiverdidad y desarollo agro-industrial (BIODESA) project in Bolivia that is funded by the French Ministry of Foreign Affairs. In this project, farmer cooperatives in rural areas extract oil from aromatic plants like eucalyptus and rosemary and sell their products to the University of Cochabamba who refines and exports the final products to international buyers. Small processing units based on technology innovation from the university are operated by farmer cooperatives. The identification of marketable products and potential buyers required a partnership between the university and an international NGO who provided its commercial network. A long-term commitment from donors has been necessary for the appropriate technology and the commercialisation to be developed simultaneously. A frequent difficulty lies in developing the right technologies without the commitment of a buyer to buy regular volumes. In this particular case, the establishment of partnerships between farmers' cooperatives, university and NGO offers new opportunities to enter the organic and fair trade niche markets.

5. Promoting deliberative institutions and inter-professional bodies

State deficiencies are usually high in less-developed countries, i.e., the lack of reliable statistical data, difficulties in organising internal negotiation with stakeholders, and pressure of foreign aid (Félix, 2003). However, negotiation processes between the State and POs are essential in creating a more enabling institutional environment for farmers' access to markets. These negotiations can lead to State decisions that foster producers' competitiveness, as reflected by the example of the Foutah Jalon potato growers in Guinea. These producers successfully succeeded in competing with European farmers after negotiations between the Federation of Foutah Jalon farmers[1] and the Government of Guinea, who agreed to limit potato imports from Europe during the period when Foutah Jalon potatoes are marketed. Foutah Jalon farmers were therefore able to develop their production through improvements in productivity, storage, and marketing. In 4 years, yields per hectare increased from 3 to 20 mt and protection measures have now been lifted[1].

Proposals are made to promote new institutions – called quaternary or deliberative institutions – that could facilitate a more participatory process in changing the institutional environment and establish new institutional arrangements (Kydd et al., 2002; Bourgeois, 2000). Within these institutions, collective discussions lead to create common knowledge over the different actors' available strategies and then, to elaborate common diagnoses and plans of action. Hence, they foster the ability of the actors to cooperate. By facilitating effective non-market coordination they can enhance investment of supply chain actors in specific assets (Kydd et al., 2002). Information and training of POs, and the strengthening of leaders' legitimacy through progressive structuring of POs are essential for establishing effective deliberative institutions.

---

[1] This Federation has 13,500 members who produce approximately 4,000mt of potatoes every year. The Federation annually markets an additional 3,000mt of non-member production. Besides support to marketing, the Federation provides members with technical advice and inputs (imported potato seeds and bags). Marketing of potatoes is managed by a group of women called *Dioulamoussous* who collect produce from 21 Federation warehouses and resell it in the capital city of Conakry. Farmers and women traders agree upon the producer price as well as the trading margin. Source: http://www.paysansdufouta.org/

Among these are the national negotiation platforms between representatives of POs, other stakeholders (representatives of the processing and trade sectors...) and State representatives. These mediating institutions should not depend on the State, but the State should act as a guarantor of efficiency (Jesus and Bourgeois, 2003). Inter-professional bodies represent another type of deliberative institutions that operate at the supply-chain level. These are private organisations grouping various stakeholders involved in the different functions of the supply chain (producers, traders, carriers, exporters...) and possibly State representatives (Gitz and Trocherie, 1998). They are aimed at resolving, in a concerted way, the constraints that hinder the competitiveness of a specific sub-sector, creating and sharing added value.

The efficiency of an inter-professional body depends on its legitimacy (the effective participation of all members, legitimacy of each group representative, transparent mechanisms of decision, funding, etc). The establishment of such a body is a long and complex process, which requires capacity building, information provision and participative analysis to effect a concerted diagnosis of the situation and to identify the common interests and the collective margins of progress. Although inter-professional bodies are part of the private sector, Gitz et al. (1998) demonstrated the important role of the State in the emergence of inter-professional bodies through the creation of an enabling legal framework. These bodes can lead to the establishment of contractual relations between the different operators and to debates with the authorities that can influence the policy-making process. They are particularly useful for quality-oriented products where standards and enforcement rules are to be negotiated.

Nevertheless, inter-professional bodies are not common in developing countries. They are emerging preferentially in short supply chains with few well identified actors, or where a dominant group of actors takes the lead in the process, i.e., in chains where there are few coordination problems are. Examples of inter-professional bodies also exist for export goods, such as cotton in Benin where POs are organised nationally after a process of transfer of responsibilities from a semi-state enterprise to POs as part of the liberalisation process of the cotton sector. If this type of organisation facilitates coordination and exchange of information among stakeholders, inter-professional organisations seem to be of more benefit to the most powerful actors of the sector, e.g., inputs suppliers or cotton ginneries in Benin (Cadot, 2003).

Conclusion

This short review of strategies and experiences aimed at pro-poor competitive policies for local, national and international markets makes clear that horizontal co-operation is an asset that cannot be ignored or underestimated. The potential of horizontal co-operation to sustain market access pathways for smallholder producers is not just a matter of cost-sharing mechanisms or economies of scale. It also deals with the dynamics of innovation and learning-by-doing, and with the stakeholders' legitimacy and capacity for priority setting, negotiation and voice. Horizontal co-operation deserves to be given high priority by donors, governments and NGOs, and involvement from the private sector in order to develop a wide array of innovative support strategies.

References

ARTE (Agroindustrias Rurales y Territorios). 2004. Memorias del Congresso internacional de Toluca (Mexico). Mexico: Universidad Autonoma de Mexico/Universidad Autonoma del Estado de Mexico/Universidad Autonoma de Chapingo, CD-Rom.

Balsevich, F., Berdegue, J.A., Flores, L., Mainville, D., Reardon, T., Busch, L. and Unnevehr, L. 2003. Supermarkets and produce quality and safety standards in Latin America. American Journal of Agricultural Economics 85(5).

Beccatini, G. 1979. Dal settore industriale al distritto industriale. Rivista de Economia e Politica Industriale, 5(1): 7–21.

Biénabe, E., Coronel, C., Le Coq, J.-F. and Liagre, L. 2004. Linking smallholder farmers to markets – Lessons learned from literature and analytical review of selected projects, Report for the World Bank. CIRAD/IRAM (Centre de cooperation internationale en recherche agronomique pour le développement/Institut de recherche et applications en methodes). Montpellier, France. 82pp.

Bonnal, P. and Sautier, D. 1998. O fortalecimento das associaçoes de productores na area do Projeto Lomaco (Mozambique). CIRAD (Centre de cooperation internationale en recherche agronomique pour le développement) – Lomaco – Agence Française de développement. Maputo, Mozambique/Paris, France. 25pp.

Bosc, P.M., Eychenne, D., Hussein, K., Losch, B., Mercoiret, M.R., Rondot, P. and Mackintosh-Walker, S. 2003. The role of rural producer organisations in the World Bank rural development strategy. Rural Strategy Background Paper No. 8. World Bank, Washington DC, USA. 161pp.

Boucher, F. 2004. Enjeux et difficultés d'une stratégie collective d'activation des concentrations d'agro-industries rurales : le cas des fromageries rurales de Cajamarca (Pérou). Thèse de Doctorat en Economie de l'Université de Versailles-Saint Quentin en Yvelines, France. 230pp.

Bourdanove, C. et Martos, F. 1992. Lexique de théorie économique: vocabulaire, concepts et éléments de théorie économique. Ellipses, Paris, France.

Bourgeois, R. 2000. La constitution des filières et institutions quaternaires – boites à idées. *in:* Fraval, P. Eléments pour l'analyse de filières agricoles en Afrique subsaharienne. Synthèse. Ministère des affaires etrangères, Direction générale de la coopération internationale et du développement, Paris, France.

Cadot, J. 2003. Preliminary study of coordination in smallholder sub-Saharan African agriculture. Coordination equilibria and institutions. Mémoire d'Ingénieur de l'Ecole nationale supérieure d'agriculture de Montpellier. Montpellier, France. 66pp.

Cerdan, C. et Sautier, D. 2001. Réseau localisé d'entreprises et dynamique territoriale : Le bassin laitier de Gloria (Sergipe, Brésil). Etudes et recherches sur les systemes agraires et le développement, 32: 131–144.

Devautour, H., Maizi, P. et Muchnik, J. 2001. Systèmes techniques, savoir-faire et innovations agro-alimentaires : Approches et méthodes. Collection alimentation et savoir-faire agro-alimentaires

Africains (ALISA), rapport n° 10. CIRAD (Centre de coopération internationale en recherche agronomique pour le développement). Montpellier, France. 35pp.

Delion, J. 2000. Producer organization – donor partnerships in project implementation in Africa – Risks and precautions from a social perspective. Agriculture Knowledge and Information Systems Discussion Paper. World Bank, Washington DC, USA. 29pp.

Dries, L., Reardon, T. and Swinnen, J.F.M. 2004. The rapid rise of supermarkets in Central and Eastern Europe: implications for the agri-food sector and rural development. Development Policy Review, 22(5): 525–556.

Félix, A. 2003. De vrais-faux obstacles. Grain de sel, 25: 15.

Gitz, V., Trocherie, M.P. et Zanker, S. 1998. Les interprofessions agricoles françaises : émergence, diversité et perspectives. Mémoire de l'Ecole nationale du génie rural, des eaux et des forêts. Paris, France. 56pp.

Jaffee, S. and Morton, J. (eds.). 1995. Marketing Africa's High-value Foods – Comparative Experiences of an Emergent Private Sector. Kendall/Hunt. Washington DC, USA.

Jésus, F. and Bourgeois, R. (eds). 2003. Reconciling actors' preferences in agricultural policy towards a new management of public decisions. CIFOR Monograph No. 44. Cereals Grains Pulses Roots and Tubers Centre. Bogor, Indonesia. 139pp.

Krugman, P. 1991. Increasing returns and economic geography. Journal of Political Economy 99: 483–499.

Kydd, J., Dorward, A. and Poulton, C. 2002. Institutional dimensions of trade liberalisation and poverty. Paper presented at Organization for Economic Cooperation and Development Global Forum on Agriculture, meeting on Agricultural Trade Reform, Adjustment and Poverty, 23–24 May 2002, Paris, France. 25pp.

Lucey, T. and Pesche, D. 1995. Synthesis of action points and key observations. Paper presented at 12 January, 1995 Workshop on Potential Supports to Private Farmer Organizations in Agricultural Sector Programs – Focus on Best Practice. AFTES. Washington DC, USA. 18pp.

Mazoyer, M. 2001. Protecting small farmers and the rural poor in the context of globalization. Paper presented at the World Food Summit 2001, held at the Food and Agriculture Organization of the United Nations (FAO), Rome. Italy.

Mazoyer, M. et Roudart, L. 2002. Histoires des agricultures du monde, du néolithique à la crise contemporaine. Edition du Seuil, Paris, France. 291pp.

Nadvi, K. and Schmitz, H. 1999. Clustering and industrialization: Introduction. World Development 27: 1503–1514.

ODI–CIRAD (Overseas Development Institute – Centre de cooperation internationale en recerche agronomique pour le développement). 2001. Sharing lessons from collaborative Franco-British–West African research and policy initiatives in West Africa: relevance to rural development policy and processes. ODI, London, UK. 84pp.

Perret, S. and Mercoiret, M.R. 2003. Agricultural producer organizations. Their contribution to rural capacity building and poverty reduction. Pages 22–29 *in:* Bosc, P.M. et al., The role of rural producer organizations in the World Bank rural development strategy. Rural Strategy Background Paper No. 8. World Bank, Washington DC, USA.

Porter, M. 1990. The Competitive Advantage of Nations. The Free Press/McMillan, New York, USA.

Reardon, T. and Berdegue, J. 2002. The rapid rise of supermarkets in Latin America: challenges and opportunities for development. Development Policy Review 20(4): 371–388.

Reardon ,T., Timmer, C.P., Barrett, C.B. and Berdegue, J. 2003. The rise of supermarkets in Africa, Asia, and Latin America. American Journal of Agricultural Economics 85(5): 1140–1146.

Requier-Desjardins, D., Boucher, F. and Cerdan, C. 2003. Globalization, competitive advantages and the evolution of productive systems: rural food processing and localised food systems in Latin American countries. Entrepreneurship and Regional Development 15: 49–67.

Richardson, G.B. 1972. The organization of industry. Economic Journal 82: 883–896.

Roche, G., Deberdt, A. et Perez, R. 2004. Organisations des producteurs et mise en marché de produits différenciés – Le cas de la filière de cacao 'Bio-Equitable' en Equateur. Congreso Internacional Agroindustria Rural y Territorio – ARTE. Toluca, Mexico, 1–4 décembre 2004. 14pp.

Rondot, P., Biénabe, E. and Collion, M.-H. 2004. Rural economic organizations and market restructuring: What challenges, what opportunities for smallholders? A global issue paper. Regoverning Markets, Phase 1: Review workshop and International Seminar, held at Konigs Institut voor de Tropen, Amsterdam, the Netherlands, 14–19 November 2004. www.regoverningmarkets.com

Stockbridge, M., Dorward, A. and Kydd, J. 2003. Farmer organization for market access: learning from success. Literature review. Briefing Paper, Wye College. University of London, UK. 42pp.

Stringfellow, R., Coulter, J., Lucey, T., McKone, C. and Hussain, A. 1997. Improving the access of smallholders to agricultural services in sub-Saharan Africa: farmer cooperation and the role of the donor community. Natural Resources Perspectives No. 20. Natural Resources Institute (NRI), Chatham, UK.

SYAL (Systèmes agro-alimentaires localisés). 2002. Systèmes agro-alimentaires localisés: entreprises, produits et territoires. Communications présentées au Colloque International de Montpellier, 16–18 octobre 2002. Centre de cooperation internationale en recherche agronomique pour le développement (CIRAD) Montpellier, France. CD-Rom.

Williamson, O.E. 1985. The Economic Institutions of Capitalism. Firms, Markets, Relational Contracting. The Free Press, New York, USA.

Enabling rural producers to understand and better satisfy the product, process and delivery standards required by buyers

David J. Walker

Summary

Standards are required for efficient trade in agricultural commodities and products. In this context the term standards is taken to encompass the term grades. Potential benefits for developing countries conforming to standards include: reduced transaction costs, access to premium markets, increased earnings, more stable markets, reduced post-harvest deterioration, improved health and safety of workers and consumers, and greater provision for worker welfare and environmental issues. There is potential for producers to access the growing local and regional food aid market.

The potential negative aspects of standards include: the creation of non-tariff trade barriers, costs of conformity that are significant and possibly prohibitive, substandard food that cannot be exported being consumed by the poor, the potential for malpractice, and the possible marginalisation of small-scale producers.

The different forms of national standards and the possibility of conflicting, unclear and inappropriate standards, some adopted from elsewhere, are discussed. There is a perception that national standards can be a barrier to external trade. Regional standards could overcome some constraints provided that they are appropriate and producers have the technical competence and the necessary infrastructure. The African Regional Organization for Standardization (ARSO) and the Commodity Market for Eastern and Southern Africa (COMESA) propose to streamline and harmonise regional commodity standards.

International and commercial standards are discussed. Commercial standards are becoming progressively more demanding and conformity is becoming more difficult and expensive. Such standards are becoming a means by which businesses penetrate markets, and assure quality and food safety criteria.

For rural producers to conform to standards of any kind it is essential that: they have access to up-to-date and understandable information to ensure standards are understood, producers have access to training and facilities to ensure that they have the technical capability to conform, the standards are appropriate for producers and end user and are applied correctly and consistently, there is a supporting and enabling environment, and they are able to meet the costs of conforming. The need for aid donor support is recognised

A list of selected researchable constraints is presented.

The need for standards

There is no doubt that standards in some form are required for trade in agricultural commodities. Agricultural commodities and products vary widely in such intrinsic characteristics as cleanliness, colour, contamination, damage, firmness, moisture content, odour, shape, taste, weight, etc. Biotic and climatic factors, soil type and cultural practice dictate that it is not possible for agricultural commodities and products to be uniform or perfect. Hence producers, exporters, buyers and end-users usually have to agree on acceptable limits or tolerances that will apply to one or more of the expected imperfections or variations. These limits will depend on the parties concerned, technical options, time available, economics, cultural implications, safety concerns, consumer interests and the intended use of the commodity or product.

A complication is that agricultural commodity quality characteristics do not remain constant. Perishable commodity quality characteristics change relatively quickly, as do even such durable commodities as cereals in adverse conditions.

An understanding of the nature and consequence of quality characteristics can be used to develop a system of classification or standardisation to assist marketing. The degree of formalisation and extent of standards depends on the nature of the trade. In developing countries, many standards are historically informal and the need for formal systems in traditional markets has been limited because buyers and sellers could bargain over products that could be assessed physically, and valued by personal appraisal of either subjective or objective characteristics.

However, global markets require formalised and recognised standards. Consumer, trader and processor purchasing power is increasing, and there is demand for a greater variety of products that are safe and differentiated by multiple quality characteristics. International trade and market liberalisation have increased competition, and products are now handled in greater volume and over greater distances. This in turn is associated with an increasing requirement for formal standards to ensure a clear and transparent understanding between trading partners (NRI, 2003). Standards are required to permit trading by specification, thereby making transactions simpler, more orderly and cheaper. Standards also increase the confidence of banks to provide credit against a known quality and therefore a known market value. Disputes over quality and performance can be more readily resolved when standards are applied.

The sanitary hazards associated with the inter-country movement of agricultural produce can be reduced if clearly defined standards are enforced, particularly in relation to preventing the spread of serious pests and pathogens.

Standards

According to World Trade Organization (WTO) agreements, standards are voluntary non-legally binding instruments approved by a recognised body that provide for common and repeated use, rules, guidelines or characteristics for products or related processes and production methods. They may also include terminology, symbols, packaging, marking or labelling requirements as they apply to a product, process or production method. Standards are distinguishable from laws and regulations that are legally binding. However, standards can be incorporated into legal regulatory frameworks.

Standards are commonly defined as 'rules of measurement established by regulation or authority' and grades are commonly defined as 'a system of classification based on quantifiable attributes' (Jones and Hill, 1994). The former are more prescriptive and regulate what is or is not permissible in the context of consumer health and national economic interest, while the latter are more descriptive measures that permit greater specificity and facilitate trade (World Bank, 2002).

Standards and grades are parameters that segregate similar products into categories and describe them in consistent terminology that can be commonly understood at a distance by market participants.

There was formerly a view that standards were the domain of the public sector and grades were the domain of the private sector. However, this differentiation is no longer clear. In this paper the term standard will be considered to include the term grade.

Potential benefits of standards

Developing countries that invest in improving food standards and related institutions can expect to achieve improved livelihoods and advances in public health, agricultural production and export markets.

Recognised standards reduce transaction costs, protect the purchaser and end user, formalise and qualify traditional systems and facilitate trade over distance. They assure health and safety for consumers by removing unsafe products and processes from the food system, and can help protect workers from harmful or socially unjust working conditions where the standards apply to processes or production methods.

As public awareness of the importance of environmental and resource use increases, standards offer a means for consumers and retailers to voice their concerns and thus create an impetus for sustainable management of natural resources, wildlife protection and improved labour standards.

Implementation of standards to access premium markets will highlight opportunities for improving quality, reducing post-harvest deterioration and losses, and draw attention to the potential rewards available. This will be particularly the case where commodities are traded by a number of grades. Thus standards should inspire producers and traders to rectify malpractices and deficiencies that previously resulted in deterioration and reduced profit margins. Hence standards could contribute to increased food security both nationally and regionally. This happened in Uganda with maize grown as a cash crop. Producers were careless and contamination with soil and stones was so common that the country earned a reputation for supplying only low-grade maize. With government support, a trade association established minimum standards in 2002 and since then maize export quality has improved, significantly strengthening its regional marketing.

The ability to determine conformity with standards provides the means and opportunity to measure and compare certain selected quality characteristics. Hence loss of standard between harvest and marketing could provide a measure of post-harvest losses. This could be a useful tool in on-farm and marketing loss-reduction programmes such that over several seasons standard achievement could be an impact indicator of agricultural research and extension support.

Standardised produce is likely to be more equitably priced than non-standardised produce. This should bring stability to market prices and to the quality of produce offered. Prices quoted against a recognised standard will assist producers and traders to market their products. Greater conformity in quality will provide processors and manufacturers with the consistency of commodity necessary for the optimum performance of processing equipment and production lines. Standards also strengthen and protect consumers' rights.

Producers in developing countries stand to benefit from improved access to additional quality-conscious markets that are prepared to pay a premium for quality. Examples of such markets include: the food-aid sector looking to procure surplus commodities locally or regionally in developing countries, niche markets associated with specific types of coffee, European supermarkets, and the organic market. Access to such markets will potentially increase economic return, enable diversification of production systems, and facilitate the growth of income and employment opportunities in value-adding enterprises. Whilst niche markets represent only a small proportion of the overall market they are locally very important to the producers and their economies.

However, these benefits are dependent on producers in developing countries investing and participating in such opportunities. There are considerable constraints to their involvement, principally in the investment and operational costs of understanding, and complying with the complex requirements.

Whilst most local and regional procurement of food aid involves cereals, cereal products and pulses, there is undoubted potential for the suppliers of sugar, salt, vegetable oil, milk powder, biscuits, dried fish and canned meat and fish, who can meet the necessary quality standards. In addition to the routine durable commodities there is unrealised potential for the supply of fresh horticultural produce for food aid.

Potentially negative aspects of standards

Standards were traditionally seen as a tool for sellers and buyers to facilitate long-distance trade. However, more recently there has been an increase in the implementation of sanitary and phytosanitary (SPS) measures to safeguard the health and safety of consumers, and to protect workers (social standards) and the environment, e.g., European Union (EU) pesticide regulations. Equally important has been the increase in requirements for conformity assessment (certification, testing and inspection) and traceability. These criteria are seen as having a significant negative impact for developing countries attempting to access premium markets because the costs of conforming to such standards can be significant and possibly prohibitive.

Box 1. Market for locally or regionally sourced food aid cereals

Studies of local and regional food aid procurement in Ethiopia (Walker and Wandschnei-der, 2005), Kenya, Sudan (Walker and Boxall, 2002) and Uganda (Wandschneider and Hodges, 2005) reveal that there is a substantial premium market for locally produced cereals and pulses. The quantity of food aid cereals procured to international standards by the United Nations World Food Programme (WFP), the Government of Ethiopia, and other international agencies and donor countries in Ethiopia was estimated at 268, 215 mt in 2001, 180,430 mt in 2002 and 261,970 mt in 2003. In Uganda the local market for food aid was 50,530 mt in 2001, 46,697 mt in 2002, 107,819 mt in 2003 and 121,266 mt in 2004.

In 2003 the European Union (EU) funded the purchase and movement of over 24,000 mt of sorghum from Sudan to Ethiopia. In 2004 the WFP organised the supply of 4,000 mt of blended cereals and soya beans from Ethiopia to Darfur, Sudan.

Access to this large and growing premium market is not easy for small-scale producers or traders. Some agencies have an open tender system; others operate a closed tendering procedure for pre-qualified organisations. Tenders are often announced in newspapers that are distributed mainly in the capital city. This could present time constraints and prevent market information reaching potential suppliers in distant regions. Tenderers are required to submit bid bonds and, if successful, performance bonds. Such financial guarantees necessitate support from the bank sector and incur a cost to producers. Procurers are commonly looking to secure supplies in lots of, say, 1,000 mt or more. Such quantities are beyond the aspirations of small-scale producers and most farmer co-operatives or associations. Even large players in the local grain trade were not familiar with the contractual requirements of such business when it boomed in the mid-1990s, but market competence has developed over the past decade. This market requires supplies of cereals and pulses that conform to specific quality standards that are similar to international cereal trading requirements.

Occasionally, procurers are prepared to consider offers of smaller quantities around the 500 mt mark and some make active efforts to include producer groups. However, participation of small-scale producers in this market has been minimal in all four countries studied by NRI. Nevertheless, this does not mean that they have not benefited financially to some extent by supplying the premium market through large-scale traders. All concerned will have become accustomed to the need to offer produce that conforms to strict quality standards.

Trade liberalisation has reduced tariff barriers, but it has exposed another layer of trade measures. There is concern that developed countries use stringent quality SPS requirements as non-tariff economic trade barriers that can prove difficult to surmount. Patricia Hewitt, UK Secretary of State for Trade and Industry, cited an example of the EU's regulations to limit the level of aflatoxins in imported groundnuts. These are far tougher than other international standards, although it was estimated that the benefit would be an annual saving of 1.4 lives per billion people. Ms Hewitt pointed out that the EU does not have a billion people and because of these standards Africa has lost exports worth US$670 million per year. This could be viewed as protectionism disguised as health and safety (Wintour and Elliott, 2005).

A consequence of developing countries accessing premium outlets for their produce, commonly global or regional markets, with more-stringent quality criteria than national standards, is that consignments with the lowest standards will be retained for the domestic market; thereby creating a two-tier standards system. It implies that local people will be deprived of the best-quality products leaving lower-quality products for the local population. An example of this is Ethiopian white haricot beans. Only beans that meet a minimum government quality standard can be exported so as to maintain the reputation of this country's commodity on the international market. In this instance there are no significant health problems. However, in other situations where cereal consignments are rejected for export because of food health concerns such as failure to meet stringent mycotoxin or microbial tolerances, there is a risk that at times of shortage these rejected consignments will be made available to the domestic market. Those sectors of the community that are already poorly nourished and seeking cheap food will be the least capable of coping with food of low nutritional quality.

Use of multiple grades within an overall standard has been observed to provide significant potential for malpractice by graders and warehouse operators in numerous countries.

The imposition of standards that cannot be achieved by small-scale producers using good agricultural practice could further marginalise them from trade and economic development.

National quality standards

National standards for agricultural products can take various forms. Most countries have a Bureau of Standards that prepares quality standards for a range of commodities. These appear to be focused on food safety and hence have detailed requirements for the commodity not to contain harmful levels of heavy metals or pesticides. Such standards would be extremely useful if doubts were raised as to whether a commodity was fit for human consumption. However, any attempt to use such standards for regular commercial trade would be doomed to failure because of the logistical, cost and time constraints of undertaking such a wide range of expensive and exacting analyses on each sample submitted.

Domestic end users of agricultural commodities are frequently country- or region-specific. Therefore national or regional standards, whether established within liberalised economies or earlier by parastatal organisations, ought to reflect the characteristics and requirements of the national agro-economic sector so as to harmonise and facilitate local trading. However, very few countries have developed standards from first principles based on criteria the producers can bring to market following good agricultural practice, the needs of the processing sector, and the requirements of the end users or consumers. It is too easy to adopt standards from another country without considering their relevance to the local agro-industry. Maize in Malawi is milled into meal; maize in Ghana is typically fermented as whole grains and then made into a wet paste product called *kenkey*. The two countries' national standards should reflect these differences. Standards should relate specifically to 'fitness for purpose', hence it is important to consider the specific end use of the product and needs of processors. Walker and Boxall (1998) reviewed existing maize quality standards in Ghana in which the quality criteria required by the end users were identified and appraised as a basis for developing a national quality standard specifically tailored to the capacity of the producers and needs of the industry and end users. A noteworthy attempt to determine standards from first principles was undertaken for maize in Swaziland (Mpanza, 2000). This work highlighted the substantial costs in terms of finance, staff time and materials in developing such standards.

In some countries there are several different and conflicting standards for the same commodity. A study of maize standards in Zambia, a country producing around one million tonnes of maize annually, revealed that following the repeal of the formal national grain standards after market liberalisation in 1989, several different standards had been developed by traders or organisations representing traders (Walker, 2000). In 1989 there were three maize standards and a large number of commercial millers each had their own customised standards. Producers were confused by the existence of so many conflicting standards. The lack of a single, appropriate and accepted maize quality standard presented a constraint to the development of the liberalised grain market.

In the late 1990s there was a similar situation with maize in Ghana, a country that also produces around one million tonnes annually. Walker and Boxall (1998) identified seven different formal standards for maize in addition to various informal standards. A single draft national standard was subsequently developed.

Developing countries often do not have the financial, technical and institutional resources to develop relevant national standards and thus have no alternative but to adopt the standards of others, irrespective of their appropriateness.

Regional quality standards

There is a perception that national standards for agricultural commodities in some developing countries are a barrier to formal cross-border and regional trade. There is no doubt that the development of regional standards would offer potential for significant trade growth in many developing countries. The supplier aims generally to meet the commercial standards of the buyer. It should be of little consequence whether or not the commercial specifications of the buyer are different from the national standards of the producer, notwithstanding impositions of national minimal standards, e.g., Ethiopian haricot beans discussed earlier.

However, there are two practical constraints. Firstly the producer might have difficulty ascertaining whether or not consignments conform to the purchaser's

Box 2. Informal standards in urban and rural maize markets in Ghana

Government sources were adamant that there were no standards in the national domestic market. However, a study revealed that maize perceived subjectively to be of poor quality will frequently command a lower price or take longer to sell, especially when competing in the market place with maize considered to be of higher standard. The price of grain judged to be of significantly lower standard would be discounted by wholesale traders, but only by 10 to 20%.

Wholesale traders in the maize-producing town of Techiman listed their quality concerns in descending order of importance:
1. Size of grain (small-grained traditional varieties preferred
2. Insect holes
3. Soil admixture/staining
4. Discolouration/disease/mould.

However, wholesale traders in Accra differentiated primarily between new and old maize, recognising that new maize is frequently inadequately dried before sale so it could lose weight and volume when it dried whilst in the hands of the trader. Additionally, inadequately dried maize is more likely to discolour because of fungal infection if kept for more that a few weeks. Maize containing a few discoloured grains will be acceptable for some end uses such as *kenkey* production.

Discolouration is less of a problem to retail traders than insect damage to which there is greater customer resistance. Retail traders who will frequently sieve grain prior to sale to remove the insects.

Market purchasers will often differentiate between traditional and new high-yielding varieties in the same condition; the latter often commanding a lower market price. This probably illustrates a preference for traditional grains that are flintier and easier to store.

It is a concern that there is little match between the standards of wholesalers, retailers and consumers. Producers might have even more or different perceptions of quality.

commercial standards. When samples are submitted to government-operated testing institutions in some countries, e.g., Egypt and Zambia, the laboratory will most likely be required by its own mandate to test for conformity with national standards and not with the commercial specifications attached to the submitted samples. There might be problems in finding a local laboratory that is recognised as competent, and has the necessary chemical reagents, to conduct the analyses. Ghana presents an example of a developing country with limited technical capability to ensure produce meets export-market requirements, e.g., there is no reliable service for analysis of detect heavy metals. In some places where facilities do exist the staff require further training.

Secondly, there could be technical or procedural constraints. The nascent maize trading sector in Uganda is developing rapidly to meet the specific needs of the WFP, which is procuring cereals and pulses for distribution as food aid within the country. The natural market growth opportunity for this sector is Kenya, which commonly imports maize from as far away as South Africa. However, the formal maize trading sector in Uganda has no experience of trading in drier grain (13.5% moisture content in Kenya as against 14.0% moisture content in Uganda) or from a position where physical stocks of grain are assembled in warehouses ready for despatch. The Ugandans view these changes in trading practice as problematic. The response to problems similar to these has been the promotion of regional standards harmonisation initiatives.

Regional trade is much more likely to be aligned with regional standards where such standards have been developed in collaboration with commercial traders and are considered by all parties to be appropriate. It is important that special interest groups do not capture the process of developing standards.

Box 3. Regional harmonisation in Africa

The African Regional Organization for Standardization (ARSO)) is an African intergovernmental organisation established in 1977, based in Nairobi, Kenya. It is the intergovernmental body mandated to promote standardisation in Africa. ARSO's programme is based on the blueprint for Africa's economic development outlined in the 1980 Lagos Plan of Action for the Economic Commission for Africa, which envisaged the establishment of an African Common Market through integration of various sub-regional economic groupings. ARSO's programme is designed towards removal of technical barriers that hinder intra-African trade and integration. One of its committees is responsible for the preparation of African Regional Standards for agriculture and food products.

The Commodity Market for Eastern and Southern Africa (COMESA) similarly proposes to streamline and harmonise food quality standards within its nineteen member countries. There appears to be some overlap between the two programmes.

The United States Agency for International Development (USAID) funded a study that developed simple common quality standards for sorghum so as to facilitate trade in four countries in southern Africa (Niernberger and Taylor, 2001).

International quality standards

A key feature of trade liberalization and removing barriers to trade has been the development of the WTO agreements on Technical Barriers to Trade (TBT) and SPS measures. These measures present a multilateral framework of rules to minimise unnecessary obstacles to trade. Although governments sign these agreements they are aimed at assisting the private sector business community. The WTO agreement requires members to base their regulations on those set by international bodies, e.g., the Codex Alimentarius for SPS measures. Strictly speaking, developing-country exporters should only have to meet the requirements of SPS and TBT to access international markets, but in reality compliance with European law and standards is the key to access the EU market. Where countries develop standards requiring higher levels of compliance the reasons for this ought to be scientifically based. The most well known international food standards organisation is the Codex Alimentarius Commission that is based in Rome, Italy. It was created in 1963 by two United Nations organisations, the Food and Agriculture Organization (FAO) and the World Health Organization (WHO). It was intended to develop food standards, guidelines and codes of practice under the Joint FAO/WHO Food Standards Programme. The main objectives are protecting the health of consumers and ensuring fair practices in the food trade, and promoting co-ordination of all food standards work undertaken by international, governmental and non-governmental organisations (NGOs).

Although the work of Codex recognises the need to facilitate international trade it focuses on sensitising the global community to the dangers of food hazards as well as the importance of food quality. Hence Codex standards can be used to positively identify fitness for human consumption.

The International Organization for Standardization (ISO) is the world's largest developer of standards. It is a non-governmental organisation that comprises a network of 148 national institutes co-ordinated by a central secretariat in Geneva, Switzerland. Its standards contribute to making the development, manufacturing and supply of products and services more efficient and safer. They aim to make trade between countries easier and fairer. ISO standards cover not just agricultural products but also related storage, processing and testing methodology. The Quality and Standards Authority of Ethiopia declaration of its intention in 2005 to develop a range of national food commodity standards under the ISO 9000 regime illustrates an example of ISO's influence.

The WTO Agreement on the Application of Sanitary and Phytosanitary Measures in 1995 identified a specific objective of harmonising SPS measures within the standards, guidelines and recommendations developed by the Codex Alimentarius Commission, the World Organization for Animal Health (Office International des Epizooties, OIE) and the International Plant Protection Convention.

The emphasis towards internationalisation of standards was illustrated further by the joint initiative of the FAO, the OIE, the World Bank, the WHO and the WTO to form the Standards and Trade Development Facility in 2004.. This is a global programme in capacity building and technical assistance that aims to assist developing countries in trade and SPS.

International standards can also be set by commodity authorities such as the International Coffee Organisation based in London, which established minimum standards for its members' exports in the 2002 Coffee Quality Improvement Plan (CQIP).

Commercial standards and procurement

There is a general perception that standards, particularly those involving health and food safety, belong in the public domain. However, the private sector has great influence in setting standards and codes of practice to meet the requirements of trade in agricultural commodities both nationally and internationally.

Some speciality or market niche commodities have established their own standards that are used by purchasers when contracting supplies. Some suppliers are so dominant in the market that purchasers will use the supplier's standards, e.g., purchasers of US grain will almost always buy grain according to US standards. Some speciality coffees that are exempted from the CQIP fall into this category.

Generally, international buyers of agricultural commodities have the option of buying to their own standards or to those of the producers whether they are national, regional or international. Where the standards of the producers meet the requirements of the procurer that is the end of the story. In other instances buyers will procure to a national standard because it presents the best means of acquiring the commodity to the highest possible local standards within the capability of the local agro-industry. This is the case with many consignments of white haricot beans exported from Ethiopia. These beans are then reprocessed in Europe or elsewhere to the standards required by the food industry and the consumer. The costs of subsequent reprocessing are factored into the purchase price. The opportunity remains for the haricot bean sector in Ethiopia to upgrade its quality standards. However, such an opportunity is constrained by the need for significant financial investment in bean sorting and cleaning technology.

The WTO has issued guidelines on the application of SPS and TBT. However, many international buyers also have the option, and frequently the leverage, to impose their own commercial standards and specifications irrespective of whatever standards might have been created nationally, regionally or internationally. Buyers in the USA will often stipulate United States Department of Agriculture (USDA) standards and European buyers will frequently use the EU standards. EU standards principally include: food hygiene and safety, genetic modification, market standards, organic production, extent of pesticide residues, phytosanitary and traceability. In the case of horticultural fresh produce the international trade is heavily dominated by large retailers who apply their own private sector standards, e.g., Marks and Spencer (Farm to Folk), Tesco (Nature's Choice) and McDonald's (McDonald's Agricultural Assurance Programme). These standards incorporate hazard analysis and critical control point (HACCP) systems and require compliance with the EU requirements and much more.

A consortium of 11 Dutch and UK retailers launched the European Retailers' Protocol for Good Agricultural Practice (EUREPGAP) Farm Gate Standard in 1996. By 2004 this consortium had grown to include 31 retailers in 14 countries, including one in South Africa. Its influence extends to the markets for fruit, vegetables, flowers, grains, meat, farmed fish and coffee. The reality in 2005 is that there are many retailer-specific standards that require EUREPGAP plus other requirements. Private-sector standards for agricultural food products principally include: environment, food safety, social welfare, wildlife and conservation. The outcome is that standards such as these often become non-voluntary for access to major markets.

Commercial standards are progressively becoming the means by which businesses penetrate markets, and assure quality and food safety criteria. Buyers are frequently setting standards with a focus on the end-user (consumer). To ensure compliance, buyers are demanding that auditing be undertaken by a third party. The buyers do not consider these and other costs of compliance as their concern, neither do they make allowances in offering price incentives for compliance since buyers consider their standards as pre-competitive minimum requirements.

The private sector and producing countries participate in the international standard setting committees of Codex and ISO. However, the ability of producers to influence the possibly more important buyer-led, standard-setting processes is constrained.

Some NGOs view government and international regulations as inadequate and have developed more demanding market-based standards or codes of practice, e.g., the Forest Stewardship Council and Fair Trade Foundation. These NGOs apply pressure on buyers to accept these standards as part of their drive for sustainable growth and development. Such standards have little to do with the intrinsic quality of products and more to do with processes of production, worker welfare and trade conduct.

How can rural producers understand and better satisfy the product, process and delivery standards required by buyers?

Many rural producers already have some experience with standards, especially those growers concerned with such traditional export crops as cocoa, coffee, cotton, flowers and tobacco. However, subsequent to market liberalisation, and the growth of buyer interest groups, many are now unfamiliar with the market standards being applied to staple and cash crop foodstuffs in national, regional and international markets. The following comments are primarily focused on access to local and regional markets because these have the most significance to small-scale producers.

Standards must be understood

Standards should be built on characteristics that the users consider important and should be easily recognisable and quantifiable. Because standards are linked to economic return it is important that they are measured objectively and are seen to be so measured. Hence procedures should be transparent and the parties concerned, especially producers, should be well informed.

For producers to conform to standards for product, process or delivery necessary for access to premium markets it is important that they understand fully all of the specific technical and procedural requirements. However, given the multi-layered nature of the standards environment, the many different buyer specific requirements, the difference in application between different commodities, and the dynamics of the commodity markets, this is not easily achieved. Many producers have an inadequate appreciation of the standard's demands and requirements. The situation is exacerbated by standards changing over time and at a rate that is likely to increase in line with product differentiation.

Understanding the status of standards can be challenging. With regard to the microbiological testing of foodstuffs there are four categories of criteria that are recognised:

- Standards – often legislated and embodied in law
- Guidelines – not legal standards, although regulatory bodies might use them
- In-house guidelines – vary from country to country, or even from company to company
- Specifications – technical requirements that form the basis of a commercial transaction (Shapton and Shapton, 1998).

It is necessary for producers to have the same perception of quality as the buyer. Hence producers require relevant and clear information that is readily accessible and in a form that they can understand and contextualise. This requires more than just being issued with printed information. There is a need for transparency and to understand the requirements of the market. Understandably, this might be difficult when the buyers, processors or consumers are in another country. In Zambia, eight grower co-operatives formed a second-tier management co-operative, the Lubulima Commercial Co-operatives Union, to ensure that they were kept well informed about buyers' standards and other requirements relevant to their exports of baby corn, mangetout, and sugar-snap peas to the EU, and green maize to the regional markets in South Africa and Zimbabwe.

Some national and regional retailers are supportive in ensuring that producers are fully informed of the requirements. However, it is more common for producers to be provided with information by their exporters or their primary marketing organisation. Some national organisations, such as the Cocoa Board (Cocobod) in Ghana, work hard to ensure that their cocoa growers are fully aware of the quality requirements. However, the broader national agricultural extension services, particularly those in Africa, often lack the necessary information themselves and are unable to inform the growers about current market standard requirements. It is possible that extension work is often ineffective because there is a mismatch of perceptions as to what constitutes an improvement in quality. It is generally believed that grain with fewer insect holes will result in improved quality standards and therefore value. In some instances the mental leap from qualitative loss reduction to value added is not justified.

Producers must have the technical capability to comply with the standards

Training small-scale producers how to produce in accordance with client standards is essential. However, this poses questions as to who pays for and delivers the training and how it is delivered.

There has been a long legacy of the commercial sector working closely with producers to raise the quality of their harvested products. In the 1960s and 1970s entry into the sector was more commonly in the form of plantation-cum-processing-for-export enclaves by firms such as Unilever, Del Monte, e.g., Libby's support to outgrower pineapple producers in Swaziland. During the past decade there has been widespread developing-country market entry by such input supply firms as Monsanto and Pioneer, by processors such as Coca-Cola and Nestlé, traders such as Cargill, and retail distributors such as Carrefour, McDonalds, Royal Ahold or Walmart (Reardon and Barrett, 2000). However, it is now unusual for large companies to invest in their international value chains by undertaking such activities as directly supporting the training of producers.

Ghana provides a good example of a statutory public body, Cocobod, working with farmers to ensure the quality of their cocoa production. In this instance this is achieved by an extension service solely dedicated to this commodity. All developing countries have some form of agricultural extension, which in principle is there to guide and support producers. However, many national agricultural extension services are ineffectual. This raises further questions as to what, if anything, is taking their place and if smallholder producers could pay for the extension advice or other trade-related services. An interesting example of generating funding is found in Jamaica where the costs of a standard pre-clearance programme for ackee fruit export to the USA are met by an export levy (Olembo, 2002).

In practice it is now more common for the public sector to be primarily concerned with the development and enforcement of minimum safety standards to protect public health, social welfare and the environment. A constraint of the public sector is its limited understanding of the regulatory demands of the regional or international market place. Private sector standards are commonly more exacting than the basic minimum and hence are of more significance to producers looking for premium markets. In some sectors the large-scale private sector is increasingly playing a very important quasi-public role with respect to the regulatory environment, promotion, advocacy, monitoring and auditing. Whilst these requirements are laudable in principle they can present practical and technical barriers to producers.

NGOs are increasingly becoming involved in supporting small-scale farmer access to premium markets. For example, CARE has established a private-sector partnership with a horticulture export company in Kenya to form a company that provides organisational support, advice and training to assist small-scale farmers conform to retail standards in Europe.

Standards cannot be diluted, but the question often facing producers is how to apply standards to their local conditions with systems that assure an equivalence of risk outcome. This frequently requires the development of appropriate management systems.

Standards must be appropriate

Standards ought to be achievable by both small-scale and large-scale growers following good agricultural practice. Ideally, it should be possible to determine conformity to standards with basic equipment on the farm, or at least in the production areas or at the primary marketing organisation. Unfortunately, the determination of many standards requires laboratory conditions and specialised equipment and competences.

Microbiological testing clearly requires a laboratory. Surprisingly, so does basic testing of coarse grain standards. The procedures for these are based on gravimetric determinations often of quantities of grains, or material present amongst the grains, that require accurate weighing. While such accurate weighing presents little difficulty in a laboratory or a well-equipped grain-grading centre, it is neither cost-effective nor feasible for producers, traders or exporters to undertake such procedures in the field. Some organisations have partly addressed this issue by means of colour charts showing examples of the different standards and grades or, for durable commodities, by the dissemination of prepared samples. Nestlé Ghana, in its attempts to purchase its required quality from within Ghana or in neighbouring Burkina Faso, has gone some way towards developing an alternative practical volumetric system of determining grain quality in the field with the aid of a plastic measuring cylinder. However, much more development would be required before such a system could be appropriate for nationwide application (Walker and Boxall, 1998). A volumetric, as opposed to a gravimetric, approach for grain standard determination would also be more appropriate for situations where grain is traded by volume and not by weight as is the case in some rural areas.

Broken grains lower the quality standard for millers because they do not yield so much flour as does an equal quantity of whole grain. The extent of 'brokens' is determined by the fact that they will fall through a sieve with holes of a certain size. Sieve sizes used for this procedure differ in aperture size and shape around the world. To be meaningful the sieve size should relate to the screens used to clean the grain at intake into the mill. If the sieve and the screen have the same-sized holes then the implementation of the standard will be directly related to the material that the miller will be unable to use in the production of flour. However, a study of standards and milling screens in Zambia found that there was often no correlation. The sieve sizes specified in some standards were frequently inappropriate as a quality determinant.

Standards must be applied correctly and consistently

Standards must not only be applied correctly and consistently, they must also be perceived to be so applied. Trust in the standards system is an important factor. However, there is widespread uncertainty in national and international commerce as to whether there are recognised and accessible competent authorities to implement, support, monitor and audit or verify commercial standards. National and regional agencies are often under-funded. They also sometimes lack skilled motivated staff, adequate infrastructure, and adequate inspection and certification capabilities. Another perceived weakness in the management of standards by developing countries is the lack in both the private and public sectors of technical capacity and available resources to engage in standards development and to assess the technical justification and economic implications of new standards and their application domestically or by export partners (Standards and Trade Facility, 2005).

To apply standards correctly it is important to understand the terminology. However, this can be difficult because what appear to be common terms can often have different meanings, e.g. the definition of a broken grain in one system of standards is frequently different from its definition in another, thus it is difficult to compare the standards for wheat in Bangladesh with those of the EU or USA. Anyone unaware of the small print of the definitions in standards could make unjustified comparisons.

Need for a supporting and enabling environment

Whilst there is no doubt that the private sector plays an important role in developing and applying standards, it is the public sector that is often best placed to provide the necessary supporting and enabling environment. National governments are well placed to lower the cost infrastructure of nascent exporters and/or value-added processors.

Different organisations with different interests have generated a standards situation that contains as much conflict as there is harmony. Multiple perspectives exist on the role of standards in the national, regional and global economy. Standards could be viewed by some as instruments and expressions of trade liberalisation, and by others as a means to reduce transaction costs and build trust. They are also viewed as ways of tackling difficult food safety hazards and of co-ordinating complex food systems. It is not surprising the producers, especially small-scale growers who have the potential to supply quality-conscious and probably premium-price markets, need support.

Producers need to be supported by accessible analytical laboratory services. Many African countries do not have the necessary laboratory support, and samples need to be couriered to regional laboratories, or on occasion to Europe, for certain aspects of quality determination, e.g., rancidity of vegetable oils, and evidence of genetic modification. The increasing need to monitor for genetically modified commodities will stretch existing expertise. Retesting or recertification of products in the importing country could be avoided if the there is mutual recognition or agreement for conformity assessment procedures used to determine compliance with technical regulations in the exporting country (ITC, 2004).

Establishing, building and maintaining the confidence of international buyers are crucial to the success of exporting countries. This confidence needs to be founded on a reliable and credible system of audit and verification of compliance with requisite standards. This is an area that commonly needs further development at national and regional levels.

Cost of conforming to standards

Conformity with standards requires investments of time, effort and probably finance. Small-scale producers, e.g., smallholder tea growers in Malawi, might have other conflicting and more immediate pressures and demands on their time, effort and resources that preclude the necessary sustained investment in developing their capacity and capability to meet the quality standard that would ultimately increase their economic return.

Changes in commodity production, harvesting and handling and processing practices often require significant financial investment. Producers are less likely to invest in conforming to standards if they are unsure as to the sustainability of the market opportunity or suspect that the standards will be changed at short notice.

There could be opportunities for producers to share costs by affiliating into associations or similar groupings.

Need for aid donor support

Producers should continue to look to their national governments and their commercial marketing intermediaries for support in linking them to their buyers and facilitating their compliance with the necessary standards. However, national governments in many cases do not have the funds or the market awareness to meet the needs of producers. Marketing intermediaries might not be prepared or willing to invest in developing the capacity and competence of would be suppliers. Some of the problems are at the public private interface. The general perception is that there is insufficient public–private dialogue and co-operation in standards development, implementation, domestic enforcement, and export market strategy (Standards and Trades Facility, 2005)

In the absence of adequate commercial sector support, there appears to be a need for continued donor assistance, especially for the small-scale sector.

Conclusions

1. Successful compliance with standards that facilitate access to premium markets has the potential to contribute sustainably to the improved livelihoods of small-scale producers, processors and traders.
2. Developing countries are reacting too late and ineffectively to the changing regulatory framework to avoid negative impact on their export markets, particularly on behalf of small-scale producers and traders who do not have the resources to monitor and react to change in market requirements.
3. It is unlikely that small-scale producers, processors and traders in developing countries will be able to take full advantage of the opportunities presented by the regional and global commercialisation of agriculture without significant donor investment.
4. There is a clear need for developing countries to develop further the necessary infrastructure required to facilitate market access for their producers. This infrastructure could include:
   • Standards formulating bodies
   • Laboratory testing facilities
   • Accreditation, certification and auditing services
   • Training services
   • Information and enquiry points.
   However, it will require significant investment to achieve access to regional and international markets.
5. The demand for local and regional procurement of food aid is growing and provides a potentially large premium market for producers who can provide

commodities and delivery performance that conform to donor quality standards.

6. Investment is required in both the public and private sectors. The public sector has critical roles in developing minimum safety standards to protect local consumers, overseeing certification processes, and ensuring that resource-poor farmers and small-scale domestic industries are not excluded from markets because of an inability to comply. Achieving standards compliance and accessing markets is a private sector issue and therefore it is essential to have the active involvement of commerce.

7. There is a need for an effective private – public sector interface so that businesses can inform public officials of their needs in the national, regional and international market place, and for them to understand the barriers that they face.

8. In-country frameworks have to be established that clearly define institutional responsibilities for developing national standards, implementation, surveillance, and for participation in international standards-setting organisation. Resources are required for pro-active participation in the committees of these organisations and in positions of influence in setting the agenda of the bodies.

9. Developing countries need the resources and capability to track, assess and react to newly developing regulations through monitoring the WTO enquiry points for each country. This could pre-empt problems in achieving compliance in export markets but requires financial and technical resources and institutional infrastructure that permit information flow to all relevant parties in both the public and the private sector.

10. It is important that the institutional framework of service providers functions within a supporting and enabling framework that specifically assists small-scale farmers and traders to achieve compliance with standards. The support that they require will include:
    • Access to the necessary information and ensuring that it is fully understood such that farmers comprehend the terminology of the standard and its status, i.e., is it incorporated into a legal regulation
    • Provision of training services to ensure technical and management competence to achieve compliance
    • Assured representative, i.e., unbiased, commodity sampling services
    • Up-graded capacity and competence of local laboratory analytical services which now have to cope with increased demand for precision and reliability
    • Independent national audit services, ideally to conduct cost-effective pre-audits.

11. Key areas for investment in developing countries include:
    • Building the capacity of government agencies
    • Promoting participatory processes for establishing standards
    • Promoting and upgrading skills and facilities of local producers and processors to ensure compliance and certification.

12. Where combined public and private sectors in individual countries lack the resources to create the necessary national infrastructure it will be necessary

to consider regional initiatives and co-operation, e.g., the establishment of regional accreditation bodies to assess national conformity assessment service providers and the equipping of regional accreditation laboratories.

13. It is possible that some national and regional standards are not fully appropriate for the producers or end users and require revision.

Selected researchable constraints

- Specific needs of individual developing countries. Not all of them have the same problems with compliance and they will have different support needs. It will be important to identify, appraise, quantify and cost the specific needs of each
- How producers, processors and traders could reduce costs of compliance by affiliating into associations or similar groupings
- The full cost of compliance with standards by individual developing countries, including the costs of: record keeping, facilities to monitor and audit, lost markets, cost in consumer health and the cost of traceability and verifying authenticity. Determine transaction costs at producer level
- How the necessary support services to small-scale producers, processors and traders could best be provided, especially in the absence of an effective agricultural extension service
- How quality perceptions along the supply chain match with those of the final buyer
- Field procedures, protocols and proxies for assessing conformity to standards, e.g., volumetric system for basic grain quality determination
- More-precise and consistent terminology when setting national, regional and international standards.
- Appropriateness of some nationally or regionally produced standards prior to investing in their widespread application
- If the export of the best quality food results in an increase in non-exportable unsafe commodities reaching the poorest
- Which standards have been more trade restrictive to developing countries than warranted by science, risk or necessity
- How to develop appropriate standards that are inclusive of the poor
- How small-scale producers can best access the premium local and regional food aid markets
- How private sector companies in developing countries are developing their own standards and ascertain the impact this will have on small-scale producers, processors and traders.

References

ITC (International Trade Centre). 2004. Improving and maintaining market access using WTO agreements on TBT and SPS. Export Quality Bulletin No. 75, ITC, Geneva, Switzerland.

Jones, E. and Hill, L. 1994. Re-engineering marketing policies in food and agriculture; issues and alternatives for grain grading policies. *In:* Padberg, D.I. (ed.) Re-Engineering Marketing Policies for Food and Agriculture, Food and Agricultural Marketing Consortium, Department of Agricultural Economics, Texas A&M University, College Station, Texas, USA.

Mpanza, T.V. 2000. The development of national grading standards for maize marketing in Swaziland. Dissertation submitted in partial fulfilment of Masters programme. Natural Resources Institute, University of Greenwich, London, UK.

NRI (Natural Resources Institute). 2003. Working paper on agricultural product standards and grades. Report for the Food and Agriculture Organization of the United Nations (FAO), Rome, Italy. NRI, Chatham, UK. (unpublished)

Niernberger, F. and Taylor, J.R.N. 2001. Development of simple common grain quality standards for sorghum to facilitate trade in southern Africa. Draft final report of Chemonics International Inc., Gaberone, Botswana. (unpublished)

Olembo, S.A.H. 2002. Regulating the agricultural sector in developing countries, who calls the tune? Paper presented at the Development Studies Association conference held at the University of Greenwich, London, UK, 9 November 2002. (unpublished)

Reardon, T. and Barrett, C.B. 2000. Agro-industrialization, globalization and international development. An overview of issues, patterns and determinants. Agricultural Economics, 23: 195–205.

Shapton, D.A. and Shapton, N.F. (eds). 1998. Principles and Practices for the Safe Processing of Foods. Woodhead Publishing Ltd. Cambridge, UK.

Standards and Trade Facility. 2005. www.standardsfacility.org (accessed 17 February 2005).

Walker, D.J. 2000.The role of agricultural food commodity standards and quality assurance systems in warehouse receipt financing in Zambia. Report by the Natural Resources Institute for the Common Fund for Commodities, Amsterdam, the Netherlands. (unpublished)

Walker, D.J. and Boxall, R.A. 2002. The development of a food market profiles map for the World Food Programme. Report by the Natural Resources Institute, University of Greenwich, Chatham, UK. 52pp. (unpublished)

Walker, D.J. and Boxall, R.A. 1998. Maize quality grading in Ghana. A component of the project on practical improvements to the liberalised grain marketing system. Report by the National Resources Institute on behalf of the Department for International Development (DFID), London, UK. (unpublished)

Walker, D.J. and Wandschneider, T. 2005. Local food aid procurement in Ethiopia. A case study for the EC PREP programme of the UK Department for International Development. Draft report by the Natural Resources Institute, University of Greenwich, Chatham, UK. (unpublished)

Wandschneider, T. and Hodges, R.J. 2005. Local food aid procurement in Uganda. A case study for the EC PREP programme of the UK Department for International Development. Final draft report by the Natural Resources Institute, University of Greenwich, Chatham, UK. 61pp. (unpublished)

World Bank. 2002. Understanding Product Grades and Standards and How to Apply Them. Giovannucci and Reardon, Washington DC, USA.

Wintour, P. and Elliott, L. 2005. EU must end world poverty to win respect says Hewitt. The Guardian, 24 January 2005, page 10, UK.

Overview

Mapping the market: market-literacy for agricultural research and policy to tackle rural poverty in Africa

Jon Hellin, Alison Griffith and Mike Albu

Introduction

Within policy, research and development agendas, there has been a re-emergence of interest in agriculture and pro-poor growth in rural areas. A number of multilateral and bilateral aid agencies, for example, the UK Department for International Development (DFID), the Asian Development Bank (ADB) and Swedish International Development Agency (Sida), have developed 'making markets work for the poor' conceptual frameworks and integrated them into their development assistance agendas at the country level. The Consultative Group on International Agricultural Research (CGIAR), a strategic alliance of members, partners and international agricultural centres that mobilises science to benefit the poor, now recognises that smallholder farmers' livelihoods depend on much more than the production of food staples. The CGIAR is now conducting research on how farmers can better access markets. Many non-governmental organisations (NGOs) that have traditionally focused on working with farmers to improve agricultural production and productivity are also broadening their activities to include processing and marketing.

In the recent past agricultural and rural poverty reduction policies have largely been influenced by one of two broad strands of thinking: trade liberalisation or technology-led solutions. The former seeks to stimulate demand for rural production through optimal allocation of resources in the agriculture sector (e.g., by removing the foreign exchange distortions, tariffs and subsidies that distort agricultural markets). The latter seeks to stimulate the supply side of the rural economy, through sustainable increases in agricultural productivity and value addition (e.g., through new varieties, improved cropping systems and better post-harvest processing). The preceding thematic papers have illustrated some of the challenges and issues that need to be addressed in order to make markets work for the poor. These include:

- Building linkages and enhancing trust between actors in the market chain (Best et al., this volume)
- Supporting small-scale producers to associate, collaborate and coordinate to achieve economies of scale in their transactions with buyers or suppliers (Biénabe and Sautier, this volume)
- Making channels of information and market intelligence accessible to rural producers (Marter, this volume)
- Enabling rural producers to understand and better satisfy the product, process or delivery standards required by buyers (Walker, this volume),

Trade liberalisation and technology-led solutions alone are unlikely to fulfil the agriculture sector's potential contribution to pro-poor growth in Africa. What is needed is a more comprehensive, market-literate framework; one that brings together and then builds on the technology-led and trade liberalisation thinking. Market literacy can be defined as the awareness, understanding and capacity to build the processes, institutions, competencies and relationships that enable market systems to work for poor producers. This paper presents a market-literate framework in the form of a Market Map. The Market Map serves two purposes: for the policy maker and rural development planner, it is a conceptual framework used to consider the commercial and institutional environment in which small-scale producers (including smallholder farmers) operate. For the practitioner, it is a practical and potentially participatory tool that can be used to facilitate pro-poor growth in rural areas through directly improving linkages and relationships between market-chain actors, and to prepare the ground for introducing or generating innovation in products, processes and market access.

Agriculture and pro-poor growth

Challenges facing smallholder agriculture

Despite rapid urbanisation, an estimated 70–75% of the world's poorest people live in rural areas where their livelihoods are largely dependent on agriculture. Many of the rural poor are smallholder farmers. In this paper, and based on Narayanan and Gulati (2002), smallholders are characterised as farmers (crop or livestock) who practice a mix of commercial and/or subsistence production, where the family provides the majority of labour and the farm provides the principal source of income. Such smallholders are often thought to be efficient users of resources, while their farming systems are often characterised as being a relatively equitable means of providing income and food directly to poor people (Kydd, 2002). Furthermore, smallholder farming is seen as strategically indispensable to development as a whole because:

- It accounts for a large proportion of agricultural production. Agriculture, however, is not only an economic activity and source of production and income; it is also an important part of rural peoples' culture and social organisation.
- Growth in this type of farming is linked to reductions in rural poverty and inequality. Growth in agricultural incomes is effective at reducing rural poverty because it has knock-on or multiplier effects on local markets for other goods and services provided by non-farm rural poor, such as construction, manufacturing and repairs (World Bank, 2001).
- These agricultural activities can provide such environmental services as the conservation of soil and water, the maintenance of bio-diversity, and a contribution to locking up carbon. These services are important to society in both urban and rural areas as well as locally and globally.

Smallholder farming is taking place in the context of a number of global drivers and meta-trends that are reshaping the global agricultural economy, providing rural producers with new opportunities, but at the same time are plac-ing the livelihoods of rural producers in the developing world under intense and increasing strain (see Table 1).

Table 1.   Global drivers and meta-trends

Global drivers	Meta-trends
What drives globalisation?	Global and local trends independent of globalisation
• Trade liberalisation	• Technological change
• Intellectual property rights	• Urbanisation, increasing incomes, population pressure
• Food safety and quality standards	
• Foreign direct investment	• Shifts in food consumption patterns
• Scale of agro-industry	• Environmental degradation

Source: Narayanan and Gulati, 2002

Faced with growing populations and inequitable land distribution, small-holders face the challenge of intensifying agricultural output without destroying the land resource (soil, water and land) upon which it all depends. Africa, however, is rather more fortunate than South Asia or Latin America, in that most countries have relatively equitable land distribution (InterAcademcy Council, 2004). What is unequal in Africa is farmers' access to new technology and access to both input and output markets.

The achievement to date has not been particularly encouraging: it has been suggested that, worldwide, approximately 12×10^6 ha of arable land are destroyed and abandoned annually because of unsustainable farming practices (Pimentel et al., 1995)

A more recent threat to smallholder agriculture, especially in sub-Saharan Africa is the human immunodeficiency virus/acquired immunodeficiency syn-drome (HIV/AIDS) pandemic. The impact of HIV/AIDS in terms of morbidity and mortality is particularly severe in the agricultural sector in Africa. According to the Food and Agriculture Organization of the United Nations (FAO) some 7 million farmers and farm workers in 25 African countries had died of AIDS by 2000 and 16 million more will die by 2020 (FAO, 2001).

There is also the growing phenomenon of the rapid growth in demand from expanding urban populations in developing countries (FAO, 2004). As a result of this demand, food systems can no longer be viewed simply as a way of moving basic staples from farm to local plates. Producers now often supply long and sophisti-cated market chains, and market processed and branded products to mainly urban consumers (Barghouti et al., 2004). This is particularly the case with the growth and increasing concentration of supermarkets (Weatherspoon and Reardon, 2003).

In the context of the global drivers and meta-trends outlined in Table 1, farming's capacity to provide the sole means of survival for rural populations is diminishing fast. There is, therefore, little justification for an exclusive reliance on primary agricultural development to improve the quality of life in rural areas (Dorward et al., 2004). Rural non-agricultural employment (RNAE) is re-emerging as a critical issue in sustaining viable rural economies and reducing rural poverty. The definition of 'non-agricultural' excludes primary production, whether in agriculture, fisheries or livestock, but covers manufacturing (including agro-processing) as well as such services as transportation (Berdegué et al., 2000).

The contribution of RNAE to rural people's livelihoods should not be underestimated. In sub-Saharan Africa, a range of 30–50% reliance on non-farm income sources is common and it may attain 80–90% in southern Africa (Ellis, 1999). The importance of RNAE is likely to increase because agriculture today requires improved linkages with input supply systems, agricultural processing chains, and systems for the distribution of fresh and processed products, particularly when farmers move into higher-value crops (Barghouti et al., 2004).

As the four thematic papers have illustrated, if the rural agricultural enterprise sector (encompassing both primary production and value-added to agricultural products) is to continue to have a major role to play in pro-poor growth[1], a number of challenges have to be overcome, these include:

- Depressed international crop prices and unfair competition in domestic markets from imported products due to subsidised agricultural over-production in the developed world
- Physical and commercial isolation from the markets and potential channels of economic growth emerging in domestic or international trade
- Inadequate access to the knowledge, technology and skills needed to diversify rural livelihoods and secure markets for increased agricultural productivity (Marter, this volume). Farmers often find it difficult to meet the market demands for quality, quantity and continuity of production as well as the standards set by Organization for Economic Co-operation and Development (OECD) countries (Walker, this volume)
- Lack of trust within the market chain (Best et al., this volume) and also between producers (Biénabe and Sautier, this volume).

Faced with these challenges, there are those who question whether there is really any future for smallholder farming (Maxwell et al., 2001), but on the other hand, the United Nations Millennium Project Hunger Task Force was established to promote immediate action towards achieving the Millennium Development Goal (MDG) of reducing hunger by half by the year 2015 (The World Bank Group,

---

[1] Pro-poor growth is growth that is good for the poor (DFID, 2004). One definition of pro-poor growth considers only the incomes of the poor and the extent to which growth is 'pro-poor' depends on how fast the incomes of the poor are rising. Pro-poor growth can be seen as the average growth rate of incomes of poor people.

2004). The Task Force is emphasising the need to renew and increase support for smallholder farming (FAO, 2004) It is generally expected, however, that in the future a smaller proportion of the population will be involved in farming and that larger numbers of people will be employed in other parts of the rural and urban economy (Tripp, 2001).

If the collapse of rural economies is to be prevented then policy mechanisms must be found to enable rural populations to share in the potential economic growth created by some of the global drivers and meta-trends outlined in Table 1. In the recent past agriculture and rural poverty reduction policies have largely been influenced by one of two broad strands of thinking: trade liberalisation or technology-led solutions.

Trade liberalisation

Trade-distorting policies by OECD countries are particularly harmful to African agriculture because of agricultural production subsidies, limited market access and export subsidies (InterAcademy Council, 2004). The trade liberalisation approach aims to stimulate demand for rural production through a more optimal allocation of resources in the agriculture sector. This involves removing foreign exchange distortions, tariffs and subsidies that distort agricultural markets. These reforms reflected the principles of what became known as the *Washington Consensus on Agriculture* (World Bank, 2001).

The argument is that market liberalisation will enable African smallholder farmers to exploit their comparative advantages in land and labour and by so doing will be able to access growing northern markets. There is evidence to back up this assertion: using economic simulation models, Runge et al. (2003) have estimated that sub-Saharan Africa stands to benefit most from trade liberalisation in terms of the share of the value of agricultural production and of GDP that such economic benefits would represent. The authors calculate that trade liberalisation would lead to sub-Saharan Africa's exports increasing by US$10.7 billion by 2025, a 45% increase. This is in contrast to the last two decades, during which Africa has lost ground in the global market place for its agricultural exports. The region's share of total world agricultural exports has fallen from about 6% in the 1970s to 3% today (Diao and Hazell, 2004).

It is also important not to focus exclusively on export markets: domestic and intra-regional food markets are another potential source of demand for Africa's agricultural products (Peacock et al., 2004). As Table 2 shows, the current value of sub-Saharan Africa's domestic demand for food staples is approximately US$50 billion. This figure dwarfs the current value of the exports. Admittedly, only some of this output is sold, but domestic demand is a growing market and one that offers real income opportunities (Diao and Hazell, 2004).

World governments regularly sound the clarion call for market liberalisation but their actions belie their rhetoric (Oxfam, 2002). In addition, market opportunities do not necessarily translate into benefits for farmers: under the Lomé Convention, for example, the European Union (EU) gave preferential market access

Table 2. Size of sub-Saharan Africa's agricultural markets

Market size (US$ billions)	East Africa	Southern Africa	West Africa	Total sub-Saharan Africa
Exports to non-African countries	4.0	5.9	6.7	**16.6**
Intra-African trade	0.4	1.1	0.4	**1.9**
Domestic market for food staples	17.6	12.1	20.1	**49.7**

Source: Diao and Hazell, 2004

to the African, Caribbean and Pacific (ACP) countries, and yet exports from these countries to the EU fell from US$23 billion in 1985 to US$20 billion in 1994 (DFID, 2000). Furthermore, new suppliers from Asia and Latin America are proving to be very competitive in the export markets for Africa's traditional export crops, and rich importing countries are becoming choosier about products quality and standards (Walker, this volume).

Others have questioned whether the *Washington Consensus on Agriculture*, with its emphasis on trade liberalisation, provides as many opportunities for smallholder development as is claimed (Kydd and Dorward, 2001; Wiggins et al., 2002). Specifically, market liberalisation may have removed price distortions, but it has done little to benefit most small-scale farmers, especially those living away from roads and markets' (InterAcademy Council, 2004). As Vorley (2003) writes 'much attention has been focused on market distortions caused by protectionist trade policies. But even if unjust trade rules were to be reformed, disparities in bargaining power, scale, market access, information or access to credit, may still entrench anti-poor and anti-rural bias in markets'. Major obstacles, such as poor road infrastructure [Africa's road system leaves about 70% of its farmers poorly connected to markets (InterAcademy Council, 2004)] mean that the rural poor are unable to build links with market chains in ways that will improve their livelihoods.

Technology-led thinking

Smallholder farming in many parts of the world reaches productivity levels that are only one third of the potential yield under optimum conditions (IFAD, 2001). Only 7% of the arable land in Africa is irrigated against 40% in Asia, and fertiliser consumption in Africa is only 9 kg/ha compared to 100 kg/ha in Southeast Asia and 206 kg/ha in industrialised countries (FAO, 2005). Meanwhile, each 10% growth in agricultural productivity in Africa has been shown to reduce poverty by 6%, with more than 110 million poor in Africa, a 10% increase in crop yields could help almost 7 million more people raise their incomes above the poverty line of US$1 per day (Thirtle et al., 2001 cited in InterAcademy Council, 2004).

Based on the above, another strand of thinking currently dominating agriculture and rural poverty reduction policy seeks to stimulate the supply side of the rural economy i.e., agricultural production, through sustainable increases in agricultural productivity and value-addition (e.g., through the use of new crop varieties, improved seed, and better crop, animal and land husbandry).

The technology-led approach, however, has certain limitations. In some cases, there is little point in pushing for higher-yielding technologies when markets do not exist for the increased outputs, or when increased productivity merely saturates existing markets and depresses farm-gate prices (Dorward et al., 2002).

Furthermore, an assessment of future agricultural technology policies for rural development emphasises that most of the new technologies that will become available to farmers will be 'information intensive', i.e., requiring increased levels of knowledge for appropriate management (Tripp, 2003). In addition to basic technical knowledge, the rural poor need to be able to operate in increasingly sophisticated input and output markets because of the global drivers and meta-trends shaping the world economy (see Table 1). As Best et al. (this volume) point out in their paper on building linkages and enhancing trust, there is growing evidence that attempts to alleviate poverty and hunger through interventions targeted at improving staple cash crop production alone are not working. This is one of the reasons why NGOs, along with bilateral and multi-lateral organisations, whose focus in the past may have been almost exclusively on increasing agricultural production, are increasingly looking at how to make markets work for the poor. There is an emerging consensus that greater market literacy is needed in development policy and practice.

Why 'market-literacy'?

Access to markets can be an incentive to improved land management and increased agricultural production and productivity but, as mentioned earlier, trade liberalisation and technology-led solutions alone are unlikely to fulfil the agriculture sector's contribution to pro-poor growth in Africa. Resource-poor farmers seldom understand how the market works. They have little or no information on market conditions, prices and quality of goods; they are not organised collectively, they have limited experience of market negotiation and little appreciation of their capacity to influence the terms and conditions upon which they engage with the market (IFAD, 2001).

What is needed is a more comprehensive market-literate framework, one that brings together and builds on the technology-led and trade liberalisation thinking. The objective of a more comprehensive approach is to bring about improvements in the livelihoods in terms of the secure income/reduced vulnerability of poor rural producers working in market-based production systems. The market-literate approach aims to promote the growth and improved functioning/performance (e.g., competitiveness, productivity, employment, value addition, linkage coordination, efficiency) of market chains in ways that benefit poor small-scale producers.

The improved functioning of market chains includes:

- Identification of market opportunities
- Greater inclusion and empowerment of women
- Better access to appropriate processing technologies
- Implementation of effective business organisation practices
- More efficient farm to market channels
- Timely access to affordable financial and business services.

In this context, Dorward et al. (2002) pose some searching questions for pro-poor analysis of rural livelihoods and markets (Box 1).

Dorward et al. (2002) point out that the questions outlined in Box 1 are both complex and challenging and could become unmanageable. They suggest that it is useful to have a unifying framework for the examination of the way that particular markets work. In the following sections an example of such a framework, the Market Map is introduced.

Box 1. Questions for pro-poor analysis of rural livelihoods and markets

- Who are the poor, what are the assets that they hold, what activities are they engaged in, what are their aspirations and livelihood strategies?
- Which markets are important for the livelihoods of the poor (or should be important for them) now or in the future, directly or indirectly?
- How well do these markets currently serve the poor, in terms of ease, security and conditions of access?
- How do these markets fit into supply and value chains? How do these chains operate, where are the constraints, where are the high returns being made?
- What stakeholders are involved in these markets and what are their roles, interests, strengths, weaknesses, opportunities and threats?
- What are the barriers to entry and the transaction costs and risks for different stakeholders?
- What is the institutional environment like and what are its effects on key markets– is it enabling or disabling? How could these be developed or modified to improve market access for the poor?
- What institutional arrangements are currently in place? Why are they in their current form? How could this environment be developed or modified to improve market access for the poor?
- How are these markets changing and how are they likely to change as a result of wider, external processes of change? What opportunities are there for support to wider process of growth?

Source: Dorward et al., 2002

The Market Map: a framework for making markets work for the poor

Meeting a development need

Earlier it was argued that a strategy for rural African poverty reduction should not only rely on trade liberalisation and processes of technological development. It requires a better understanding of how markets for smallholder produce in rural areas actually function, and the identification of appropriate innovative responses to this at the level of services and institutions. This in response to the fact that while markets can indeed provide a very efficient mechanism for exchange, coordination and allocation of many resources, goods and services, they do not always work has effectively and efficiently as we would like.

The aim should be to focus more attention on the processes and institutions, competencies and relationships that enable markets to work for poor rural producers. Awareness and understanding of these issues are called 'market-literacy' for short, and it is argued that this is an important requirement in the design and implementation of both agricultural research and rural development programmes that aim to reduce rural poverty generally.

The Market Map serves two purposes. For the policy maker and rural development planner, it is a conceptual framework for thinking about the commercial and institutional environment in which small-scale producers (including smallholder farmers) operate. For the practitioner, it is a practical and potentially participatory tool that can be used to represent and communicate knowledge about specific producers, their market chains, and institutional environments and service needs.

The thinking behind the Market Map reflects changes in the policy context over the last 40 years. In over-simplified terms, there has been a change from an emphasis on supporting supply (through state provision of extension, input supply and credit services) to an almost exclusive focus on stimulating demand as part of structural adjustment and liberalisation (Peacock et al., 2004). The pendulum is now moving back towards a growing interest in institutional issues around market failures and service delivery problems facing smallholder producers.

The more market-literate approach illustrated by the Market Map provides development practitioners with a conceptual and operational tool to facilitate pro-poor growth in rural areas and to close the wealth gap between Africa and other parts of the world. As can be seen later, processes of elaborating the Market Map, if conducted in a participatory way, can be a vital intervention in themselves – directly improving linkages and relationships between market-chain actors, and preparing the ground for introducing or generating innovation in products, processes and market access.

Antecedents of the Market Map

One of the Market Map's strengths is that it is the product of an inter-disciplinary initiative drawing together practitioners from several fields, including small enterprise development, natural resource management, fair trade, agricultural marketing and community development. It is considered that the Market Map will be particularly useful in broad-based multidisciplinary programmes, where winning adherence to a coherent shared conceptual framework can often be very difficult.

Practical Action (the new name for the Intermediate Technology Development Group, ITDG) developed the Market Map initially at a workshop involving international staff from Africa, Latin America and South Asia in 2002. Since then the framework has been adopted and adapted as training tool by such organisations as TraidCraft and Oxfam. These, and other experiences, will be discussed further in section 3. Readers will almost certainly recognise aspects of other tools and approaches in this work. The formative ideas that have contributed to Practical Action's thinking include:

- Sub-sector Analysis, as originally conceived (Haggblade and Gamser, 1991) and subsequently adapted (Lusby and Panlibuton, 2004)
- The Sustainable Livelihoods Framework approach[2] and the recognition that in the conceptualisation and application of 'livelihood approaches' there is often a lack of emphasis on markets and their roles in livelihood development and poverty reduction (Dorward et al., 2002)
- Value-chain analysis (Kaplinsky and Morris, 2005), particularly participatory approaches (Mayoux, 2003).
- The territorial approach to rural agro-enterprise development (Lundy et al., 2005) used by Centro International de Agricultura Tropical (CIAT) and discussed in one of the thematic papers seminar (Best et al., this volume).

The Market Map: an initial orientation

The Market Map is designed to be used after particular product groups (or sub-sectors), that appear to offer growth potential for poor producers/smallholders, have been identified. Appropriate criteria for selecting appropriate products or sub-sectors have been described extensively by others, e.g., CIAT (Best et al., this volume) and Action for Enterprise (AFE) (Lusby and Panlibuton, 2004) so these are not covered here. The Market Map is made up of three inter-linked components (see Figure 1).

The market chain actors

The central component of the framework is constructed by mapping the economic actors who actually own and transact a particular product as it moves through the market chain from primary producer to final consumer: smallholders and larger-scale producers, traders, processors, transporters, wholesalers, retailers etc., see Figure 2.

In many cases, the market chain comprises more than one channel and these channels can also supply more than one final market. A comprehensive mapping therefore describes interacting and *competing* channels (including those that perhaps do not involve smallholders at all) and the variety of final markets into which these connect. As far as possible, information about product volumes and values,

---

[2]   e.g., DFID's version at Livelihoods Connect website www.livelihoods.org

Figure 1. The Market Map: an overview

Source: Albu and Griffith, 2005

and numbers of enterprises or livelihoods supported at each point in the chain is overlaid on the map – as for a standard sub-sector analysis (Haggblade and Gamser, 1991). Information about patterns and trends in the data is also incorporated.

Defying convention, the typified framework schematic (see Figure 2) reverses the direction of the chain. It shows the flow of *income* from markets along the chain to primary producers, rather than (as is conventional) the flow of *goods* in the opposite direction. This counter-intuitivism is introduced deliberately to emphasise a demand-led perspective. It provokes users of the Market Map to consider how market chain linkages and functions can be improved so as to facilitate the flow of income to target producers who are perhaps furthest from end-markets. Instead of asking 'how can these smallholder farmers get more income for this crop?' it suggests the question, 'How might a greater share of (say) urban expenditure on this product reach these farmers?' be asked This mindset can help preclude

Figure 2. Market chain actors and channels of demand

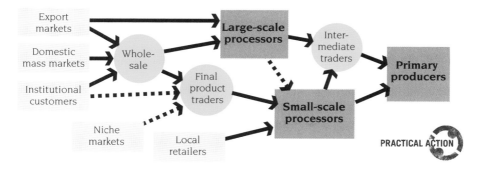

Source: Albu and Griffith, 2005

negative presumptions about the role of intermediaries, and increase understanding of competitive pressures from other channels.

A critical early step in applying the Market Map lies in selecting which markets and channels offer the best prospects for enhancing poor producers' livelihoods. This decision – informed by an overview of the prospects and relationships between competing channels – determines the focus applied to developing the Market Map further. At this stage, the potential for establishing new linkages in the market chain can also be considered.

Once the potential of a specific market channel (or a number of alternative channels) has been identified the analysis moves into a more-detailed consideration of how value accumulates along the market chain. By better understanding the contribution each actor in the chain brings to the product, the aim is to identify inefficiencies, inequities and losses that could be remedied, or added value that could be captured, particularly by poor producers. A comprehensive market-chain analysis will explore how the chain is 'governed' since this influences how profit margins are divided up through the chain, i.e., which actors or other institutions: a. define the conditions for participation in the chain, b. ensure compliance with these rules, and c. provide assistance with meeting these rules.

While many market chains are characterised by inequitable relationships between actors, a clear objective of the Market Map approach is to help stakeholders realise mutual benefits by improving the 'systemic efficiency' of the chain. Helping stakeholders become more aware of the functions and processes that are needed along the chain in order to satisfy more lucrative or reliable markets is key to this. The advantages and challenges of participatory approaches – in all aspects of constructing the Market Map – will be discussed.

The enabling business environment

The second component of the Market Map is a charting of the critical factors and trends that are shaping the market chain environment and operating conditions, but may be amenable to change. These 'enabling environment' factors are generated by structures (national and local authorities, research agencies etc.) and institutions (policies, regulations and practices), that are beyond the direct control of economic actors in the market chain.

The purpose of charting this enabling environment is not simply to map the status quo, but to understand the trends that are affecting the entire market chain, and to examine the powers and interests that are driving change. This knowledge can help determine avenues and opportunities for realistic action, lobbying and policy entrepreneurship.

In thinking about the very wide range of factors, it may be useful to distinguish those that relate to *market demand*, i.e., prices, quantities, qualities and timeliness of supplies required by buyers; those that bear on *transformation* activities, i.e., costs of producing, processing, storing and moving produce; and those that affect *transactions* activities, i.e., costs of doing business (Kydd, 2002). The latter include such costs as:

- **Contracting:** building linkages, agreeing terms, monitoring performance and enforcing contracts
- **Securing finance:** costs of providing (or not being able to provide) collateral
- **Legal recognition:** licensing and business formalities
- **Quality assurance:** information and skills needed to understand, monitor and certify adherence to buyer's standards.

Transformation costs are naturally a prominent theme in current policy initiatives on rural African poverty. It is widely hoped that agricultural productivity could be significantly improved by technological development – in improved seed and livestock breeds, farming inputs, storage and processing techniques – and infrastructure investment, e.g., in roads, electricity or irrigation.

However, in market chains based on smallholder agriculture, transactions costs can easily outweigh the potential benefits of participation in the market – and thus render irrelevant the productivity increases achieved by investment in infrastructure and technological development.

The costs of transactions in market chains in rural African economies tend to be adversely high due to: diseconomies of dispersed low-intensity production, inaccessible legal systems, unclear title to property, and low levels of trust generally. In contrast to more-developed economies, transactions-cost-reducing institutions and structures (e.g., contract enforcement mechanisms, communications infrastructure, land registries, trading standards, organisations of producer collaboration) are very weak.

Even more problematically, many of the institutions that do exist often hinder and block rather than facilitate people's own efforts to move out of poverty – being simply misused to extract administrative rents from producers, processors and traders. Some of these blockages are legally sanctioned, such as by-laws, licensing regulations and local-level taxes; and others take the form of arbitrary small-scale abuses of power by people in authority[3]. It is common to find abuse of procedures from authorities responsible for: policing transport, ensuring public health, licensing business premises, or protecting the natural environment, to identify just a few. As a result the local-level policy environment often remains inimical to self-employment and start-up business. Local enterprise often arises 'outside' the regulations, i.e., as an unrecognised informal-sector activity, and depends on paying off local officials to allow continued operation (Ellis, 1999).

A particularly pervasive institutional factor that needs to be considered often takes the form of socially enforced gender roles. In many communities, these roles obstruct women smallholder farmers and entrepreneurs from participating in certain kinds of financial transactions, block their access to markets and/or deny them ownership of property or control of income. To reiterate then, the factors that are

---

[3] Ellis and Harris (2004), list for example: payments required in order 'to stay on the right side of authority' when in business; fake prohibitions on livestock movements or fishing boats created in order to extract fees; gratuities demanded by chiefs for rights of access certain resources; and fees required to secure public services that should be delivered free.

likely to be important in the enabling environment for specific agricultural market chains in Africa include those relating to:

Market demand
- Consumption trends (volumes, prices and quality expectations)
- Tax and tariff regimes

Transformation activities
- Infrastructure (constraints and investment policies)
- Technological development (seeds, breeds, inputs, processing etc.)
- Transport licensing and regulation

Transactions activities
- Systems for agricultural finance
- Gender roles in business and financial affairs
- Registration of land and property
- Commercial law and practices (including contract enforcement)
- Business licensing and regulation
- Product standards and quality assurance.

In using the Market Map specific factors, issues and trends that are identified as significant influences on market-chain operations are recorded above the market chain itself. Priority is given to identifying and unpacking issues that are likely to cause significant impact on market-chain operations or are relatively amenable to change themselves (see Figure 3).

As before, a key objective in applying the Market Map approach is to help market-chain stakeholders become more aware of these factors and trends. Action to improve the enabling environment usually depends on concerted lobbying, coordinated campaigns or advocacy.

Figure 3. Factors in the enabling business environment

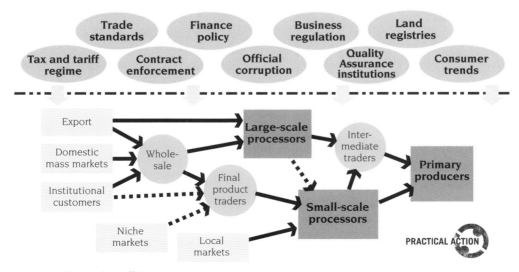

Source: Albu and Griffith, 2005

Clearly, if the process of charting the enabling environment is participatory, it is more likely to build the trust, coordination and collaboration between actors in the market chain needed to achieve this.

Business and extension services

In most effective market chains the economic actors who actually form the chain (i.e., transact the main product) are supported by services from other enterprises and support organisations. As Best et al. (this volume) note, once an enterprise has been established, there is an on-going need for it to access services of different types, both market and technical, that will allow it to grow and maintain its competitiveness.

The third component of the Market Map framework is concerned with mapping those services that support, or could potentially support, the market chain's overall efficiency. Such services can be referred to as business development services (BDS), business services, or even livelihood development services (Miehlbradt and McVay, 2004). The range of services that can potentially add value is huge and includes:

- Input supplies (seeds, livestock, fertilisers, etc.)
- Market information (prices, trends, buyers, suppliers)
- Financial services (credit, savings or insurance)
- Transport services
- Quality assurance – (monitoring and accreditation)
- Technical expertise and business advice
- Veterinary services
- Support for product development and diversification.

Mechanisms of service delivery can differ substantially. In exploring what already exists, it is important to recognise that the options are not confined solely to conventional government *extension services* and private *fee-based services* or input providers. There are also *embedded services*, where services are incorporated within a commercial transaction for another product, e.g., pest control advice offered by a trader to a contract farmer. And finally there are *informally provided services* where the service, such as information or advice, is negotiated through social networks and reciprocal relationships, which may be 'invisible' to outsiders (Hitchens et al., 2004).

At this stage mapping 'services' involves identifying particular service needs and their locations within the market-chain in order to get an overall picture of the opportunities for using services to improve market-chain efficiency or equity (see Figure 4). This mapping is a precursor to subsequently assessing the most appropriate mechanisms for delivery of services, in terms of outreach, sustainability and cost-effectiveness.

Where fee-based service delivery looks broadly feasible, much can be learned from small enterprise development. Since the mid 1990s the BDS market development' approach to business services for small enterprises has accumu-lated a persuasive body of experience about creating diverse, sustainable,

Figure 4.   Business and extension services

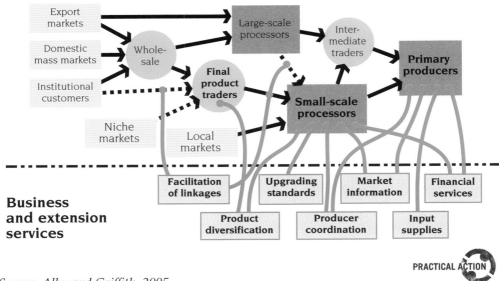

Source: Albu and Griffith, 2005

client-responsive services even where existing markets are weak or under-developed. The goal of the approach is to enable small enterprises to buy the services of their choice from a wide selection of (primarily) unsubsidised private-sector suppliers in a competitive and evolving market (Miehlbradt and McVay, 2003). The role of governments and donors is then seen to be one of facilitating this process through interventions that build sustainable market institutions and social structures – but not to undermine the emergence of these institutions and structures by directly delivering or subsidising services.

As a direct result of the emergence of the BDS market development field, significant work has been done to elaborate practical methods of assessing the market for services. These methods enable one to gauge what services are potentially viable and understand the demand or supply-side constraints that have to be addressed to develop a vibrant and sustainable market.

BDS market development approaches were initially applied most successfully to services needed by small and medium-sized enterprises (SMEs), often urban-based, rather than rural micro-enterprises or smallholder farmers. SMEs may, of course, be important actors in market chains that involve smallholder farmers and rural enterprises. More recently however, it has been suggested that BDS market development approaches have direct relevance even to rural producers in weak economic environments (Hitchens et al., 2004).

An important point is that even where fee-based services are not commercially viable – for example, because of the high transactions costs encountered in financing services and contracting services on a micro-scale, a market development approach may still be relevant. Embedding services within other commercial transactions is a common and effective way to reduce transaction costs, particularly those related to financing inputs. Examples include:

- Inputs (seeds, fertilisers) provided by buyers of crops
- Advice on grading and packaging products from traders
- Training in pest management provided by input suppliers
- Contract farming in bananas, cacao and coffee.

But embedded services can create their own problems of control and coordination with associated risks for the service provider. For example, how does the trader who provides a farmer with valuable technical advice to improve his/her crop yield, ensure the crop is not sold elsewhere? It could be argued that these risks can be mitigated by building greater mutual understanding between actors along the market chain: greater awareness of the rewards of raising overall market chain (systemic) efficiency can contribute to achieving the necessary levels of trust and collaboration (see examples in the following section and Best et al., this volume).

Finally, there are informally provided services. These are not merely reciprocal arrangements between individuals. In many situations, for example, the requirement for systemic efficiency is better collaboration between large groups of producers to achieve economies of scale in: bulk purchasing of inputs; assembling produce for storage and transport; group commissioning of specialist fee-based services, and access to intelligence on prices, market and technology trends (Biénabe and Sautier, this volume). This co-ordinating function is often best achieved informally by producers collectively working for themselves – as a kind of 'service' provided by their own social networks and institutions of voluntary collaboration.

The point to note here is that as one moves away from purely fee-based services to services that are embedded in other transactions or organised through collaborative institutions, there are substantial advantages to be gained by strengthening relationships and mutual understanding among small-scale producers and between actors along the market chain. The Market Map can be used to help this happen by: a. representing and communicating shared knowledge about specific market chains, and b. by fomenting on-going dialogues between different actors participating in the process of its research and construction.

Participatory Market Mapping

The Market Map in its entirety (see Figure 5) has proved to be a very useful way to visually represent and succinctly communicate knowledge about specific market chains' actors, operations, contexts and needs to different stakeholders. These stakeholders include farmers, traders, project managers and policy makers.

Furthermore (and more importantly), the process of mapping the market-chain structure and actors, diagnosing the key enabling environment issues and assessing service needs can – if conducted in participation with market-chain actors themselves – be a powerful way to build understanding and trust between stakeholders. Best et al. (this volume) point out that following sub-sector selection, a more in-depth analysis of the supply chain for selected product or products is required, through which specific actors are identified and characterised, relationships

Figure 5.   The Market Map complete

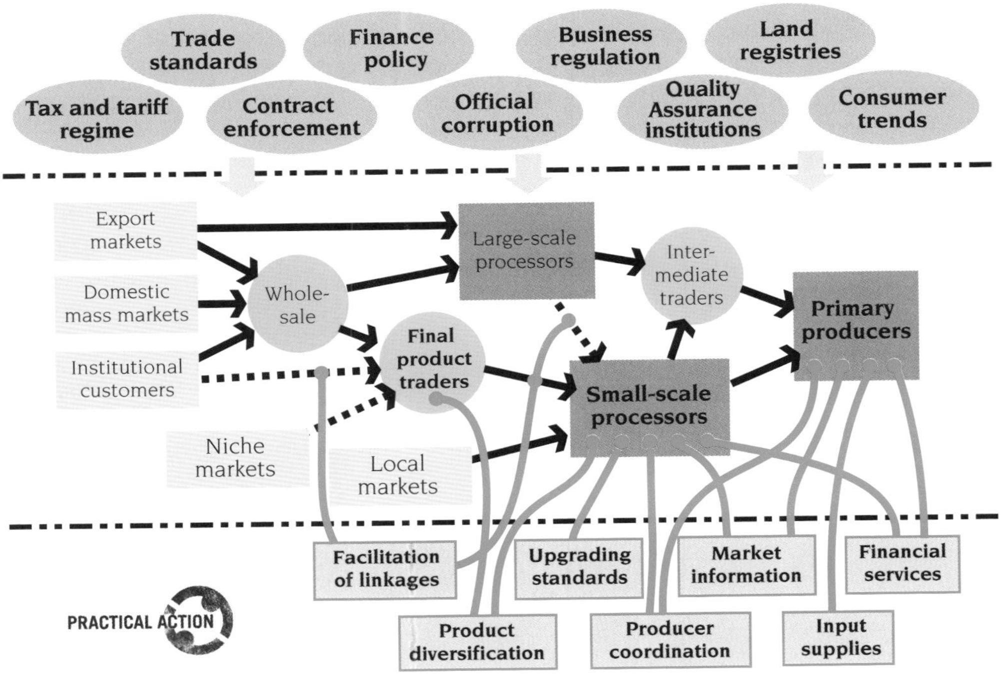

Source: Albu and Griffith, 2005

among actors are understood, bottlenecks are identified and actions proposed for overcoming them.

Participatory market chain analysis (PMCA) has been used by a number of organisations including the Centro Internacional de la Papa (CIP) in the Andes where it is seen as a method of involving market-chain actors in sharing knowledge and building trust in order to generate joint innovations (Bernet et al., 2005). Participatory approaches to market chain analysis contribute to Market Maps that are more likely to be accurate and to represent a wider range of knowledge. More importantly, the participation provokes interest and builds trust. Ultimately it can facilitate the collaboration that is necessary for improving linkages and efficiencies within the market chain, for effective lobbying on enabling environment issues, and for coordinating collective action around services (see Boxes 2 and 3).

The Market Map therefore needs to be seen as a tool for action as well as a framework for thinking about agricultural research agendas and rural development programme strategy. Application of the Market Map could be part of the process of institutional development that needs to happen (with smallholder farmers and others in the market) – introducing market literacy at all levels – alongside technological development and economic liberalisation. In the following section ways to make the map and framework operational and some of the challenges likely to be encountered are discussed.

Box 2. Blackberries and participatory market chain analysis in Colombia

There is a demand for blackberries as a fresh fruit and as an input to the growing fruit pulp industry in Colombia. In the Cabuyal watershed in 2001, blackberry production was managed by an estimated 65 small-scale producers located in and around four villages. Work by Corporación para el Fomento de los Comités de Investigación Agropecuaria, a local NGO, revealed a rustic production system with limited use of appropriate techniques, serious pest and disease problems, and low yields. Inappropriate post-harvest management and packing led to important product quality degradation, and as a result, much of the fruit produced did not meet quality standards for higher-priced markets. Furthermore, no local organisation existed through which support for blackberry marketing could be effected.

By bringing together producers, truck owners, intermediaries, and input providers, it became clear that a major limitation to improved competitiveness in the market chain lay in the lack of farmer organisation. A production system composed of individual farmers plays into the hands of intermediaries who can use their access to information to maintain low farm-gate prices, and also increases costs for such services as inputs and transportation, with few checks on the quality of the services. Interestingly, these points were raised not by the farmers but rather by truck owners, input providers, and intermediaries who said that they would be willing to provide better support services at more competitive prices if there were a local producer's organisation with which they could negotiate.

Following discussions, blackberry producers formed a community business organisation through which farmers would not only sell their fruit, but also access bulk quantities of inputs such as organic fertiliser, classify their production, and group their fruit for travel to the market.

Source: CIAT, 2001

The Market Map and operational challenges

The previous section explained how the framework has been developed for application and adaptation in different and unique contexts. By sharing learning about the application of the Market Map it is hoped that users, whether policy makers or practitioners, will be better able to adopt the principles of the framework. This section gives some examples of how the framework has been used to date (albeit in a limited way), explores challenges, and draws initial lessons from those experiences.

Making the Market Map work

Within Practical Action the Market Map has been an invaluable framework for strategic development of the International Markets and Livelihoods Programme. It has provided a common language and approach to develop coherent programme objectives. Operationalising it at project level has been challenging for the

Box 3. Bamboo and participatory market chain analysis in Ecuador

In Ecuador, local NGOs, government officials and larger entrepreneurs expressed interest in exploring the opportunities to reduce poverty offered by bamboo. Supported by the Netherlands Development Organisation [Schweizerische Normen-Vereinigung (SNV)] they came up with a strategy for supporting the entire bamboo production chain. This would benefit a range of market-chain actors, including smallholder producers and traditional bamboo gatherers, as well as small traders, lorry drivers, manufacturers and exporters.

SNV conducted an evaluation of the bamboo production chain. This diagnosis was based on the participation of actors across the chain and revealed a number of problems. The process and its findings encouraged the actors to jointly discuss their problems. The Ecuadorian Ministry of Agriculture subsequently institutionalised this forum by creating a Bamboo Advisory Council (CCB). This was a vital step, as institutionalisation meant that the forum was more resilient and also that the sector now had an official mechanism for influencing sector policy.

SNV organised a strategic planning workshop that was attended by the main market actors. The participants drew up a document setting out the CCB's strategic objectives, activities, values and principles, as well as the roles and responsibilities of the various actors. The PMCA brought together groups who otherwise may never have had an opportunity to work together. One challenging problem at the outset was to overcome the lack of trust between the actors. Used in a participatory way, the PMCA enables actors to have a shared understanding of the market chain in terms of costs and benefits. This creates transparency, improves trust and creates more equal relationships.

The SNV is now helping to forge an alliance between on the one hand, small-scale producers, whose assets are: land, labour and bamboo production skills, and agro-industrialists, with their management and investment capacities and commercial contacts, on the other. Such an alliance has much more viability and impact than a new market chain consisting solely of small-scale producers. SNV facilitates the drawing up of long-term contracts between small-scale suppliers and agro-industrialists. Both parties stand to benefit from these: the small-scale producers will benefit in terms of higher prices, security of sales, provision of inputs, and information. The agro-industrialists will benefit from a secure supply of inputs, i.e., produce of the right quality delivered in sufficient quantities and in time.

Source: Marlin, 2004

international team, since using the Market Map in the design and implementation of projects involves adopting a new approach and inevitably it takes time to build capacity. Progress is being made, evident in a recent project in Kenya and this section benefits from the emerging lessons of that work. By sharing the Market Map with other organisations Practical Action has also learned from its application in different ways (see Box 4).

Box 4.   Using the Market Map

An early adaptation of the framework was for a study commissioned by the Southeast Europe Enterprise Development (SEED) programme of the International Finance Corporation (IFC) for work in the Balkans to support the medicinal plants sector[4]. The team[5] responsible for making recommendations used the framework to look at the sub-sector in a holistic way and structure their proposals for interventions in the sector. Using the Market Map to guide an analytical process produced a set of issues affecting the market chains of medicinal herbs, for example, weak regulation of the sector. By developing an understanding of the market chains and the issues affecting the actors in those chains the team were able to make recommendations. For example, the team considered that the private sector should be engaged in ensuring better regulation of the trade since it has the leverage to promote better standards of practice (e.g., through embedded services). Therefore their recommendation was self-regulation by the private sector, including the development of best-practice standards for sustainable harvesting and fair trade. This included determining minimum prices to be paid to collectors for particular species.

Source: Donnelly and Helberg, 2004

Initial analysis and mapping

As discussed earlier one of the strengths (and indeed primary purpose) of the Market Map is that it lends itself to participatory analysis of market chains. For this approach to be effective a two-stage analytical process is helpful:

- Initial mapping by the facilitator – produces a Market Map that shows the market-chain(s) actors, the services they require (actual and potential) and the enabling environment issues. One way of gathering information is to create an 'Interest Group'[6] that consists of stakeholders and key informants. The information gathered at this stage is used to facilitate the PMCA.
- PMCA, bringing together the specific actors in the chain (see below).

In Kenya a new project in the herbal products sector is using the framework to explore alternative livelihood options for marginalised pastoralists (see Box 5). It is a learning project researching approaches that enable producers and other market-chain actors to identify solutions to market-chain issues, regulatory constraints and service needs. The project team have produced the initial analysis, created a Market Map (Figure 6), and are now proceeding to PMCA, where the mapping exercise will be completed with market-chain actors who will develop solutions and innovations.

The initial analysis produced a Market Map (see Figure 6) that will be further developed by the market-chain actors during PMCA. By beginning to identify costs and added value at each stage of the chain the facilitators can challenge commonly

---

[4] Balkans Herbal Development Initiative – Phase 1 Final Summary Report
[5] Robert Donnelly, Traidcraft, UK; Ulrich Helberg, Helberg Consult, Germany; Flora and Fauna International, UK; Dragana Pecanac, Bosnia and Herzegovina
[6] CIAT Rural Agro-enterprise Programme have explored using 'Interest Groups' comprised of market actors; service providers and local decision makers.

Box 5.   Market Mapping in the herbal products sector, Kenya

Context – improving livelihoods of marginalised pastoralists
Pastoralists in northern Kenya have been facing the long-term erosion of their traditional livelihoods as a result of declining livestock prices, environmental degradation and conflict. Technology-led solutions were failing to improve livelihoods in the experience of Practical Action who have been working with pastoralist communities in Kenya for over 10 years. The areas they inhabit contain potentially valuable natural resources, including herbal products that were showing increasing demand in export markets. In 2004 a project[7] was initiated to learn about approaches to successfully integrating marginalised producers into viable market chains. For the first phase the project selected an area, West Pokot, which characterises the typical aspects of the product sector. The initial mapping exercise by the project team has highlighted a number of challenges and issues at each of the three levels of the Market Map.

Improving linkages in the market chain
The project team carried out preliminary research that identified herbal products as a viable and growing sub-sector. Further research identified a product group – aloe – as important to the livelihoods of communities, and that there is growing demand on world markets. The project approach is to:
- Enable producers (harvesters and boilers) in West Pokot to establish a 'Market opportunity group'
- Facilitate further market exploration to select the most promising market channels
- Conduct a PMCA (with market actors in the selected channels) to identify and tackle bottlenecks and opportunities.

Challenges include:
- Harvesters of aloe are disparate and disorganised
- Harvesters have misconceptions about what happens to their product; its value and destination
- Market-chain actors are very secretive about the trade because of the unresolved regulatory issues.

Creating an enabling environment
Key issues have been identified by interviewing key informants (including market-chain actors), producing a preliminary analysis of the local policy and regulating issues preventing effective participation by the communities in trade in aloe. Research into international trade issues (regulations, barriers) has been initiated. Examples of issues emerging from the analysis so far include:

---

[7] The project partners are Practical Action, Traidcraft and Kenya Gatsby Trust, funded by Ford Foundation and Comic Relief. The project includes coastal communities producing neem for export and learning about the approaches in different contexts.

Trade restrictions – The Convention on International Trade in Endangered Species of Wild Flora and Fauna (CITES) requirement on aloe export since 1999 has pushed the trade 'underground' and considerably reduced the earning potential. All exports now illegally go via South Africa 'hidden' with other products. The so-called 'Presidential Ban', which never actually became law, has created further confusion making market-chain actors even more secretive.

Corruption is endemic throughout the chain, adding costs and creating distortions of power and interests, e.g., boilers pay bribes to local chiefs to enable them to negotiate lower prices (chiefs negotiate prices on behalf of harvesters).

Prejudice against Somali traders causes a high degree of mistrust and a lack of co-operation.

Access to better business services

Initial analysis has indicated that some embedded services exist in the chain, for example:

- **Quality checking** – boilers have devised a system to test the sap before purchase (based on it's absorption); they also advise on best harvesting methods
- **Storage and bulking** – urban traders buy regularly from many boilers, taking higher quantities in the rainy season
- **Market information** – an order from the exporter triggers action in the chain and information is passed down
- **Transport** – market-chain actors absorb the cost of transport.

Additional services which actors could require:

- **Harvester co-ordination** – the current arrangement of relying on the local chief leaves harvesters vulnerable to exploitation
- **Technical extension services** to harvesters, e.g., sustainable harvesting techniques (to protect supply since the source is getting depleted in many areas); advice on harvesting methods to improve quality, e.g., technology which extracts sap through gravity
- **Energy efficient technology** for boiling, to reduce fuel costs
- **Other stakeholders (such as the National Environment Management Agency (NEMA) require environmental impact assessment**
- **Certification** by Kenya Wildlife Service (KWS) to get CITES Appendix II.

Potential for services (assessing potential demand and supply) will be explored during the PMCA.

held misconceptions around disproportionate shares of revenue in the chain, as highlighted by the example in Box 6.

The challenges encountered during the mapping phase have included:

- Developing the capacity of the project team to do the analysis (see below) – the approach was 'learning by doing'
- Time and resources required to collate information about a market chain that stretches from remote northern Kenya to Mombasa and onwards to South Africa

Figure 6.   Aloe market chain into West Pokot, Kenya

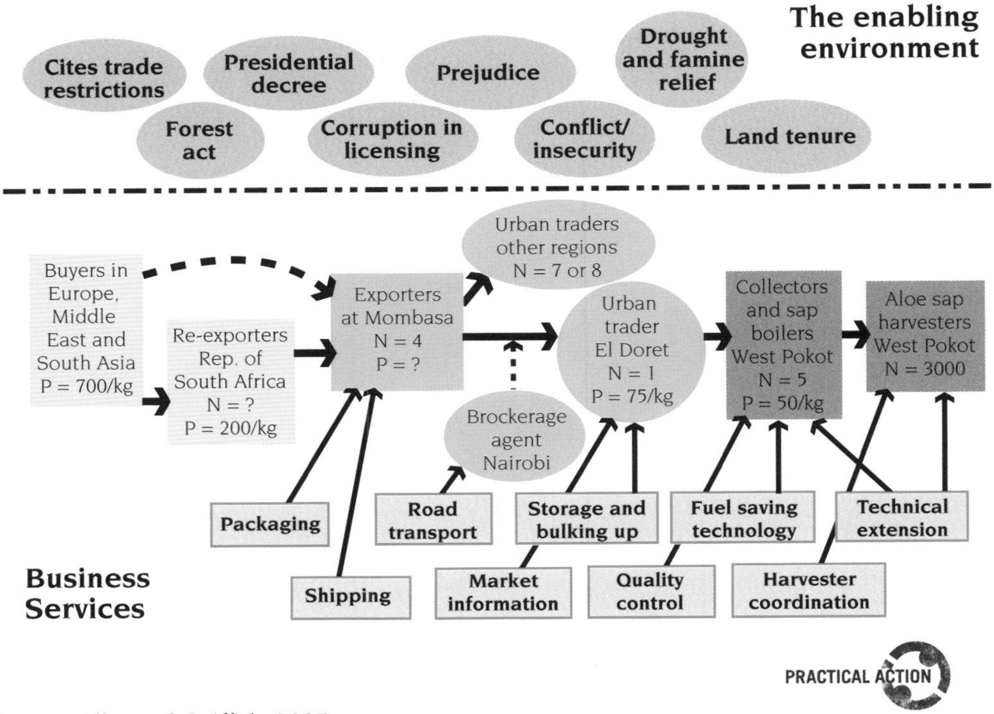

The enabling environment

Cites trade restrictions · Presidential decree · Prejudice · Drought and famine relief · Forest act · Corruption in licensing · Conflict/insecurity · Land tenure

Buyers in Europe, Middle East and South Asia P = 700/kg → Re-exporters Rep. of South Africa N = ? P = 200/kg → Exporters at Mombasa N = 4 P = ? → Urban traders other regions N = 7 or 8 · Urban trader El Doret N = 1 P = 75/kg · Brockerage agent Nairobi → Collectors and sap boilers West Pokot N = 5 P = 50/kg → Aloe sap harvesters West Pokot N = 3000

Business Services

Packaging · Shipping · Road transport · Market information · Storage and bulking up · Quality control · Fuel saving technology · Harvester coordination · Technical extension

PRACTICAL ACTION

Source: Albu and Griffith, 2005

Box 6.   Developing trust in the aloe market chain

Harvesters generally believe that boilers take an unreasonably high margin, whereas the reality is apparently quite different. The main issue affecting revenue and margins for actors in the chain is trade regulation (linked to 'unsustainable' supply issues). A strategy to tackle this problem is to apply for CITES certification, which requires a high degree of co-operation and co-ordination. In this case it would be in the interests of exporters and central agents to work with actors to address issues of sustainable harvesting at the other end of the chain, by for example, ensuring that harvesters and processors have access to the services they need to produce certified high-quality aloe.

- Building the trust of local stakeholders (particularly important because of the on-going conflict in the area)
- Managing expectations of not only the market-chain actors but also other stakeholders (e.g., those in the Interest Group). Producers often have an expectation of immediate benefits, such as higher prices. This can be partly mitigated by moving swiftly to the PMCA stage, taking account of the suggestions in Box 7.

The initial mapping of the aloe market chain enabled the project team to develop a systemic orientation and, more practically, prepare for the PMCA exercise. A key learning point to emerge is investment in this stage is important, since subsequent interventions will be more targeted and strategic.

Challenges and innovative approaches in PMCA

PMCA is at the heart of operationalising the market. It shifts from being an abstract framework and becomes a practical tool, which can facilitate improved efficiency (such as better co-ordination), innovation and improved trust within the market chain. However many practitioners are hesitant to try a PMCA approach because they believe that it will be difficult, if not impossible, to get market-chain actors together to achieve mutual objectives. Their reticence is not unfounded. Bringing together disparate, competing, demanding business people is undoubtedly challenging. This section shares some ideas on what the challenges are likely to be[8] and offers suggestions on how to address those challenges. The boxed examples relate to the herbal products project in Kenya.

Attracting market chain actors – find a 'Hook'. Very few market-chain actors (particularly those at the market end of the chain) are likely to attend a 'development project' meeting (even if they are being offered a free lunch). They are likely to be suspicious of the motives, e.g., they might suspect pressure to give their

---

Box 7.   Finding a 'hook' in the aloe market chain

The aloe Market Mapping exercise identified two issues that the project team are now testing with market-chain actors:

- Exploring the potential for a specific market chain to acquire certification from sustainable harvesting to accredited exports. This involves all actors from harvesters in West Pokot to the exporter in Mombasa and a number of key stakeholders, such as the Kenya Wildlife Service (KWS) who manage CITES certification. The 'hook' in this case is that certified exports would enable direct sales to final buyers and therefore considerably more value will flow into the chain (US$10/kg instead of US$2/kg paid by the South African buyers). Exporters and agents cannot achieve this without harvesters and boilers following sustainable harvesting techniques

- Quality improvements: quality issues affect all market-chain actors, though there are certain stages in the chain where they may be critical. The processing stage (boiling) converts sap to bitters, which is the stable form of the product for export. Improvements in efficiency and subsequent increased revenue in the chain depends on this vital stage.

---

[8] This section is based on a brainstorming exercise by the Practical Action International Markets and Livelihoods team in September 2004, using experience from Bangladesh, Kenya, Peru, Sri Lanka, Sudan and Zimbabwe.

suppliers a higher price. By identifying very specific common issues that concern all market actors, facilitators can turn these into an 'offer' that will 'hook' actors into the process (Box 7). Even if they are initially wary they will be more likely to attend if they can see a commercial benefit. Ideally the 'offer' should be achievable and directly relate to specific market-chain issues. Vague and overly ambitious offers such as 'finding new markets' may be less likely to keep actors engaged.

Balance of power in the chain. The actual and perceived imbalance of power within the value chain can be an impediment to PMCA. The perception that actors at the market end of the chain hold all the power is commonly held by facilitators, and very often by producers and small traders as well. They tend to believe that such an exercise would be a 'waste of time' because either the 'big players' would not be persuaded to come, or if they did, they would dominate the process.

This perception is not unfounded, but there are lessons emerging on how to create meaningful engagement that leads to positive changes. The more powerful actors in the chain often rely on the others further down the chain to provide a high-quality product, on time and to order, and they may need to invest to make this happen efficiently. Research in Kenya on smallholder co-operation and contract farming in the horticultural sector indicates that even the powerful actors (the contractors) needed to address issues of trust and collaboration, or else they could expect a high rate of default, which increases costs and reduces profit margins (Coulter et al., 1999). For a PMCA exercise facilitators can prepare producers in advance to understand their role in these events, and understand expectations of event results (Box 8).

Box 8. Preparing producers for a PMCA

Aloe harvesters are part of pastoralist communities (often the women and youth) who are living in relative isolation, with little exposure to commercial environments. The facilitator is working with them to create 'Market Opportunity Groups' which prepare the harvesters to engage with other market players in a constructive and informed way, and in time, to be proactive so they can explore new market links and respond to a dynamic market environment.

Mistrust between actors. Building up trust between market actors is important to facilitate open sharing of information. This is likely to take time and there may be a challenge to overcome hostility between different groups of actors. Possible strategies include:
- Facilitators visit and interview individual market actors as preparation for bringing the different groups together
- Facilitators adopt an incremental, iterative approach – engaging on one issue helps to build trust, information exchange and therefore further analysis of more complex or contentious issues.

Physical limitations to effective PMCA. When market chains stretch over long distances facilitators should consider several exercises in different places (Box 9).

Box 9. Challenge of a long-distance market chain

The aloe market chain is dislocated with actors spread over 1200 km, from remote northern Kenya to the coast, so the project is addressing this problem by holding initial partial market chain participatory meetings between such interacting actors as:

- Harvesters and boilers
- Boilers and traders/central agents
- Central agents and exporters.

These segments of the market chain overlap, so boilers, for example, will interact with both harvest and urban traders. The next step is to bring together as many representatives as possible from all groups in a central location to explore solutions and innovations to the issues they have identified in their market chain sub-section. This incremental approach also builds up trust (see above).

Minimising the impact of external influence, i.e., those not in the chain. To the extent possible it is important to try to minimise the 'visibility' of an NGO's role as facilitator. Possible strategies could be to get key actors with power and influence that are well organised themselves (e.g., exporters' federation) to organise discussions; however it would be important to mitigate for the dangers of introducing bias. Similarly it may be possible to exploit government agencies that have a mandate to promote particular sub-sectors, although the facilitator would need to be aware of perceptions of 'political' biases.

Establishing a local 'Interest Group' not only gives facilitators vital information for the initial mapping phase but also makes a clear and useful distinction between those actors involved in the PMCA, i.e., only those who are part of the chain, and the other key stakeholders who are vital players in that they create the enabling environment and provide services (Box 10).

Box 10. Aloe interest groups

The Aloe Interest Group is very focused but includes a wide range of local decision makers, service providers, research institutes, regulatory bodies, e.g., local chiefs, KWS, KEFRI, the Forestry Department, as well as selected market-chain actors (boilers and representatives from women's groups involved in harvesting). The West Pokot Aloe Interest Group links with a national stakeholder group the Kenya Working Group on Medicinal and Aromatic Plant Species, which has a specific working group on aloe. These groups are distinct from, but will be vital to, the successful aloe PMCA.

Advice for facilitators of PMCA workshops. Facilitators should:
- Have a good overview/information about the sub-sector in order to anticipate conflicts and grievances but........
  ....beware of pre-empting what the map will look like
- Work ahead to 'sell' the advantages of participatory analysis to different market actors
- Anticipate complaints and grievances of particular groups that may dominate the interactions, so.......
  ....negotiate 'norms' for running workshops through individual mediation, e.g., establishing clear agenda's in advance
- Understand that market actors may expect rapid results or changes as a result of the analysis process so........
  ....try to ensure interactions lead to rapid activities – gaining credibility for process
- Avoid being seen as 'extractive' process – drawing out knowledge from market actors, without giving much back

Developing 'in house' capacity for Market Mapping and PMCA

Market Mapping and the associated PMCA approach is likely to require investment in developing the necessary skills and experience within an organisation, particularly one that is focused on poverty alleviation and is used to directing it's focus towards the needs poor communities. In the first instance there may be a need to explore misconceptions and/or a lack of understanding about how market chains work. To address this an interactive training tool for programme and field staff called the *Value Chain Game* has been developed by Traidcraft and Oxfam, using the framework of the Market Map (Box 11). The purpose of the training tool is to 'unpack' the framework for project managers and show how a holistic approach to market development involves a full understanding of all the actors in a value chain, and the issues that affect them, in terms of services and the environment in which they operate.

In some agencies there has been a tendency to promote alternative value chains, often on the premise that 'exploitative' middlemen are the primary reason for inadequate incomes at producer level. The training tool can be an important part in challenging that perception. It may also be necessary to challenge the inclination some agencies have to conduct the full analysis (often employing consultants for the task) so that they can decide what the interventions should be. To determine specific interventions a participatory approach has significant advantages (as discussed earlier), and it should be expected that the extra resources required would be justified by the quality of information and interventions that the process yields.

PMCA builds on the participation and facilitation skills that most development staff will already have acquired in other work, but with different actors. Beginning with the premise that it is the participants themselves who can most appropriately develop solutions and innovations, will be a familiar and comfortable approach (possibly unlike business consultants who are more likely to problem-solve on

Box 11.   Value Chain Game

The Value Chain Game involves participants (development workers) mapping out a rice value chain and identifying the value added by each member of the chain. For example, a trader adds value to both the farmer, from whom s/he buys and the rice miller to whom s/he sells, for example:

Value added by a trader to a rice farmer:

- May often provide general market information, e.g., contacts, developments
- Will provide specific market information for the product s/he wants to buy
- Provides market for the product
- Often provides transport
- Will feedback on satisfaction with product and service.

Value added by a trader to a rice miller:

- Amalgamates small quantities into larger ones that make economic sense for the next buyer
- Often transports it to mill
- Carries out quality control
- Differentiates between different classes of product
- Presents product in form and at price specified by mill.

Some participants take the role of market-chain actors; others become service providers or actors in the operating environment (e.g., tax regulator). The service providers and regulators then approach actors in the chain to try and sell services or impact on their business with a 'requirement'.

The main messages participants receive from the training include:

- 'Middlemen' add value to the product and often have an important role in the chain
- Service provision is important at various points in the chain if it is to work efficiently and effectively, so when considering interventions don't focus just on the service needs of producers
- The enabling environment can seriously impede the chain and market-chain actors all have a strong interest to address this (leading to more effective PMCA).

behalf of the market-chain actors). Project staff may lack confidence with the bigger, more commercial actors in the chain but by employing the strategies described above they can develop confidence that they have positive reasons for engagement, taking an incremental approach to build up relationships.

The tendency to 'out- source' analysis and more commercial aspects of a project should also be challenged. Lessons from the BDS field indicate that there are considerable benefits to staying involved in market assessment of, for example, services. In the process of gathering information about markets, practitioners build their understanding of how the market works and start to develop relationships with market players. There is increasing recognition amongst agencies that formal surveys conducted by research firms are less effective than positive engagement at a local level[9]. The learning for donors and practitioners then is to ensure that sufficient time is given to developing capacity for the processes involved in the analysis of and engagement with market chains.

Beyond analysis: challenges for developing interventions

The purpose of PMCA is to facilitate positive changes at the three levels of the market. The previous section described how the process of developing a Market Map through PMCA could result in changes to the functioning of the market chain, e.g., better co-ordination and improved linkages etc. Changes and improvements to the other two sections of the map, access to services and a better enabling environment, are more likely to require additional interventions over a period of time, involving facilitation of market-chain actors, service providers and decision makers. The PMCA process will be the first step in identifying what those interventions should be, and engaging actors in the potential solutions. The involvement of the market-chain actors is key since they will be the customers of services and the 'voice' of the affected. The final part of this section considers some of the practical issues and challenges associated with this.

Developing sustainable service markets. A challenge for practitioners is how to gather accurate information about weak service markets to make assessments that will stimulate the supply of services that are in demand. The PMCA is potentially a valuable way to conduct market assessment, particularly in market chains where there is usually a high incidence of embedded service provision. Practitioners are using different strategies to gather information in weak markets including focused interviews with market actors on problems, potential solutions, and business benefits that services can provide, rather than on actual services. This can then lead to product concept tests for new services in a group discussion setting[10]. The example given in Box 12 shows that the Market Map framework and subsequent PMCA process could be a way to achieve this engagement that leads to new services or service packaging.

Enabling environment analysis: developing a practical plan. Market Mapping and PMCA provide information about what is constraining the development of a particular market chain. To tackle those constraints and bring about systemic change

---

[9] For example, Practical Action's learning from Enterprise Development Innovation Fund (EDIF) funded Network Brokers project 2002–2004

[10] Developing Commercial Markets for Business Development Service – Pioneering Systemic Approaches (Miehlbradt and McVay, 2004)

Box 12.   PMCA and assessing service needs

Market information services in the aloe market chain are currently embedded; each market-chain actor passes down information to the next. The whole chain responds to orders from the exporter, although this becomes more dislocated further down the chain and is smoothed out by the actors who bulk and store. The initial analysis indicates that there is a need to improve market information services, highlighted by the example of a group of harvesters who, discovering the world market price of aloe bitters, refused to sell to the boilers at their offer price, even though in reality the boilers find it hard to make a profit.

The PMCA process will facilitate the discovery of new solutions as the market-chain actors consider how information can be passed down the chain more accurately. It will be important to assess demand for 'stand alone' services to strengthen or complement the embedded ones, and explore how these might be developed as a commercially viable service. Members of the wider 'Interest Group' are key stakeholders in assessing the potential for developing market information services.

agencies need to develop strategies that target decision makers (local, national, and in some cases, international). In the natural resource and enterprise development fields learning is emerging about the potential effectiveness of advocacy activities that mobilise the voices of the poor and marginalised to bring about change. Examples include the donor community's growing interest in issues of governance as well as the increasing importance of farmers' juries as a means of rural producers to articulate their concerns, needs and frustrations (Coupe et al., 2005).

Policy implications

Market literacy at the micro, meso and macro levels

In the first section of this paper, it was argued that technological change and trade reform are not sufficient to generate poverty-reducing growth in agriculture. It was suggested that an injection of 'market literacy,' i.e., awareness, understanding of, and capacity to develop the processes, institutions, competencies and relationships that enable markets to work for poor producers – is necessary to realise pro-poor benefits.

In the next section a simple three-tiered framework called the Market Map that can be used for representing, analysing and planning interventions in markets that embodies this market-literate approach was explained. And in the third section three some examples of the application of market-literacy and the Market Map framework in the real world were described. These examples illustrate the benefits in terms of communicating knowledge and building linkages and coordination among diverse participants along actual market chains.

In this final section, the implications and challenges of adopting the market-literacy concept for policy-makers, organisations and programme managers concerned with pro-poor agricultural development are considered on three levels:

- **Micro** – strategies, alliances and practices of smallholder farmers, other producers and intermediaries, economic actors in the market chain
- **Meso** – strategies and operational structures of agricultural research institutions, government rural development agencies and NGOs
- **Macro** – broad agricultural and rural development policy, the operational approaches of multi-national agencies and national ministries.

Challenges for resource-poor producers and their economic partners (micro level)

The concept of market literacy as a key factor in development outcomes. It poses some major challenges for poor producers (smallholder farmers), other economic actors in market chains, service providers and other agencies working to encourage pro-poor growth. It emphasises that their fortunes are bound up with the capability of the whole market chain to respond (systemically) in a pro-active and agile manner to changes in the competitive environment and to emerging market signals (Best et al., this volume). Successful market chains that sustain, grow and generate income for producers will be ones that can find effective mechanisms for:

- Collaborating in production, procurement of inputs and services, and marketing activities, etc.
- Investing in market intelligence capabilities and market-information systems
- Communicating with and influencing the meso-level institutions that provide support services and infrastructure, or that can influence the business environment.

Market Mapping and PMCA provide information about what is constraining the development of a particular market chain. To tackle those constraints and bring about systemic change, agencies need to develop communication strategies that target decision makers. The preceding thematic papers outline many of the issues, challenges and ways forward with respect to each of the above points. Biénabe and Sautier (this volume) discuss the role of producer organisations. They emphasise the need to build organisational and negotiating capabilities over the long term. However, group formation is not a particularly useful strategy where this is independent of market-chain linkages. The most successful collaborative groups are formed around direct market linkages, for example, contract farming relationships. This gives producer groups a focus, reduces the demands of collective decision-making and makes it easier to define and absorb external assistance, e.g., help to achieve technical compliance with a buyer's contract.

In his discussion of market intelligence and market information systems, Marter (this volume) emphasises the value of involving producers in the design of systems, especially if they are to raise the confidence and negotiating skills of women. He notes the importance and difficulty from a sustainability perspective of establishing market mechanisms to pay for such semi-public goods. This raises the question of how fundamental producer groups are in enabling smallholders not only to afford market information access, but also to have the skills to interpret and use information.

Best et al. (this volume) also recognise the value of market intelligence capabilities (as opposed to simply market information systems) at the micro-level. CIAT's agro-enterprise development approach employs a multi-stakeholder interest group to develop at a common vision and plan of action based on analysis of market opportunities. This paper compares various tools for achieving participation in market chain analysis – all of which implicitly value participation not only as a way to achieve better-informed analyses, but also as a means to build a form of indigenous market literacy. Box 13 outlines other approaches to empowering farmers to take advantage of market opportunities.

It is important to acknowledge that all these approaches take time and resources. Cost has been a major argument against wider promotion of FFS and CIAL approaches (see Box 13). CIAT's agro-enterprise development approach also requires methods that are intensive in the use of time and recognises the need for facilitation by persons with an appropriate level of technical knowledge and social skills. On a positive note, these costs can be seen as genuine investments in market development, with inherently more potential for reducing dependence and creating sustainable impacts than past strategies that created dependency on subsidised extension services. However, adopting market-literacy goals will clearly

Box 13.   Empowering farmers

Experience in Latin America, with a range of participatory extension and research models such as farmer field schools (FFS) and local agricultural research committees Comité de Investigación Agrícola Local (CIALs) demonstrate that these may be effective in empowering farmers and providing them with some of the skills needed to take advantage of market opportunities. FFS is a training approach that was developed to help farmers understand integrated pest management as an alternative to chemical control. The format is now being extended to help farmers learn about market demand and product requirements as well as how to negotiate in new markets. CIALS develop farmers' research and learning capacities; they aim to encourage farmers to learn by doing, to criticise their own and others' work, and to adapt their processes to changing conditions.

These participatory methods can stimulate local innovation, because the emphasis is on principles and processes rather than recipes or technology packages. In some cases, farmers who participate in CIALS are learning how to manage funds, plan time, launch microcredit schemes, prepare proposals to access external resources, and deal with outside agronomists and professionals on a more equal basis (Sherwood et al., 2000) A number of CIALS have launched small businesses involving the production and marketing of seed, and selling fresh or processed food products (Braun et al., 2000). Suitably empowered, farmers are better able to influence formal research and extension systems to their own benefit and to gain access to potentially useful skills, information and research products.

create major challenges for the people, skill-sets and structures of the meso-level organisations aiming to encourage pro-poor agricultural growth.

Challenges for agricultural research institutions and rural development agencies (meso level)

At the meso level a market-literate approach requires institutionalising a new way of thinking throughout organisations. Many meso-level organisations, such as NGOs, are shifting from a production focus to a market focus and this will require a new set of priorities (this also applies at the macro level – see Box 15 below). This commitment should lead to changes in allocation of resources. In the theme paper on linkages, Best et al. (this volume) suggest that meso-level organisations would find it useful to be clearer about their role as facilitators or providers , and in many cases where there is a change (usually from provision to facilitation) then there will be a need for support. Equipping staff to adapt to a market orientation is a process that will take time and needs commitment at all levels of an organisation. Priorities for organisations aiming to develop successful market chains that sustain, grow and generate income for producers include:

Using a systematic analysis of market needs and opportunities. A framework, such as the Market Map, used in different ways can assist organisations to design market literate programmes, projects and interventions.

Building capacity (people, skills and structures) for market-literate working practices. In the aloe example it was noted that a considerable challenge was building the capacity of the project team to conduct the analysis and facilitate the PMCA. Many organisations adopt a 'learning by doing' approach that has some drawbacks. It is important for practitioners to learn from others and also to invest in developing capacity to understand and apply a market-literate approach (including the use of appropriate analytical and participatory tools and methods).

Promote an inter-disciplinary ethos. New approaches in organisations can understandably be received with hesitance and scepticism. It is important to value and maintain the skills in, for example, natural resource management, but to complement them with stronger business and market skills.

Inform and influence at the macro-level. For example, in relation to identified enabling environment issues, in the second theme paper, Biénabe and Sautier (this volume) highlight the role of meso-level organisations acting as catalysts for producer representation on the specific issues affecting their product sectors and market chains.

Support and empower at the micro-level, e.g. participatory market-chain analysis. The third section discussed the challenges and innovation approaches to PMCA and ways to build the confidence and experience of facilitators so that the

Box 14. The market development approach to BDS

Donor and development programme strategies in the field of small enterprise development have radically altered since the mid-1990s – most dramatically in the realm of non-financial services (or BDS). Starting with a series of conferences sponsored by the Committee of Donor Agencies for Small Enterprise Development, the field coalesced around a set of core principles for BDS delivery, sometimes referred to as the market development paradigm. This reversed previous heavily subsidised strategies in which small enterprise support agencies typically tried to push free services out to their target clients. Instead, it rapidly came to be accepted that the role of donor-funded agencies should be to act as facilitators of the market for services – stimulating demand for a variety of services among customers and building the capacity of private service providers to fill that demand.

The widespread change in strategy among donors and practitioners, internationally, was achieved through a variety of ventures and activities that built momentum and enough consensuses to support a new set of principles. The support for innovating and learning in this field is considerable, indicated by the new BDS Knowledge website (http://bdsknowledge.org), which contains information from over 100 agencies working in 70 countries. The initial investment required to bring about such a significant change was considerable and involved significant, co-ordinated and sustained support from donors. Examples of this support include the International Labour Organization (ILO) BDS seminar, which is an important annual event for practitioners from over 90 countries; practitioner learning programmes such as the SEEP programme on BDS Market Assessment funded by USAID; and comprehensive training programmes for decision makers, managers and specialists such as the Springfield Centre's 3-week intensive course that has trained over 300 people from 30 countries.

To stimulate parallel processes in the agricultural development sector might involve some of the following activities:

- Establish a supporting framework from key donors [e.g., USAID, DFID, Swiss Development Co-operation (SDC)] with resources to influence the field
- Cultivate an identifiable community of practice among policy makers, donors, researchers and practitioners to network innovation and experience about market literacy in the agricultural sector
- Build this community around a high-profile recognised annual event (e.g., a seminar)
- Allocate donor funds for action research that consciously brings together researchers and practitioners from around the world to share practices and stimulate South – South learning
- Establish a dedicated website to collate knowledge, papers and articles describing market-literacy practices, project experiences and toolkits
- Create high-quality training course(s) to disseminate knowledge among field practitioners and project managers, and establish benchmarks for best practice.

exercise develops relationships in market chains and results in tangible positive outcomes for producers.

Co-ordinate and collaborate. It is important to have a shared vision and objectives, for example, for a territory or sub-sector (Best et al., this volume) to ensure that the approach to market development is consistent (so that interventions to build a market are not undermined) and to negate to the extent possible gaps in, for example, service provision. Collaboration also promotes learning that is vital in a relatively new area. This can be formalised, through learning alliances or project partnerships, or it can be less formal, creating networks of those developing expertise in the area. A good example of this is the BDS market development field that has a variety of fora for practitioners to share learning. The lessons from the BDS market development field show how many macro- and meso-level organisations can work together to bring about a radical and lasting change in development approaches (see Box 14).

Challenges for governments and donor policy (macro level)

At the macro level, recognition of the market-literacy concept involves an orientation and commitment similar to that described for meso-level organisations above. Gibson et al. (2004) set out four clear priorities for governments and donors that involve embedding a more market literate-approach (Box 15).

Box 15. Making Markets Work for the Poor (MMW4P): an objective and an approach for governments and development agencies

While there are no easy formulae, there are clear priorities for organisations seeking to make sense of MMW4P in their work:

- **Recognise MMW4P as a key objective:** put MMW4P explicitly at the heart of organisations' strategies and aims; this is the first step to operationalisation
- **Understand the key stages in MMW4P as an approach:** build a thorough understanding of markets; develop a transparent (and shared) picture of how markets could work in the future; and ground interventions in these analyses is the essence of the MMW4P approach – in doing so, take cognisance of emerging principles of good practice
- **Internalise MMW4P:** take the broad objective and approach into organisations' realities. Using different tools (some of which are listed at the end of this paper), begin the process of aligning organisations' work with a credible view of market development
- **Engage with other players on this basis:** MMW4P requires that different players in markets know their respective roles and commit themselves to undertaking these effectively. Markets cannot be built by one organisation alone.

Source: Gibson et al., 2004

Lessons for governments and donors include:

- By introducing and emphasising 'market-literacy' in rural poverty-reduction policy it is possible, necessary even to make market analysis a prerequisite in agricultural research initiatives and rural development programmes (so that the analysis becomes as common-place and well established as environmental and social impact assessments)
- Embedding a market-literate approach requires investment and allocation of resources to develop the necessary skills
- Donors must be willing to lose some control over project design i.e., determining the specific interventions – these will not be known at the start of the project if the market approach (or similar) is taken, with full participation
- Investment in the analytical stage and in PMCA is important since subsequent interventions will be more strategic and targeted. Donor should encourage, rather than discourage, programmes that plan for this type of analysis.
- Consistency of approach is important. As Best et al. (this volume) point out 'confidence is strained when conflicting approaches are espoused among and even within donor… agencies'
- Encourage joined-up government vis-à-vis enabling environment issues
- Developing-country governments need to be committed to confront inequality and find solutions (such as to corruption) – they need global institutions such as the World Bank, the United Nations, or the World Trade Organization (WTO) to tackle these issues – so that all move towards mutual understanding about the problems and how to address them (Best et al., this volume).

References

Albu, M. and Griffith, A. 2005. Mapping the Market: a framework for enterprise development practitioners. Guidelines from Practical Action (formerly ITDG). Available at http://www.bdsknowledge.org

Barghouti, S., Kane, S., Sorby, K. and Ali, M. 2004. Agricultural diversification for the poor: guidelines for practitioners. Agriculture and Rural Development Discussion Paper No. 1. World Bank, Washington DC, USA.

Berdegué, J., Reardon, T., Escobar, G. and Echeverría, R. 2000. Policies to promote non-farm rural employment in Latin America. Natural Resource Perspectives, No. 55. Overseas Development Institute (ODI) London, UK.

Bernet, T., Devaux, A., Ortiz, O. and Thiele, G. 2005. Participatory Market Chain Approach. BeraterInnen News 1/2005. Available through www.sfiar.ch

Braun, A.R., Thiele, G. and Fernández, M. 2000. Farmer field schools and local agricultural research committees: complementary platforms for integrated decision-making in sustainable agriculture. Agricultural Research and Extension Network (AgREN) Paper No. 105. Overseas Development Institute (ODI), London, UK.

CIAT (Centro Internacional de Agricultura Tropical). 2001. Integrated Agro-enterpises Project, CIAT Report 2001. Cali, Colombia.

Coulter, J., Goodland, A., Tallontire, A. and Stringfellow, R. 1999. Marrying farmer cooperation and contract farming for service provision in a liberalising Sub-Saharan Africa. Natural Resource Perspectives, No. 48. Overseas Development Institute (ODI), London, UK. 64pp.

Coupe, S., Hellin, J., Masendeke, A. and Rusike, E.A. 2005. Farmers' Jury: the Future of Smallholder Farming in Zimbabwe. ITDG Publishing, London, UK

DFID (Department for International Development). 2000. Eliminating World Poverty: Making Globalisation Work for the Poor. DFID, London, UK. 73pp.

DFID (Department for International Development). 2004. Pro-poor growth briefing note 1. DFID Policy Division, London, UK.

Diao, X. and Hazell, P. 2004. Exploring Market Opportunities for African Smallholders. 2020 Africa Conference Brief No.6. International Food Policy Research Institute (IFPRI), Washington DC, USA.

Donnelly, R. and Helberg, U. 2004. Balkans Herbal Development Initiative – Phase 1 Final Summary Report – Serbia and Montenegro, report for IFC SEED Project. TraidCraft, UK.

Dorward, A., Poole, N., Morrison, J., Kydd, J. and Urey, I. 2002. Critical linkages: livelihoods, markets and institutions'. Paper presented at the seminar on Supporting Institution, Evolving Livelihoods. Held at Bradford Centre for International Development, University of Bradford, Yorkshire, UK, 29–30 May, 2002.

Dorward, A., Fan, S., Kydd, J., Lofgren, H., Morrison, J., Poulton, C., Rao, N., Smith, L., Tchale, H., Thorat., S., Urey, I. and Wobst, P. 2004. Rethinking Agricultural Policies for Pro-poor Growth. Natural Resource Perspectives, No. 94. Overseas Development Institute (ODI), London, UK.

Ellis, F. 1999. Rural Livelihood Diversity in Developing Countries: Evidence and Policy Implications. Natural Resource Perspectives, No. 40. Overseas Development Institute (ODI) London, UK.

Ellis, F. and Harris, N. 2004. New thinking about urban and rural development. Keynote paper for DFID Sustainable Development Retreat, University of Surrey, UK.

Gibson, A., Scott, H. and Ferrand, D., 2004. Making Markets Work for the Poor an Objective and an Approach for Governments and Development Agencies. Report for ComMark Trust, Woodmead, South Africa. 36pp.

FAO (Food and Agriculture Organization of the United Nations). 2001. The impact of HIV/AIDS on food security. Twenty-seventh session of the Committee on Food Security, Rome 28 May–1 June 2001. Available at http://www.fao.org/docrep/meeting/003/Y0310E.htm. (accessed September 2004).

FAO (Food and Agriculture Organization of the United Nations). 2004. The State of Food Insecurity in the World 2004. Annual report by Economic and Social Department, FAO Rome, Italy

FAO (Food and Agriculture Organization of the United Nations). 2005. FAO News Release 05/18e. February 2005. FAO, Rome, Italy.

Haggblade and Gamser. 1991. A Field Manual for Subsector Practitioners, GEMINI, Washington DC, USA.

Hitchins, R., Elliot, D. and Gibson, A. 2004. Making business service markets work for the poor in rural areas: a review of experience, report for Department for International Development (DFID). Springfield Centre, Durham, UK. www.springfieldcentre.com.

InterAcademy Council. 2004. Realizing the Promise and Potential of African Agriculture. report for InterAcademy Council, Amsterdam, the Netherlands.

IFAD (International Fund for Agricultural Development). 2001.The challenge of ending rural poverty. Rural Poverty Report No. 2001. IFAD, Rome, Italy

Irz, X., Lin, L., Thirtle, C. and Wiggins, S. 2001. Agricultural productivity growth and poverty alleviation. Development Policy Review, 19(4): 449–466.

Kaplinsky, R. 2000. Spreading the gains from globalisation: what an be learned from value chain analysis? IDS Working Paper No.110, Insitute for Development Studies (IDS), University of Sussex, Brighton, UK.

Kaplinsky, R. and Morris, M. 2005. A Handbook for Value-chain Research. Insitiute of Development Studies, University of Sussex, Brighton, UK.

Kydd, J. 2002. Agriculture and rural livelihoods: is globalisation opening or blocking paths out of rural poverty?' Agricultural Research and Extension Network (AgREN) Paper No. 121. Overseas Development Institute (ODI), London, UK.

Kydd, J. and Dorward, A. 2001. The Washington Consensus on poor country agriculture: analysis, prescription and institutional gaps. Development Policy Review 19(4): 467–478.

Lundy , M., Gottret, M.V., Best, R. and Ferris, S. 2005. A guide to developing partnerships, territorial analysis and planning together. Territorial approach to rural agro-enterprise development, Manual 1. CIAT, Colombia. http://www.ciat.cgiar.org

Lusby, F. and Panlibuton H. 2004. Promotion of Commercially Viable Solutions to Subsector and Business Constraints, Action for Enterprise, USAID Office of Microenterprise Development. Available at http://www.bdsknowledge.org

Marlin, C. 2004. The bamboo product chain: creating opportunities for small producers in Ecuador. Capacity. org Newsletter 22, 9, July 2004. SNV, the Netherlands. Available at http://www.capacity.org

Maxwell, S., Urey, I. and Ashley, C. 2001. Emerging issues in rural development. Overseas Development Institute (ODI), London, UK. 10pp. (mimeo)

Mayoux, L. 2003. Trickle-down, Trickle-up or Puddle: Participatory Value Chain Analysis for Pro-Poor Enterprise Development, Women in Sustainable Enterprise (WISE). Available at http://www. enterprise-impact.org.uk

Miehlbradt, A. and McVay, M. 2003. Developing Commercial Markets for Business Development Services – a BDS Primer, International Labor Organization (ILO) Small Enterprise Development Program, Washington DC, USA.

Miehlbradt, A. and McVay, M. 2004. Developing Markets for BDS: Pioneering Systemic Approaches, International Labor Organization (ILO) Small Enterprise Development Program. Available at http://www.bdsknowledge.com

Miehlbradt, A. 2001. Guide to Market Assessment for BDS Program Design, FIT Manual, International Labor Organization (ILO), Washington DC, USA.

Narayanan, S. and Gulati, A. 2002. Globalization and the smallholders: a review of issues, approaches and implications. Markets and Structural Studies Division Discussion Paper No. 50. International Food Policy Research Institute (IFPRI) and World Bank, Washington DC, USA.

Oxfam. 2002. Rigged rules and double standards: trade, globalisation, and the fight against poverty. Report by Oxfam, Oxford. UK.

Peacock, C., Jowett, A., Dorward, A., Poulton, C. and Urey, I. 2004. Reaching the poor, a call to action. investment in smallholder agriculture in sub-Saharan Africa. FARM-Africa, London, UK.

Pimentel, D., Harvey, C., Resosudarmo, P., Sinclair, K., Kurz, D., McNair, M., Crist, S., Shpritz, L., Fitton, L., Saffouri, R. and Blair, R. 1995. Environmental and economic costs of soil erosion and conservation benefits. Science 267: 1117–1123.

Runge, C.F., Senauer, B., Pardey, P.G. and Rosengrant, M.W. 2003. Ending Hunger In Our Lifetime: Food security and globalization. International Food Policy Research Institute (IFPRI) and The Johns Hopkins University Press, Baltimore, USA.

Sherwood, S., Nelson, R., Thiele, G. and Ortiz, O. 2000. Farmer Field Schools in potato: A new platform for participatory training and research in the Andes. Newsletter of the Center for Research and Information on Low External Input and Sustainable Agriculture (ILEIA) 16 (4): 24–25.

The World Bank Group. 2004. 'Millenium Development Goals'. Available at http://www.development-goals.org/. (accessed December 2004).

Thirtle, M., Lin, L. and Piesse, J. 2001. The impact of research-led agricultural productivity growth on poverty in Africa, Asia and Latin America. Working paper, Department of Environmental Science and Technology, Imperial College of Science, Technology and Medicine, University of London, London, UK.

Traidcraft and Oxfam. 2003. How to Improve Oxfam Work in Market-Based Projects. Traidcraft, Gateshead and Oxfam, Oxford, UK.

Tripp, R. 2001. Seed Provision and Agricultural Development: the institutions of rural change. Overseas Development Institute (ODI), London, UK 182pp

Tripp, R. 2003. The enabling environment for agricultural technology in sub-Saharan Africa and the potential role of donors. Natural Resource Perspectives, No. 84. Overseas Development Institute (ODI), London, UK.

Vorley, B. 2003. Food, Inc.: corporate concentration from farm to consumer. UK Food Group. London, UK.

Weatherspoon, D.D. and Reardon, T. 2003. The rise of supermarkets in Africa: implications for agrifood systems and the rural poor. Development Policy Review 21(3): 333–355.

Wiggins, S., Keilbach, N., Preibisch, K., Proctor, S., Herrejón, G.R. and Muñoz, G.R. 2002. Agricultural policy reform and rural livelihoods in Central Mexico Journal of Development Studies 38(4): 179–202.

Winrock International. 2002. Agriculture: increasing farm productivity and incomes using market strategies. http://www.winrock.org/what/PDF/agriculture.pdf (accessed February, 2005).

World Bank. 2001. World Development Report 2000/2001: Attacking Poverty. The World Bank, Washington DC, USA.

Discussions

Discussions

The workshop that was held on 28 February and 1 March 2005 in Westminster, London was based on five key papers that were commissioned and prepared in advance, i.e., the four thematic issues papers and an overview. These, together with the keynote perspectives, formed the starting point for the discussions that followed. The aim was to present a broad summary of the state of research knowledge in the area of access to markets, but more importantly, to build upon it to gain some sense of the priorities that future researchers and policy makers should attach to the constraints that need to be addressed.

A series of discussions were held following the thematic presentations, and resulting from this, a series of 'leading questions' were formulated with the aim of defining these priorities. A further set of discussions examined the questions in order to define some guiding principles for further work in priority areas, in a form that could be taken up and acted upon by various parties: donors, the private-sector, governments, research agencies and other related organisations. The commentary that follows is therefore a synthesis based on the extensive contributions made, in plenary discussions and in separate working groups, followed by some bulleted points that make practical suggestions for policy makers and practitioners.

Q1 Focus of interventions. Where should resources be focussed? On supporting the most marginalised majority to take the first steps up from subsistence farming, or on graduating a select minority into mature, commercially viable agro-enterprises?

This question had two underlying components. The first was whether a reduction in rural poverty was indeed best approached by attempting to upgrade smallholder agriculture; and secondly, if a more active commercial agro-enterprise sector is desired, are smallholder farmers the best starting point? And at the heart of this lies the familiar dilemma of whether poverty-focussed approaches can be reconciled with commercial, private-sector methods; a debate that is led by donor beliefs and partners' values as much as by informed evidence. There was also a clear sense of urgency; that the steady rise in poverty indicators (in Africa) allows only a limited window of opportunity, felt to be of the order of a decade, to demonstrate whether large-scale access to markets is a realistic option for drawing smallholder farmers out of poverty.

An agreement on the strategic approach is necessary if the best use of resources is to be achieved, since the challenges of engaging smallholder farmers in market systems are many and varied, but the resources available to apply to them are limited, as is the capacity to absorb and apply donor investment. The theme papers, especially those on creating linkages and on the role of producer organisations drew comments on these points. There is relevant research in other disciplines to be taken into account (the work of Jonathan Riggs at the Durham University Geography Department was cited). Such research questions the intuitive assumption that since most of the poor are rural small-scale farmers, improved smallholder agriculture is the preferred route for addressing rural poverty reduction, as opposed to non-farm rural income generation. Smallholder farmers can gain some resilience when organised into producer groups, but even these groups can prove fragile when investments in their strengthening are attempted, and experience shows that donor-funded producer organisations find it hard to shift their focus from food security concerns to more commercial approaches. Or as many put it; "Can we turn smallholder farmers into small-scale business people?"

The main characteristic of the workshop's conclusions was to avoid hard prescriptions and unhelpful labels, but to recognise the varied and shifting nature of small farm enterprises, and to favour flexible and responsive solutions.

- Since the majority of smallholders are poor, it is important to work directly with them in order to reduce poverty. The poor are not a homogeneous group, however, people move in and out of poverty and innovations and enterprise development will catch on unevenly amongst those of the poor who are better equipped or better able to adopt them. Differentiating between 'winners' and 'losers' is unhelpful and can serve to perpetuate poverty. To some extent the dilemma can be tackled by using different organisations to work with different groups of producers.
- Conversely, not all of the rural poor are farmers, and strategies are needed to help non-farmers to become agro-entrepreneurs.
- Smallholders should be encouraged and assisted to expand their enterprises, not to stay small. Whilst the focus must remain on overall benefits to the poor, strategies will need to target – initially at least – those who show entrepreneurial potential. Successful local role-models are known to be a strong influence on others in their community.
- Similarly, an ability to innovate may only be found in a small minority of producers, and project interventions may need to work with this sub-set, but mixed approaches are probably of most benefit.
- Over the long term, some sections of the poor community may be more risk-averse than others. A process approach, including differentiated strategies that address risks to which the very poor are extremely averse, is most appropriate. Producer organisations also need ways of buffering risks, particularly financial risks, to assist the long-term sustainability of production.

Q2 Private sector involvement. How can the private sector be interested and engaged in working with small-scale producers; that is, how can 'champions' (as Best et al., describe them) be fostered, and business with smallholders be made attractive?

Given that markets are strongly populated by private-sector players, the discussions rapidly moved on to considerations of how the resources, knowledge and skills of the private sector could be harnessed in enabling smallholder farmers to connect with the market. Existing market chains and actors are already in place, and can prove to be more efficient than they seem, so one obvious strategy is to direct investment to them, rather than trying to establish new or parallel structures. In particular, much could be learned from the experience of the branded commodity sector, where strong links with buyers and commercial agents seem to be a success factor.

Evidence seems to indicate that increasing transparency between the actors in the market chain confers increased trust and strengthens the relationships in the chain. More consideration needs to be given to the challenge of creating that increased transparency; often not an easy concept for commercial partners, whilst maintaining a poverty-focussed approach. Again, a poverty-focussed approach requires giving attention to how the primary producers – small-scale farmers – can be given a voice in deciding how services are delivered, and the converse question of ensuring that information providers gain an accurate understanding of clients' needs, based on competent market analysis. These are all part of the particular issues of how to move to demand-led services in weak and remote markets.

- One set of precepts was cited from a recent DFID private-sector partner meeting:
  - Only work with partners who put something at risk
  - Don't get academics to do market surveys – get people who really know the business
  - Avoid workshops – real businesses can't afford the time to attend!
  - Incentivise business development service suppliers.
- Private enterprise will only act in concert with small-scale producers when there is a profit to be made, but engaging with a multiplicity of smallholders entails high transaction costs. To reduce this deterrent, growers need to be helped by development agencies and programmes to organise themselves. Farmers and small-scale producers who enter the market are of course private-sector workers, but need to be organised in a form that other members of the sector can deal with in terms that make sense.
- The possibilities of linking venture capital to smaller producers need exploring. Contract farming is one way to make the links, as is understanding consumers' needs as they develop.
- A change is needed in the general attitude of the public, NGOs and the public sector towards private traders and entrepreneurs. Similarly, the private sector needs to discard a prevailing negative view, and understand that the poor are also discerning consumers, and that with trust and a willingness to share risk, there is profitability in working with them.
- Governments need to address the importance of creating a positive enabling environment. This can lead to wider benefits of capital and business development in-country, retained added value, and possible political benefit.

- The private sector will need incentives to engage more strongly with the poor both as consumers and producers. Ethical trading attributes may provide this in export markets (for example the current interest in 'organics'), but in domestic markets consumers are seeking quality, low costs, reliability and assured supply. Informal markets need to be taken into consideration as a part of the market chain.
- The benefits of group organisation are many. They include the reduction of transaction costs, bulking, quality assurance, certainty of supply, access to guarantee funds, easier market entry, and support from government. While the main attraction is the opportunity for profit, there are also gains in social responsibility reflecting the mutual benefits of building trust and dependency, and ensuring contract performance within the commercial relationship.

Q3 Government. What legitimate role should governments realistically assume in supporting or delivering human and social capital development?

Various new skills, knowledge, capabilities and social institutions are needed for farmers and agro-entrepreneurs to participate and compete successfully in market systems. Much of this can be facilitated by governments providing the appropriate enabling and supporting environment. At many points, the discussions threw up examples of these opportunities: Removing the bureaucratic obstacles to supplying the minor ingredients, packaging and presentation materials that otherwise inhibit the development of food-processing businesses. Ensuring donor policy coherence that, for example, allows imported food aid to undermine local markets. Enabling special-interest groups to become effective commodity associations. The creation of more-appropriate information exchange mechanisms in market intelligence, beyond the traditional provision of written information. And generally, that governments should focus more on facilitating the development of human and social capacity rather than taking on the implementation role.

- Governments need to plan strategically, and be prepared to offer sustained and integrated support to market development initiatives. An example of the success of this approach was cited in the case of the 'Operation Flood' milk scheme of India's National Dairy Development Board in Gujarat, which integrated infrastructure development, market regulation, and the establishment of milk-collection centres.
- Governments should promote a bottom-up leadership approach that ensures that knowledge from the grass roots is integrated into policy development.
- More diagnostic work on systems and supply chains is required.
- Governments can play a key role in funding training and education programmes and in ensuring their delivery to those who need them the most. They must support access to local education and training programmes led both by themselves and by private-sector organisations. Such programmes should include vocational training.

- The Comprehensive Africa Agriculture Development Programme (CAADP) is production-oriented. A market- and demand-oriented element would enhance its plans and directly benefit all stakeholders.
- In order to aid the development and viability of small-scale businesses, and thus to reduce the tendency for small business people to shift in and out of poverty, governments need to reduce the excessive regulation and to provide stronger incentives for business start-up.
- Governments should ensure that they have the infrastructure in place to aid the delivery of social capital. This includes the infrastructures for information and communications technologies (ICT), mobile networks, regulation of chains, monopolies and financial services. The private sector should be seen as an essential investor in developing these infrastructures.
- In order to strengthen partnerships between the private sector and smallholder producers, governments should address ways in which contracts can be stronger and more robust in rural settings.
- Government can empower development in some of the poorest areas by providing economic support – for example by reducing local taxation and promoting rural infrastructure – and by fighting corruption.
- Whilst governments might be moving to a more facilitative role in private industry, smallholders still need extension support and financial service regulation. State agents are ill-informed about local markets and often cannot provide the level of service that well trained extension agents might. Governments should therefore invest in providing marketing training for field-based extension agents. Agricultural training curricula need revision to incorporate the new skills needed today.

Q4 Market literacy. How can agricultural research institutions and rural development programmes transform themselves to become market-literate?

A major contention from the discussions was the need for more understanding of the functioning of commercial market systems; and that this need for market literacy (a 'paradigm shift') was most acute among those actors and stakeholders who are traditionally out of contact with private-sector workings. Typically, this would be traditional research institutions, government agencies and many NGOs. Market literacy demands a new range of staff skills, capabilities and operational processes from all agencies that aim to facilitate rural development.

Not only research institutions, but agricultural extension services were also noted as needing to be re-oriented away from production concerns towards a greater focus on value-addition and marketing. The challenge is to identify for policy makers the directions and interventions that will lead to the right enhancements in the enabling policy environment. Useful tools do exist, and the Michigan State University experience in Mozambique was cited, where a typology of agro-enterprises (processors) capable of distinguishing those that had the right linkages and potential for enhancing poverty-focussed growth has been developed.

- Collaborative partnerships need to be formed between the private sector and research institutions to allow the private sector a role in leading the research agenda. This should include commercial representation on research boards at council, institutional and national levels. In many countries an agricultural research council determines the research agenda, but farmer/market concerns indicate there should be representation from private trade and not just government on the boards of such councils.
- Research institutions can often appear to be out of touch with the reality of the private sector. Marketing specialists should be contracted or added to research station staff to aid a research agenda that includes the concerns of key market players. Research bodies should undertake market intelligence and work in multi-disciplinary teams to give them a stronger understanding of their market place. That said, it is recognised that such surveys are not the distinctive competence of agricultural research centres. Concerns of market players should influence the agenda of research institutions and rural development organisations
- It is important to acknowledge that it is a very difficult process to go from being a facilitator to a provider in the market. Transformation happens when there is pressure and incentive to make changes. For example, setting commercial objectives and targets for researchers would directly link research to the private sector. And incentives should be designed to encourage problem solving.
- Whilst research should be of commercial use, care needs to be taken to ensure that producers influence but do not control research bodies and create conflicts of interest. One way to do this is to set the targets for researchers in terms that are related to commercial objectives. Another option is to give producers some control over research bodies (as in the case of the banana industry in Jamaica, where the research centre is funded by a producer group). But it is important to avoid distorting research outcomes through an unbalanced or inappropriate incentivising of agricultural research.
- A stronger emphasis on contract research and the role of applied research is needed to enable rural development programmes and research institutions to directly benefit from the private sector.

Q5 Future research priorities. What are priority researchable issues at national and international levels? How important is new research, compared to building on existing knowledge and capabilities?

There are clearly still gaps in current knowledge of the issues that matter most in making market systems work for smallholder agriculture. Future research providers will still be concerned with targeting research to ensure its greatest effectiveness.

One perpetual concern is the need to achieve a balance between strategic or 'blue sky' research that may generate knowledge capable of making profound differences in widespread application over the long term, and applied research aimed at mobilising knowledge closer to the market with more immediate benefits to poor communities.

Whatever the balance, two principles were apparent from the discussions: firstly, that all research (including strategic research) must ultimately be action-oriented, and must produce outputs whose relevance can be understood by farmers. Secondly, that research to date has created a large body of useful knowledge on post-harvest management, and there is considerable potential still unrealised for transforming that knowledge into more applicable forms, and setting up the tools, techniques and intermediaries by which it can be delivered to users.

- Research at national and regional levels and below is important in order to 'ground truth' existing knowledge, mobilise it, and generate lessons on how research outputs can be effectively delivered to poor users in the field. This needs to be complemented by research at an international level that can focus on longer-term strategies, and policy constraints that prevent agricultural and post-harvest knowledge being put to use in ways that reduce poverty. Long-term international trends (the example of the importance of the supermarkets' importance in the demand chain was cited) also require decision tools and methods to be researched and developed in order to improve small-scale farmers' integration into the market system.

- There is a need to understand how to add value at community level, how partnerships and supply chains work, and how NGOs are dealing with marketing issues.

- Research to gain an understanding of the future for smallholder agriculture is needed, and to determine the directions for development that are realistic in different contexts. Such research needs to be set in a livelihoods approach, in order to be informed by an understanding of the needs and priorities of beneficiary groups.

- Domestic mass markets for agricultural produce are large and growing and they are, moreover, more readily accessible to smallholders than export markets. More surveys of such markets are needed to determine their requirements, and to understand the behaviour of such key players as commission agents.

- Work needs to be done on standards appropriate to poor consumers, and consumers need to understand the impact of standards they set on producers. With the focus on consumers should come an understanding of how partnerships of various types work and can be replicated.

- There is need to understand what are the blockages that prevent better use of existing knowledge within the supply chain; transparency and accountability are vital components of this.

- What is already working should be identified and the knowledge shared, particularly on marketing and market access for low-value, high-volume crops. A practical step would be to resource the development of 'How To' guides, and to provide national repositories of information extracted from projects, government, private sector, etc.

- A methodology for involving local stakeholders in carrying out market research and market information surveys is needed, together with funding for process-oriented projects.
- The Market Map framework merits careful consideration.

Contributors and participants

Contributors

Mike Albu is an international project manager, policy researcher, trainer and strategic planner with 15 years' experience in international non-governmental organisations working to reduce poverty in African and South Asian countries. He trained as an engineer, and specialised at MSc-level in science and technology policy, focusing in particular on small enterprise development policy. In recent years, Mike has worked for the Intermediate Technology Development Group (ITDG) in East African countries and Bangladesh, testing market development strategies for improving the business and extension services needed to support sustainable livelihoods from micro-enterprise. His areas of expertise include training and application of sub-sector and value-chain analysis methodologies; monitoring and evaluation; strategic planning and project management.

International Projects Manager (Enterprise Development Advisor), Practical Action, The Schumacher Centre for Technology and Development, Bourton-on-Dunsmore, Rugby, Warwickshire, CV23 9QZ, UK
Tel: +44 (0)1926 634400, Fax: +44 (0)1926 634401, Email: mike.albu@practicalaction.org.uk

Frank Almond trained as a Chemical Engineer and practised initially in the steel, process and petrochemical industries, specialising in process modelling, combustion engineering and issues of toxic waste, pollution and emission control. In the late 1970s he joined Fritz Schumacher's Intermediate Technology Development Group (ITDG), the organisation set up to promote the development and introduction of smaller-scale technologies, and was their Chief Executive for 8 years up to 1995. Following that, he joined the World Wildlife Fund as a Director of WWF-UK, where traditional species and habitat conservation was linked to human development, education, and market-based interventions. He now operates as an independent consultant and Partnerships Adviser to DFID Crop Post-Harvest Programme (CPHP).

Independent Consultant, 6 Bowen Road, Rugby, Warwickshire, CV22 5LF, UK
Tel: +44 (0)1788 574528, Email: frank@almondconsult.com

Rupert Best holds a PhD in Chemical Engineering from the University of Birmingham, UK and initiated his professional career with the Tropical Products Institute in London in 1975. Currently he is a Senior Program Specialist with the GFAR Secretariat responsible for Research Partnership Programmes. His expertise is in the area of rural enterprise development, with special interest in research and capacity development on the post-production handling, processing and marketing of tropical crops. Previously he worked for the Centro Internacional de Agricultura Tropical (CIAT) in Colombia and Uganda. From 1996–2004, Rupert co-founded and managed CIAT's Rural Agroenterprise Development Project, which with national and local partners in Latin America, East and Southern Africa and South-East Asia, developed the territorial approach to rural business development. In the period 1982–96, he was Leader of CIAT's Cassava Program (1990–1996) and Head of the Cassava Utilisation Section (1984–1989). While working in Peru (1977–1981) he was responsible for formulating the Andean Pact's Technology Development Project for the Rural Sector.

Senior Program Specialist, Global Forum on Agricultural Research (GFAR) Secretariat, c/o FAO, SDR, Viale delle Terme di Caracalla, 00100 Rome, Italy
Tel: +39 06 57054475, Fax: +39 06 5705 3898, Email: rupert.best@fao.org

Estelle Biénabe is an economist involved in research at the French Centre de coopération internationale en recherche agronomique pour le développement (CIRAD), where she is working on organisational issues in local agriculture and food systems and on product-differentiation processes based on quality-oriented practices and territorial specifics. Estelle holds a PhD in Environmental Economics from the University of Montpellier, France. Estelle has experience in commodity chains, resource management and environmental policy analysis in the developing world, notably in Central America, with the Inter-American Institute for Cooperation on Agriculture (IICA) and Centro Agronomico Tropical de Investigacion y Ensenanza (CATIE), Costa Rica.

Research Economist, CIRAD-Tera, TA 60/15, 34398 Montpellier cedex 5, France
Tel: +33 4 67 61 59 09, Fax: +33 4 67 61 44 15, Email: estelle.bienabe@cirad.fr

Shaun Ferris is currently Manager of the International Centre for Tropical Agriculture (CIAT)'s Rural Agroenterprise Development Project, where he is responsible for project activities in Latin America, Asia and Africa. The project portfolio is based on the concept of empowering service providers from research and development and rural communities with skills in market analysis and developing new agro-enterprise projects and is currently working with partners in over 30 countries. Shaun has worked in the area of marketing and post-harvest innovation since 1989 on a combination of long- and short-term contracts for both research and development agencies, including the Consultative Group on Inernational Research (CGIAR), World Bank, European Union, United States Agency for International Development (USAID) and numerous partner agencies. He was the regional coordinator of FOODNET, a marketing and agro-enterprise project, providing support to 10 countries in Eastern Africa. As part of this work, he developed local, national and regional market information and market intelligence products.

Manager, Rural Agro-enterprise Development Project, Centro Internacional de Agricultura Tropical(CIAT), PO Box 6247, Kampala, Uganda
Tel: +256 77221163, Fax: +256 41 567670, E-mail: s.ferris@cgiar.org

Alison Griffith started her career in the UK agricultural sector (following a BSc in Agriculture and Food Marketing) and subsequently moved to East Africa where she was involved in developing services to livestock farmers. After a Masters by Research in fair trade in food (examining issues for small-scale farmers exporting to niche markets) Alison worked for Traidcraft, as a consultant and as East Africa Programme Manager. Having joined ITDG in 2001 as Market Access Specialist she created a Community of Practice to develop ITDG markets work and has provided support and inputs to programmes in Africa, Asia and Latin America Since 2003 she has been co-ordinating the Markets and Livelihoods team and has recently been appointed International Team Leader. Her particular areas of expertise and interest include participatory market chain analysis and business development services market assessment.

International Team Leader – Markets and Livelihoods, Practical Action, Schumacher Centre for Technology and Development, Bourton-on Dunsmore, Rugby, Warwick-shire, CV23 9QZ, UK
Tel:+44(0)1926634467,Fax:+44(0)1926634401,E-mail:alison.griffith@practicalaction.org.uk

Sue Hainsworth has spent over 35 years helping scientists to communicate their research results to potential users. An Agricultural Sciences graduate from Nottingham University, she worked in the Centre for Overseas Pest Research of the then Ministry of Overseas Development editing Tropical Pest Management and other publications. After a 2-year stint in Rome as a consultant editor to FAO and the International Plant Genetic Resources Institute (IPGRI, then IBPGR); in 1982 she joined the International Crops Research Institute for the Semi-Arid Tropics in Hyderabad, India as Research Editor; leaving 18 years later when Head of Publications. She has recently spent 5 years in Hyderabad running her own editorial and publishing services and coordinating the production of many Green Ink publications in India. In early 2005 she returned to the UK to become a full-time member of Green Ink Publishing Services Ltd.

Editor, Green Ink Publishing Services Ltd, Chaucer House, Mill Lane, Othery, Bridgwater, Somerset TA7 0QT, UK
Tel: + 44 (0)1823 698848, E-mail: s.hainsworth@greenink.co.uk

Jon Hellin has a PhD in Geography from Oxford Brookes University where he is also an Honorary Research Associate. He has an MSc in Forestry and its relation to land use and a BA in Modern History from Oxford University. He has worked in Latin America, the Caribbean, East Africa and South Asia. He is the author of *Feeding the Market: South American Farmers, Trade and Globalization* (ITDG Publishing, 2003) and from 2003 to 2005 he led ITDG's Markets and Livelihoods Programme. He now works as a Poverty Specialist with the Centro Internacional de Mejoramiento de Maiz y Trigo (CIMMYT) based in Mexico.

Poverty Specialist, Centro Internacional de Mejoramiento de Maiz y Trigo (CIMMYT) Apartado Postal 6-641, 06600 Mexico DF, Mexico
Tel: +52 55 5804 2004 ext 1153, Fax: +52 55 5804 7558, Email: j.hellin@cgiar.org

Alan Marter is a marketing and development economist with wide-ranging commodity and geographical expertise. He has over 30 years' working experience in developing countries, especially in Africa covering commodity and marketing analysis, small enterprise development, agricultural processing, institutional development, sector appraisals and policy analysis. He has skills in the development, monitoring and management of both research and development projects and has undertaken market studies, project and sector appraisals and evaluations both with institutions in developing countries and with international bodies including those concerned with marketing and trade issues.

Independent Marketing and Development Economist, 'Bankview' Albany Road, Rochester, Kent, ME1 3ET, UK
Tel: +44 (0)1634 846317, Email: alanmarter@aol.com

Richard Mkandawire is a socio-economist; a graduate of the University of Malawi, with MA and MSc degrees from the University of Missouri, USA and a PhD from the University of East Anglia, UK. He is currently Advisor on Agriculture to the New Partnership for Africa's Development (NEPAD) and member of the Technical Advisory Board of the Global Environmental Change and Food Systems (GECAFS). Having previously taught in the Universities of Malawi, Zambia, and Venda in South Africa, and served as an external examiner in a number of universities in Southern and East Africa, he worked with the Commonwealth Secretariat as the Commonwealth Youth Programme Regional Director for Africa. Richard has extensive experience in development initiatives having undertaken a wide range of research and consultancy in such varied areas as: food policy and agriculture, gender and development, irrigation development, youth policy analysis and development, artisan fisheries and development, land tenure systems and agrarian development, youth and reproductive health, youth livelihoods and employment etc. He has in written and published extensively in these and other areas.

Agriculture Adviser, New Partnership for Africa's Development (NEPAD), PO Box 1234, Halfway House, Midrand 1685, South Africa
Tel: +27 11 313 3338, Fax: +27 11 313 3450, Email: Mkandawirer@nepad.org

Mandivamba (Mandi) Rukuni is currently Program Director with the W. K. Kellogg Foundation's Africa Program and is based in Pretoria, South Africa, where his main focus is on promoting models of integrated rural community development. A graduate of the Universities of Zimbabwe (PhD) and Reading (MSc) his career has been largely as an academic associated with several universities including Zimbabwe, where he was Dean of Agriculture for 6 years, Michigan State, USA and Pretoria, South Africa. His work has spanned: food security issues in Africa; institutional development and transformation for agriculture and rural development; smallholder irrigation development in Africa and agricultural and R&D policy. More recently he has focused on business strategy models for Africa and on low-cost and effective educational and skills enhancement in Africa, and has published extensively across these fields. Some of his best-known work has been on land tenure, especially in enhancing tenure security in traditional systems and community-based natural resources management. Rather an un-conventional academic he has worked with a wide array of developmental organsations including centres of the Consultative Group on International Agricultural Research (CGIAR) where he currently sits on the Boards of the International Food Policy Research Institute (IFPRI) and Centro Internacional de Agricultura Tropical (CIAT). He has done considerable board work for the corporate sector in Zimbabwe, where he chaired the Commission of Inquiry into Land Tenure Systems.

Program Director, W K Kellogg Foundation, 3rd Floor, Sanlam Building, 353 Festival Street, Hatfield, Pretoria, 0028, South Africa
Tel: +27 12 342 3003, Email: mvr@wkkf.org

Denis Sautier is a research scientist at the French Centre de cooperation internationale en recherche agronomique pour le developpement (CIRAD), where he heads a research unit working on food qualification and territories. With an MD in Agriculture and a PhD from the University of Paris, he focuses his research on poor farmers' access to markets and on the relationships between markets and social development. Half of his career has been spent in Latin America working with national research systems, universities and non-governmental organisations involved with collaborative research and training with producer organisations. His current work and publications focus on the organisation of local food systems and the rise of values-based food labels in several developing countries.

Research Scientist, CIRAD-Tera, TA 60/15, 34398 Montpellier cedex 5, France
Tel: +33 4 67 61 71 18, Fax: +33 4 67 61 44 15, Email: denis.sautier@cirad.fr

Antonio Schiavone is working for the Global Forum on Agricultural Research (GFAR) as a Programme Officer. He is currently facilitating the development of a Global Post Harvest Initiative with a strong market entry point, in collaboration with the Food and Agricultural Organization of the United Nations (FAO). Prior to this position he was awarded a 2-year Research Scholarship by the Italian Ministry of Foreign Affairs and was seconded to GFAR to conduct studies on the development of small and medium-sized enterprises in poor rural areas. An Italian and British citizen he holds a degree in Economics from the University of Florence in Italy, where he specialised in Economics for the Developing Countries.

Programme Officer, Global Forum on Agricultural Research (GFAR) Secretariat, c/o FAO, SDR, Viale delle Terme di Caracalla, 00100 Rome, Italy
Tel: +39 06 5705 4475, Fax: +39 06 5705 3898, Email: antonio.schiavone@fao.org

David J Walker is Grain Management Adviser (Food Aid) at the University of Greenwich, Natural Resources Institute, UK. He has 33 years of international field experience with the harvesting, handling, storage, quality and marketing management systems for grains, seeds, and other agricultural food commodities in both small- and large-scale sectors. David has considerable expertise in management of food aid commodities with emphasis on quality assurance provision in drought and famine operations; design and development of commodity quality grading systems, and appraisal of damaged food commodities and ships' cargoes. Having undertaken long-term assignments in Ethiopia, India, Malawi and Swaziland, and shorter missions in many countries in Africa, Asia and South America he has wide experience in: expert reports and expert witness, training-needs assessment, development and delivery of training courses, project identification, management, implementation, administration, and monitoring and evaluation.

Grain Management Advisor (Food Aid), Food Management and Marketing Group, Natural Resources Institute, University of Greenwich Medway Campus, Central Avenue, Chatham Maritime, Kent, ME4 4TB, UK
Tel: +44 (0)1634 883760, Fax: +44 (0)1634 883386, Email: D.J.Walker@gre.ac.uk

Participants

Ambrose Agona
Head, National Post-Harvest Research Programme, National Agricultural Research Organisation (NARO), Uganda
aagona@hotmail.com

Farhad Ahmed
Associate Director, IT Transport Ltd., UK
farhad.ahmed@ittransport.co.uk

Kerry Albright
Social Development Advisor, DFID Crop Protection Programme (CPP), Natural Resources International Ltd., UK
k.albright@nrint.co.uk

Mike Albu
International Projects Manager, Practical Action, UK
mike.albu@practicalaction.org.uk

Frank R. Almond
Independent Consultant, UK
frank@almondconsult.com

Barrie Axtell
Director, Midway Technology Ltd., UK
AxtellE@aol.com

Andrew Barnett
Independent Consultant
The Policy Practice Unit Ltd., UK
Andrew@thepolicypractice.com

Greg Beeton
Managing Director, Intermediate Technology (IT) Consultants, UK
Greg.Beeton@itdg.org.uk

Thomas Bernet
Research Fellow, Centro Internacional de la Papa (CIP), Papa Andina Project, Peru
t.bernet@cgiar.org

Rupert Best
Senior Program Specialist, Global Forum on Agricultural Research (GFAR) Secretariat, c/o FAO, Italy
rupert.best@fao.org

Geoff Bockett
Director, International Business Development Services Traidcraft Exchange, UK
geoffb@traidcraft.co.uk

Mpoko Bokanga
Executive Director, African Agricultural Technology Foundation (AATF), Kenya
m.bokanga@cgiar.org

Adam Brett
Company Director, Tropical Wholefoods, UK
adam@fmfoods.co.uk

Markus Buerli
Junior Professional Officer – Agricultural Economist, International Center for Agricultural Research in the Dry Areas (ICARDA), Syria
m.buerli@cgiar.org

David Bright
Livelihoods-Markets Adviser, Oxfam GB, UK
dbright@oxfam.org.uk

Bob Carlisle
Research Manager, Department for International Development (DFID), UK
b-carlisle@dfid.gov.uk

Alfredo Chamusso
Project Manager, CARE International, Mozambique
alfredo@carevila.org.mz

Mark Clayton
Research Manager, Department for International Development (DFID), UK
m-clayton@dfid.gov.uk

Derek Cox
Director, Step Systems Ltd., UK
dcposthi@aol.com

Ben Dadzie
Regional Coordinator, West Africa, DFID
Crop Post-Harvest Programme (CPHP)
Natural Resources International Ltd., Ghana
nrintl@tnsgh.org

Alex Daniels
Programme Development Manager
APT Enterprise Development, UK
alex.aptuk@tiscali.co.uk

Peter de Groot
International Centre for Underutilised
Crops (ICUC), UK
peter@degroot.me.uk

Tim Donaldson
Manager, DFID Crop Post-Harvest
Programme (CPHP), Natural Resources
International Ltd., UK
t.donaldson@nrint.co.uk

Cynthia Donovan
Assistant Professor, International Development, Michigan State University, USA
donovanc@msu.edu

Andrew Dorward
Reader, Agricultural Development
Economics, Imperial College of Science,
Technology and Medicine, University of
London, UK a.dorward@ic.ac.uk

David Elliott
Consultant, The Springfield Centre, UK
delliott@springfieldcentre.com

Simon Ferrigno
'Moral Fibre' Cotton Project Coordinator
Pesticide Action Network–UK (PAN–UK), UK
simonferrigno@pan-uk.org

Stephanie Gallat
Post-Production Systems Officer, Food and
Agriculture Organization of the United
Nations (FAO), Italy
stephanie.gallat@fao.org

Alessandra Giuliani
Socio-Economist, International Plant Genetic
Resources Institute (IPGRI), Syria
a.giuliani@cgiar.org

Sarah Godfrey
Programme Coordinator, DFID Livestock
Production Programme (LPP), Natural
Resources International Ltd., UK
s.godfrey@nrint.co.uk

Ann Gordon
Rural Development Programme Officer
Aga Khan Foundation, Switzerland
ann.gordon@akdn.org

Andrew Graffham
Senior Scientist, Food Management
and Marketing, Natural Resources
Institute, UK
a.j.graffham@gre.ac.uk

Vino Graffham
Assistant Manager, DFID Crop Post-
Harvest Programme (CPHP), Natural
Resources International Ltd., UK
v.graffham@nrint.co.uk

Alison Griffith
International Team Leader – Markets and
Livelihoods, Intermediate Technology
Development Group (ITDG), UK
alison.griffith@practicalaction.org.uk

Jayantha Gunasekera
Team Leader – Markets and Livelihoods
Programme, Practical Action South Asia,
Sri Lanka
jayanthag@itdg.slt.lk

Nazmul Haq
Director, International Centre for
Underutilised Crops, UK
haq@soton.ac.uk

Sue Hainsworth
Editor, Green Ink Publishing Services Ltd,
UK
s.hainsworth@greenink.co.uk

Jim Harvey
Head, Livelihoods Advisers Group,
Department for International Development
(DFID), UK
jim-harvey@dfid.gov.uk

Jonathan Hellin
Poverty Specialist, Centro Internacional de
Mejoramiento de Maiz y Trigo (CIMMYT),
Mexico
j.hellin@cgiar.org

John Hollands
Editor, LEISA Magazine, global edition
Centre for Information on Low External
Input and Sustainable Agriculture (ILEIA),
the Netherlands
j.hollands@ileia.nl

Raul Hopkins
Regional Economist, International Fund for
Agricultural Development (IFAD), Italy
r.hopkins@ifad.org

Claire Ireland
Development Consultant and Environment
Portfolio Manager, The In Development
Group (IDL), UK
Claire.Ireland@theIDLgroup.com

Hannah Jaenicke
Deputy Manager, DFID Forestry Research
Programme (FRP), Natural Resources
International Ltd., UK
h.jaenicke@nrint.co.uk

Andrew Jowett
Director, Harvest Help, UK
andrew@harvesthelp.org

Richard Kachule
Research Fellow, Bunda College of
Agriculture, Malawi
richardkachule@yahoo.com

Patrick Kalunda
Research Officer (Agricultural Economics)
National Post Harvest Programme,
Kawanda Agricultural Research Institute
Uganda
karihave@starcom.co.ug

Joseph Karugia
Research Manager, African Economic
Research Consortium, Kenya
joseph.karugia@aercafrica

Pascal Kaumbutho
Executive Coordinator, Kenya Network for
Draught Animal Technology (KENDAT),
Kenya
Kaumbuthos@wananchi.com

Menno Keizer
Agricultural Economist/Marketing
Specialist, International Plant Genetic
Resources Institute (IPGRI), Malaysia
m.keizer@cgiar.org

Dan Kisauzi
Regional Coordinator, East Africa DFID
Crop Post-Harvest Programme (CPHP)
Natural Resoues International Ltd, Uganda
dfidnr@nida.or.ug

Ulrich Kleih
Marketing Economist, Natural Resources
Institute, UK
u.k.kleih@gre.ac.uk

Gopal Komandur
Director, Centre for Environment Concerns
India
hyd2cenvicon@sancharnet.in

Linda MacLeod
Chair, International Development
Enterprises (IDE), UK
Linda.1209@virgin.net

Tafadzwa Marange
Regional Coordinator, Southern Africa
DFID Crop Post-Harvest Programme
(CPHP) Natural Resoues International Ltd.,
Zimbabwe
tafadzwa@cphpsa.org.zw

Elaine Marshall
Senior Programme Officer, United Nations
Environment Programme (UNEP)
World Conservation Monitoring Centre, UK
Elaine.Marshall@unep-wcmc.org

Alan Marter
Independent Consultant – Marketing and
Development Economist, UK
alanmarter@aol.com

Edward Millard
Senior Advisor, Sustainable Landscapes
Conservation International, USA
e.millard@conservation.org

Richard Mkandawire
Agricultural Adviser, New Partnership
for Africa's Development (NEPAD), South
Africa
Mkandawirer@nepad.org

Mike Morris
Rural Livelihoods Specialist, Natural
Resources Institute, UK
M.J.Morris@gre.ac.uk

Alex Mugova
Programme Team Leader, Practical Action
Southern Africa, Zimbabwe
alexm@itdg.org.zw

Mutizwa Mukute
Secretary General, Participatory Ecological
Land Use Management (PELUM), Zambia
mutizwa@pelum.org.zm

Michael Muleba
Executive Director, Farmer Organisation
Support Programme (FOSUP), Zambia
fosup@zamnet.zm

Patrick Mulvany
Senior Policy Adviser, Practical Action, UK
patrick.mulvany@practicalaction.org.uk

Miles Murray
Emergency Programme Officer, CARE
International UK, UK
milesmurray620@yahoo.co.uk

Henry Musoke
Executive Director
Volunteer Efforts for Development Concerns
(VEDCO), Uganda
vedco@infocom.co.ug

Guru Naik
Director, Livelihood Programme
Christian Children's Fund (CCF), India
guruzi@ccfindia.com

Agnes Nayiga
Assistant Regional Coordinator, East Africa
DFID Crop Post-Harvest Programme
(CPHP), Natural Resources International
Ltd., Uganda
agnesnayiga@nida.or.ug

Gabriel Ndunguru
Principal Food Scientist, Tanzania Food and
Nutrition Centre (TFNC), Tanzania
ndunguru@africaonline.co.tz

Gideon Onumah
Senior Economist, Natural Resources
Institute, UK
g.e.onumah@gre.ac.uk

Joseph Oryokot
Technical Services Manager, National
Agricultural Advisory Services (NAADS),
Uganda
joryokot@yahoo.com

Kwasi Oware
Managing Director, Amasa Agro Processing
Co. Ltd., Ghana
amasaagro@yahoo.com

Emmanuel Owusu-Bennoah
Director General, Council for Scientific and
Industrial Research (CSIR), Ghana
eobennoah@ucomgh.com

Kumar Patel
Publishing Director, Research Information
Ltd., UK
kumarpatel@researchinformation.co.uk

Christie Peacock
Chief Executive, FARM–Africa (Food and
Agricultural Research Management), UK
christiep@farmafrica.org.uk

Wisdom A Plahar
Director, Food Research Institute, Ghana
fri@ghana.com

Guy Poulter
Director, Natural Resources Institute, UK
R.G.Poulter@gre.ac.uk

Colin Poulton
Research Fellow, Imperial College of
Science, Technology and Medicine,
University of London, UK
c.poulton@imperial.ac.uk

Shambu Prasad
Director, Centre for Research on Innovation
and Science Policy (CRISP), India
s.prasad@cgiar.org

Wyn Richards
Manager, DFID Livestock Protection
Programme (LPP), Natural Resources
International Ltd., UK
w.richards@nrint.co.uk

Abdur Rob
Team Leader, Markets and Livelihoods
Programme,Practical Action Bangladesh
rob@itb.bdmail.net

George Rothschild
Independent Consultant, UK
george.rothschild@btopenworld.com

Tunga Rukuni
Director, Development Technology Centre,
University of Zimbabwe, Zimbabwe
rukuni@agric.uz.ac.zw

Mandi Rukuni
Program Director, W K Kellogg Foundation
South Africa
mvr@wkkf.org

Amitabha Sadangi
Chief Executive Officer, International
Development Enterprises (India) (IDE-I),
India
amitabha@ide-india.org

Cerstin Sander
Enterprise Adviser, Pro-Poor Growth Team
Department for International Development
(DFID), UK
c-sander@dfid.gov.uk

Denis Sautier
Research Scientist, Centre de cooperation
internationale en recherché agronomique
pour le developpement (CIRAD), France
denis.sautier@cirad.fr

Antonio Schiavone
Programme Officer, Global Forum on
Agricultural Research (GFAR) Secretariat,
c/o FAO, Italy
antonio.schiavone@fao.org

Andrew Scott
Policy and Programmes Director,
Practical Action, UK
andrew.scott@practicalaction.org.uk

Benedikte Siderman Wolter
Communications Manager, Natural
Resources International Ltd., UK
b.wolter@nrint.co.uk

Peter Smith
Client Director, Booker Tate Ltd., UK
psmith@booker-tate.co.uk

Georgina Smith
Communications Assistant, Natural
Resources International Ltd., UK
g.smith@nrint.co.uk

Paul Spray
Head of Central Research, Department for
International Development (DFID), UK
p-spray@dfid.gov.uk

Graham Thiele
Liaison Scientist, Centro Internacional de la
Papa (CIP), Papa Andina Project, Ecuador
g.thiele@cgiar.org

Susanna Thorp
Director, WRENmedia, UK
s.thorp@wrenmedia.co.uk

Karen Twining
Director, International Development
Enterprises (IDE-UK), UK
karentwining@ide-uk.org

Jonathan Wadsworth
Rural Livelihoods Adviser, Department for
International Development (DFID), UK
j-wadsworth@dfid.gov.uk

David Walker
Grain Management Advisor (Food Aid)
Natural Resources Institute, UK
d.j.walker@gre.ac.uk

Hilary Warburton
International Team Leader, Reducing
Vulnerability Programme, Practical Action, UK
hilary.warburton@practicalaction.org.uk

Andrew Ward
Deputy Manager, DFID Crop Protection
Programme (CPP), Natural Resources
International Ltd., UK
a.ward@nrint.co.uk

Elizabeth Warham
Research Manager (Energy and
Environment), Department of Trade and
Industry, Innovation Group, UK
elizabeth.warham@dti.gsi.gov.uk

Duncan Warren
Crop Production Director, National
Smallholder Farmers' Association of Malawi
(NASFAM), Malawi
dwarren@nasfam.org

Ruth West
Project Director, Herb Trade Enterprises
Pro-Natura UK, UK
ruthwest@gn.apc.org

Andrew Westby
Director of Research, Natural Resources
Institute, UK
a.westby@gre.ac.uk

Christine Wheeler
PA to DFID Crop Post-Harvest and Crop
Protection Programmes (CPHP and CPP),
Natural Resources International Ltd., UK
c.wheeler@nrint.co.uk

Steve Wiggins
Research Fellow, Overseas Development
Institute (ODI), UK
s.wiggins@ODI.org.uk

Karen Wilkin
Deputy Manager, DFID Crop Post-Harvest
Programme (CPHP), Natural Resources
International Ltd., UK
k.wilkin@nrint.co.uk

Sileshi Zinash
Senior Resource Person, Research Forum
for Agriculture Research in Africa (FARA),
Ghana
szinash@fara-africa.org